# Employability Skills for Undergraduate Business Students

# Pearson

At Pearson, we have a simple mission: to help people make more of their lives through learning.

We combine innovative learning technology with trusted content and educational expertise to provide engaging and effective learning experience that serve people wherever and whenever they are learning.

We enable our customers to access a wide and expanding range of market-leading content from world-renowned authors and develop their own tailor-made book. From classroom to boardroom, our curriculum materials, digital learning tools and testing programmes help to educate millions of people worldwide — more than any other private enterprise.

Every day our work helps learning flourish, and wherever learning flourishes, so do people.

To learn more, please visit us at: www.pearson.com/uk

# Employability Skills for Undergraduate Business Students

Selected chapters from:

*Employability Skills*
Second Edition
Frances Trought

*The Business Student's Handbook*
Sixth Edition
Sheila Cameron

*Employability Skills*
First Edition
Frances Trought

*Graduate Career Handbook*
Third Edition
Judith Done and Rachel Mulvey

*How to Succeed In any Interviews*
Third Edition
Ros Jay

*The Interview Book*
Third Edition
James Innes

*Management & Organisational Behaviour*
Eleventh Edition
Laurie J. Mullins

*Passing Psychometric Tests*
Rachel Mulvey

Pearson

Harlow, England • London • New York • Boston • San Francisco • Toronto • Sydney • Dubai • Singapore • Hong Kong
Tokyo • Seoul • Taipei • New Dehli • Cape Town • São Paulo • Mexico City • Madrid • Amsterdam • Munich • Paris • Milan

Pearson
KAO Two
KAO Park
Harlow
Essex CM17 9NA

And associated companies throughout the world

Visit us on the World Wide Web at:
www.pearson.com/uk

© Pearson Education Limited 2019

Compiled from:

*Employability Skills*
Second Edition
Frances Trought
ISBN 978-1-292-15890-7
© Pearson Education Limited 2012, 2017

The Business Student's Handbook
Sixth Edition
Sheila Cameron
ISBN 978-1-292-08864-8
© Sheila Cameron 2009, 2016

*Employability Skills*
First Edition
Frances Trought
ISBN 978-0-273-74993-6
© Pearson Education Limited 2012

*Graduate Career Handbook*
Third Edition
Judith Done and Rachel Mulvey
ISBN 978-1-292-15887-7
© Pearson Education Limited 2014, 2016

*How to Succeed in any Interviews*
Third edition
Ros Jay
ISBN 978-1-292-08108-3
© Pearson Education Limited 2002, 2015

*The Interview Book*
Third Edition
James Innes
ISBN 978-1-292-08651-4
© James Innes 2012, 2016

*Management & Organisational Behaviour*
Eleventh edition
Laurie J. Mullins
ISBN 978-1-292-08848-8
© Laurie J. Mullins 2012, 2016

*Passing Psychometric Tests*
Rachel Mulvey
ISBN 978-1-292-01651-1
© Pearson Education Limited 2015

ISBN 978-1-787-64526-4

Printed and bound in Great Britain by CPI Group.

# CONTENTS

# Part 1:
# The Management
# Professional

# Introduction

## Every year 400,000 students in the UK graduate with a degree: what makes you stand out?

Whether you are studying for an English, history, business or engineering degree, the one thing you will all have in common is the fact that you all need to know how to market yourself. If your goal is to secure employment at the end of your degree or to start your own business, you will need to be able to convince a potential employer or investor that you are the perfect candidate. This is essential whether you wish to work in the private, public, third sector or become self-employed. Regardless of your field, there will always be competition and the need to stand out.

## Marketing and graduate development

Marketing is often seen as a business-related activity, but it is essential for every successful graduate. While at university you are developing your own individual brand. When employability is viewed in its crudest form, we are all products attempting to sell our skills in the graduate marketplace. Consider the definition of a product as:

*Anything that can be offered to a market for attention, acquisition, use or consumption that might satisfy a want or need.*

*(Kotler et al., 2016)*

If we place this in the context of employability, the market would be the graduate employment market and the skills we seek to develop throughout our degree would represent 'anything that can be offered to a market', and we would hope that these skills would 'satisfy a want or need' of a potential employer.

As a result, strong analogies can be drawn between the development of a product and the development of graduates. The skills developed throughout a degree can be seen as the product features, the elements by which you seek to differentiate yourself from the competition – the other graduates in the marketplace.

If this analogy is extended and the marketing mix is considered, further correlations can be seen. The marketing mix is 'the set of tactical marketing tools – product, price, place and promotion – that the firm blends to produce the response it wants in the target market'. (Kotler et al., 2016, p. 78) The four 'P's (product, price, promotion and place) are used by firms and graduates to bring about their desired outcomes – recruiting the best graduates and gaining employment respectively. If we review all of these elements in this context, strong correlations can be drawn.

By definition, price relates to 'the amount of money charged for a product or service or the sum of the values that customers exchange for the benefits of having or using a product or service'. (Kotler et al., 2016, p. 324)

Salary is representative of price as it relates to the amount an employer is willing to pay for graduate services. As with price, salary is influenced by supply and demand and correlations can be drawn between surpluses and shortages in the marketplace dependent upon disciplines and skills. Competition also affects price and graduate recruiters will vary their price in order to make their offer attractive.

Salary, just like price, is influenced by the value a customer, in this case a graduate recruiter, attributes to acquiring new graduates. How important do companies see the acquisition of graduates to the development of their business and how much can they afford to pay?

Promotion in essence relates to how the value/benefit of a product is communicated to the target audience – in this instance, the way a graduate promotes his or her skills by the use of curriculum vitae, application forms, interviews and online profiles. Do not forget that graduate recruiters also want to recruit the best and so, in turn, adopt a promotion strategy in order to make their offer attractive to graduates by attending graduate recruitment fairs, advertising their graduate schemes and inviting students to career open days.

Place, as with product, relates to the distribution and the availability of the product. When looking for employment you will determine how far you are willing to travel and the location within which you are prepared to work. Graduate recruiters also distribute graduates throughout their organisation both locally and globally, representing a wide distribution network.

## The career life cycle

The product life cycle (PLC) charts the progress of a 'product's sales and profits over its lifetime'. (Kotler et al., 2016) This model can also be modified to chart the development of a career. In the figure below, the PLC has been modified to represent the various stages of your career. At each stage, just as with a product, a strategy needs to be devised in order to sustain a positive result through continued career development represented by promotion, increase in salary or responsibility.

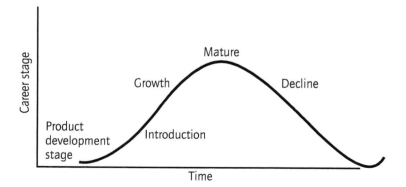

The product development stage represents the time you attend university and develop your skills prior to launching your product into the graduate market. The growth period represents the continued development of your career. It is at the mature stage that you have to make important career decisions in order to keep your career moving upwards.

Often companies in the mature phase will release an updated product with additional features to boost sales. At this stage the market has developed either due to the introduction of new technology or new processes and you have to update your skills or risk your skill set becoming outdated. To update skills students will often re-enter higher education at this stage to study for additional qualifications, either a Masters degree or professional qualifications. Others may return to education as a mature student to gain their first degree in order to enhance their career development.

The decline phase represents a shift in the market and highlights the fact that your skill set is not aligned with the job market. In many cases, this will result in redundancy. This can often kick-start the career life cycle, forcing a return to the product development stage.

---

## ? brilliant question

What stage are you at in your career life cycle? Are you still developing your product or returning to education to enhance your product? Or following redundancy, seeking to kick-start your career in a new direction?

Due to the increasingly competitive graduate market, and the increasing number of graduates in the marketplace, it has become imperative that graduates engage with the marketing of their skills in order to succeed. Employers can no longer differentiate between candidates based solely on their degree. You now have to consider what else you have to offer a potential employer.

As stated by McNair (2003), graduate employability has increased in importance 'because of the changing nature of the graduate labour market, mass participation in HE, pressures on student finance, competition to recruit students and expectations of students, employers, parents and government (expressed in quality audits and league tables)'.

What do we mean when we talk about employability?

 **brilliant** definition

**Employability**
'a set of achievements – skills, understanding and personal attributes – that makes graduates more likely to gain employment and be successful in their chosen occupations, which benefits themselves, the workforce, the community and the economy'
(Mantze Yorke, 2006)
'a set of attributes, skills and knowledge that all labour market participants should possess to ensure they have the capability of being effective in the workplace – to the benefit of themselves, their employer and the wider community'
(CBI, 2011)

The CBI builds on this definition and identifies a set of employability skills, including:

- self-management
- communication and literacy
- team-working

- application of numeracy
- business and customer awareness
- application of information
- technology (IT)
- problem-solving
- positive attitude
- entrepreneurship/enterprise.

Source: Adapted from CBI, 2009

These skills are repeatedly identified as the core skills and attributes graduates need to be able to demonstrate upon graduation. The Global Graduates into Global Leaders Report (Diamond et al., 2008) stipulates that before graduates can even begin to consider developing the skills needed to compete on a global scale they need to ensure that they have developed the core skills and attributes listed above.

These skills are a prerequisite and are reinforced by the CMI report '21st Century Leaders' (2014), when employers were asked to identify the skills required from graduates. Communication (67%), problem-solving (48%) and team-building (47%) were listed as the top three skills valued by employers. As a result, the skills identified in the CMI report are still very relevant for graduates entering the market in 2017.

## The I Brand employability model

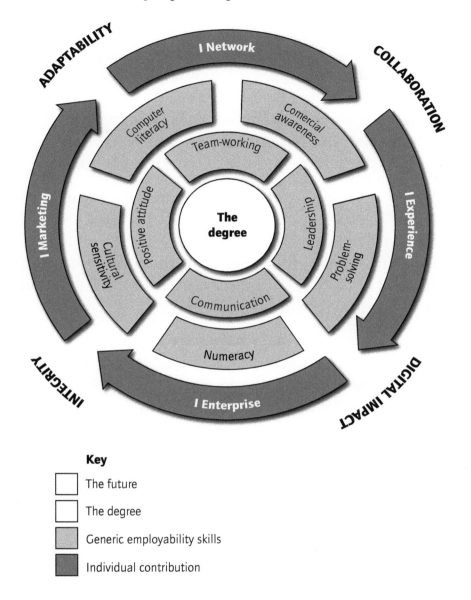

**Key**

☐ The future

☐ The degree

◻ Generic employability skills

◼ Individual contribution

The I Brand employability model incorporates these skills but recognises the importance of an individual's network, experience, enterprise and marketing skills. The model has been further developed to recognise the continually transforming and changing landscape within which organisations operate. It is important for graduates to not only develop their employability skills, but to also review how they can sustain their place within the marketplace.

A further four additional skills and attributes have been added to the I Brand employability model: integrity, adaptability, collaboration and digital impact. These four skills and attributes provide the students with the skills needed to future-proof their career development. The currency of experience is priceless when looking for a position. Repeatedly, employers will ask: 'Do you have any experience?' Often you can find yourself caught in a cycle whereby you can't get a job because you don't have any experience, but you can't get any experience because you don't have a job.

Essentially you are building your own individual brand to increase your employability – a brand being defined as 'a name . . . that identifies the products or services of one seller . . . and differentiates them from those of competitors'. (Kotler et al., 2016, p. 691) Your brand will help you stand out from the competition – other graduates in the graduate market.

Developing your I Brand encourages you to develop your own skills and differentiate your product, to communicate your brilliance to potential employers. From day one at university you need to think about how you will complete your course, but also how you will become a successful graduate. The difference is that being a successful graduate is not merely limited to gaining your degree but also includes developing additional skills that make you more marketable and as a result increase your employability.

The definitions of employability reference the development of skills and attributes that cannot be developed overnight. To attain these skills graduates cannot leave it to chance or leave it to the day before graduation. Students often believe that graduation is far away, but the three or four years will pass very quickly. Students need to actively engage with their career development to ensure that upon graduation they have developed a brand employers want to buy.

 question

If your name was a brand, what would it stand for? What is your unique selling point (USP)? Reliability? Honesty? Trustworthiness?

## The graduate market

Every year approximately 400,000 (HESA, 2015) UK graduates enter the job market, creating a situation where the demand for jobs far outstrips the supply. The market has surpassed pre-recession levels and *The Times*' top 100 graduate employers aim to increase their level of recruitment in 2016 by 7.5%.

Graduate recruiters have increased their expectations of graduate hires and are continually raising the stakes. In the summer of 2015, 77% of graduate employers required a 2:1 degree or above (AGR, 2016). The graduate recruitment market is competitive, but your time at university can be used to develop your skills to ensure you stand out.

## How to use this book

This book is aimed at students studying at levels 4 and 5 of the National Qualifications Framework (first- and second-year university students) to encourage them to get involved in university and all that it offers. The exercises and information are still applicable to final-year and Masters students.

The book provides a range of exercises focused on self-exploration and self-development, in order to increase students' marketing potential. Students are encouraged to evaluate their current skills and devise an action plan to develop additional skills while at university through extracurricular activity.

Chapters 11 and 13 provide an overview of the job market and how to navigate your way through it. Students are presented with a number of options to gain work experience while at university and also research alternative avenues to enter their first-choice career. Focuses on how you can market your skills to potential employers and highlights the dos and don'ts of applying for jobs. Encourages students to recognise that this is not a one-off process but, to have a truly brilliant future, students need to continually review their skill sets to ensure they remain employable.

# CHAPTER 1

# Employability skills valued by employers

The man (woman) who has no imagination has no wings

Mohammed Ali

When completing an application form or attending an interview, employers need evidence of your abilities: your competences. It is essential that on the application form you are able to demonstrate your skills through your experiences, and the more varied the situation the better. Judge for yourself: Is hearing about a group exercise where students fundraised and trekked to Kilimanjaro more interesting to read about than a group exercise where students completed a presentation?

Students need to consider how they build their skills and where. University presents the opportunity not only to develop your skills but to challenge yourself and develop a wide set of experiences which set you apart from other graduates. Those students who fail to engage with extracurricular activities run the risk of not only limiting their development but also the range of examples they can use when completing an application form.

The development of soft skills has become increasingly important in today's economy. It is argued that soft skills contribute £88 billion to the UK economy and it is forecast to rise to £109 billion. The importance of soft skills is reflected by employers: 97% of employers believe that soft skills (in particular teamwork and communication) are essential to business success and are becoming increasingly more important than academic results. (Development of Economics Ltd, 2015)

This chapter will help you not only identify the skills valued by employers, but will also provide examples of how you can build these skills.

# Self-management

Are you good with meeting deadlines? Are you organised? Do you use your own initiative?

If you can answer yes to these questions that's great, but if you can't manage yourself how can employers expect you to manage at work? Employers will expect you to be organised, punctual, working to deadlines and a self-starter. How you manage yourself and your approach to your work is key to being employable. Your first management role is self-management.

So what do we mean when we talk about self-management?

The CBI (2011) defines self-management as the 'readiness to accept responsibility, flexibility, resilience, self-starting, appropriate assertiveness, time management, readiness to improve own performance based on feedback/reflective learning'.

So how can you demonstrate you are good at self-management to an employer? The best way to demonstrate self-management is to look for examples in your current roles.

Do you work part time? Do you have responsibilities at home? Are you a mentor? These are excellent examples to demonstrate your ability to be responsible.

Employers will expect you to manage your time effectively and use your own initiative. Think of examples of where you have had to balance several assignment deadlines. How did you achieve this? Preparation, planning and organisation are essential for effective time management.

You can always learn from your experiences, so it is important to use feedback and reflection to see how you could have performed a task better. There is always room for improvement.

 tip

## Ask around and use feedback

You can gain valuable personal insight by gathering feedback from other students, your tutors or professors, mentors, friends and even family members. Ask them to think about both your strengths and areas you could improve on. For example:

- What should you do more of/keep doing?
- What should you do less of/stop doing?

Often others see you differently to how you see yourself and their answers will help you identify and build on your skills and areas of possible weaknesses.

Jo Blissett, Career Development Consultant, Career Quest

 example

Worried about juggling a new volunteer role alongside your existing study commitments?

First, do not fret, as flexible volunteering where you offer your services as a volunteer as and when it suits you is now increasingly common. Second, your commitment to a volunteer role demonstrates not only motivation and drive to a potential employer, but organisational skills including planning and time management.

Meeting and dealing with new people through voluntary work will not only develop your patience and empathy towards others, but will demonstrate your ability to negotiate new and sometimes stressful scenarios. Being able to remain calm under pressure and think positively will help you to stand out both during the recruitment process and in the workplace. To get    ▶

involved with a cause you're passionate about that has you jumping out of bed on a rainy Sunday morning, take a look at Do-it.org (https://do-it. org/), a national volunteering database.

Jamie Ward-Smith, CEO, Do-it.org

---

Self-management is an excellent indicator for an employer of how you will cope in the workplace. You will have many tasks to manage and demonstrating that you can multi-task successfully is a great skill. The ability to balance a commitment alongside your academic studies is an excellent demonstration of your time management, organisational and self-management skills.

## Teamworking

What do Barcelona FC, the United Nations and Great Ormond Street Hospital have in common? They all achieve success through teamwork. Each member of the team plays a vital role, and that ensures their success.

The CBI (2011) stated that at the heart of teamworking is 'respecting others, cooperating, negotiating/persuading, contributing to discussions, an awareness of interdependence with others'.

In today's workforce this has become even more prevalent, and as a result employers include teamworking exercises in their selection processes to assess how well new graduates work in teams. An assessment centre will often include a group exercise, centred around a team of potential candidates working together to find a solution to a problem. This provides the recruiters with a good indication of how candidates work with others, as often within the work environment, teams are formed across the organisation.

## Why is teamworking important?

So why is teamworking important? In today's rapidly changing marketplace organisations are faced with challenges, which cannot be addressed by one department. The challenge affects the organisation as a whole, and so teams are drawn from both across functions, but also globally. When devising solutions an organisation will need to have the knowledge from within its organisation and possibly from an expert consultant drawn from within its particular sector.

Collaboration is key in developing competitive advantage within the marketplace. This can involve collaborating externally with suppliers to develop new processes or new products. Working in teams enables an organisation to harness the expertise which exists both internally and externally. A team is much better placed to respond to the challenges faced in the competitive marketplace, as it enables the organisation to consider the challenge from many perspectives at once, and develop a solution that incorporates the needs of all of the business.

Teams come in different shapes and sizes. One size does not fit all. Throughout your time at university students will experience many different types of teams. As a member of a student society or club, students may find themselves working as a team to organise events, recruit members and fundraise. Other opportunities to work within a team are through sports, volunteering or even a group assignment.

## Developing teamworking skills

University is the perfect place to develop teamworking skills. Often students work part time, which presents the opportunity to develop teamworking skills in a live environment, and the experience will enhance many other employability skills such as communication.

Whether you work in retail, fast food or tourism you will be part of a team and begin to understand the dynamics of working collectively towards a common goal. This goal could be to meet sales targets, to fundraise a specific amount or to collectively work together to enhance the customer experience.

Within the work environment teams exist in varying formats. Project teams will be created to address a specific business challenge. Often a team can be created virtually in order to capture the knowledge and experience of co-workers located nationally or even globally. Technology, in particular Skype and Google Hangouts, facilitate the ability to speak with teams virtually.

When working virtually and internationally communication skills become even more important, especially if the team is drawn globally. Time zones, cultures and customs become important factors to ensure the team works effectively and respectfully together.

---

 example

Virtual teams

Virtual teams are now commonplace and I have run them for many years. In a global business coupled with cost pressures, virtual team-working is now a business necessity and doing this right can add a huge competitive advantage. Here are my top five tips for managing a successful team.

- **Manage cultural dynamics:** Many virtual teams will incorporate different cultures and there is a need to manage conscious and unconscious biases to ensure the right behaviours and expectations.

- **Communication:** Always have a clear agenda and appropriate lead time for pre-reading meeting documents. Allocate who will manage minutes, actions and general communications.

- **Time zones:** There is a need to be sensitive regarding time zones, if possible. Try to rotate times so that alternate time slots can be scheduled to limit individuals being subjected to regular early mornings or late night calls.

- **Respect:** Set out clear rules to ensure all team members can be heard and the team actually listens. The chair has to carefully manage engagement.

- **Technology platform:** The communication platform has to be stable and accessible. It can be very disruptive to have platforms that are unreliable. This will hamper the progress but also the overall morale in the team.

Virtual teams are invaluable in the workplace, but it must be set up for success. The above dynamics are just a handful of critical success factors to manage a virtual team.

Carol René, Enterprise Lead Information and
Data Architect, Shell International Petroleum Company

---

## What role would you play in a team?

Teams are created to provide a collective response to challenges faced by the organisation. What role do you think you would play in a team? Review these team roles and see which role reflects your skills.

- The project manager manages the team and takes on the responsibility of ensuring the project is delivered on time.

- The expert, as the name suggests, is a specialist in their field and highlights the impact of any solutions to the organisation and end-users.

- The innovator challenges the status quo and adopts a creative approach to tasks.

- The analyst evaluates all of the proposed solutions and highlights possible risks.

● The finisher ensures that all of the documentation and other outputs from the team tasks are submitted.

To review your role within ask your careers service to conduct a Myers Briggs test, which will highlight your position of strength in a team.

Certain skills and attributes are needed for a team to perform effectively. Respect is essential as you will not always be working with people you know or even like. Teams are often required to present their results or write a progress report, which will require good communication skills. The ability to negotiate or persuade is central to sourcing resources or convincing the team of a particular course of action. The success of the team is dependent on members sharing their knowledge and skills. A 'critical friend' asking challenging questions ensures that solutions are debated in full.

 example

## Conflict management and problem-solving

First, let me start by saying that when working in a team I believe conflict is inevitable and therefore unavoidable – even for those who really try their hardest to avoid it. Preparing yourselves in advance for any potential clashes by practising conflict management skills is a must if you wish to succeed in your chosen career.

One of the best ways to help you develop a constructive approach to conflict really begins long before you are even involved in one – by 'accepting' that conflict is inevitable and will occur at some point, as it will help you to positively prepare yourself. The ability to manage conflict in a constructive and positive manner is increasingly becoming a sought after 'soft skill' in the work environment.

How you manage the conflicts you face at work will play a huge part in your successes in life, as when carried out effectively, you will be able to create harmonious and respectful relationships which enhance the working environment around you. You will therefore increase your employability skills and begin to progress at work.

The top five qualities needed when managing conflict are the following:

- patience
- respect (for others)
- empathy
- (active) listening
- think win–win.

Lex A Showunmi, Company Director and
Conflict Management Trainer/Practitioner,
3S Partnerships Ltd

---

Teamworking is a vital part of any organisation. The structure and size of the team is dependent upon the nature of the task. Each member of the team plays a different role, which is equally important and contributes to the success of the project. In order for teams to work effectively team members must have a range of skills.

## Business and customer awareness

Business and customer awareness is important to an employer as your opinions demonstrate how you can add value to their organisation. Employers will expect you to understand their markets, their customers and the challenges they face.

As stated by the CBI (2011) 'graduates should have a basic understanding of the key drivers for business success – including the importance of innovation and taking calculated risks – and the need to provide customer satisfaction and build customer loyalty'.

How do you develop specific sector knowledge?

An insight to your chosen industry sector can be gained by reading newspapers, journals and newsletters from professional bodies. This will not only help you with your employability skills, but you will find you have a better understanding of your lectures and assignments. Your industry knowledge will be more apparent in the conversations you have about your sector and the responses you give in interviews. Below are a few examples of how to stay abreast of your industry:

- Create a Google Alert to refer to a page.
- Company websites provide an insight into the industry and the challenges they face in the competitive market.
- Industry-specific events can help you meet people who work in the industry and give you an insight into the structure of the organisation and the various roles which exist.

Ultimately the best way to gain an insight into an industry is to gain work experience. Work shadowing, internships and placements all provide opportunities for you to not only understand the industry but to see if you want to work in it. As a result, you will gain an insight into how companies manage the users' experience and build brand loyalty. You can develop this knowledge by reflecting on your own experiences with companies. Customer retention is important for businesses as without customers there is no business. Review company websites and how they build loyalty with their customers.

## Problem-solving

The CBI defines problem-solving as 'analysing facts and situations and applying creative thinking to develop appropriate solutions'.

Organisations continually face challenges from advancing technology, competitors and changing markets so they need employees who can develop innovative solutions that will keep them ahead of the competition. Graduates who are creative, innovative and use their own initiative are essential to developing solutions to the challenges of the future.

## How do you develop problem-solving skills?

You already have problem-solving skills. You are faced with challenges every day in both your academic course and your personal life. The skills you use to address these problems are transferable to the workplace. Essentially all problem-solving revolves around 'gap analysis', the difference between a desired outcome and the actual outcome. Regardless of whether it is an academic problem or organising an event such as your brother's wedding you will need to follow a number of steps. These are defined by Bransford and Stein (1984) in their IDEAL problem-solving model, which can be used within a range of contexts.

**I**dentify the problem. What are the essential elements of the problem?

**D**efine the problem through thinking about it and sorting relevant information.

**E**xplore solutions. What are the advantages and disadvantages of each solution?

**A**ct on strategies.

**L**ook back and evaluate the effects of your activity.

Finding a solution may need you to develop additional employability skills. For example, you may need to create a diverse team, use your communication and IT skills to present your ideas or use your numeracy skills to calculate the financial impact of your solutions. As a result, it is important that you recognise the employability skills that you are developing while completing your academic assignments and solving your daily life challenges.

 example

## Do some problem-solving

Need to learn how to think on your feet? It's time to say hello to a voluntary role.

As a leader at your local youth club not only will you be entrusted with the safety of the children, but you may need to resolve misunderstandings between members.

As a charity shop supervisor you could be called upon to address customer concerns or negotiate weekly staff rotas. The beauty of volunteering? Things may not always go to plan but you're sure to be supported by a team of passionate people all working towards the same goal. While it may feel tough at the time, approaching a problem calmly is an important workplace skill that demonstrates your personal resilience and adaptability. Added bonus? Your volunteer experience will leave you ready and raring to go when faced with that old interview chestnut: 'Tell me about a situation where you had to overcome a difficult problem'. To find a voluntary role near you head to Do-it.org, a national volunteering database.

Jamie Ward-Smith, CEO, Do-it.org

Another tool to develop solutions to challenges is the '5 Whys' developed by the Toyota Motor Corporation in 1950. Toyota developed a method where, by repeating 'why' five times, the problem and the solution are revealed through the questioning process. The 5 Whys is used to unveil the root cause of a problem. Once the root has been identified, a solution is developed, which ensures that the problem doesn't reoccur.

It is important through the questioning phase that the key stakeholders are invited to participate in the process, i.e. all those affected by the problem or the situation. Once the team members have been identified, it is important to drill down at least five levels to identify the root cause of the problem, but initially the problem needs to be clearly defined for the process to work.

The five key stages in the 5 Whys process:

1  Identify the key stakeholders – those affected by the problem.

2  Assign a team leader to lead and document the process.

3  Ask 'why' five times.

4  Define the solution and assign responsibilities.

5  Communicate the outcomes with all stakeholders.

## brilliant dos and don'ts

What to do and what not to do when problem-solving

✔ Be as specific as possible when thinking and investigating the problem – pinpoint the actual issues using factual information.

✔ Find the most important parts of the problem – what are the biggest issues or risks?

✗ Don't blame others, poor processes or systems for the problem – remain open-minded about the problem and its causes.

✗ Do not immediately assume you know what the problem is and the solutions are.

✗ Do not go straight to solve the problem before thinking, investigating and gathering information about it (facts, inference, speculation and opinion).

Mindmaps can give you an overview of a large subject while also holding large amounts of information. They can be an intuitive way to organise your thoughts, since they mimic the way our brains think – bouncing ideas off of each other, rather than thinking linearly.

Jo Blissett, Career Development Consultant, Career Quest

# Communication

Communication in essence is the sending of a message by sender A to receiver B. The format of the message can take different forms and the language will vary dependent on the context. There are several different options available.

## Face to face

Despite face to face appearing to be the easiest form of communication, messages can still be misinterpreted by the choice of words, body language, tone and the person delivering the message.

## Telephone call

Without the aid of visual expression, the choice of words and tone become even more crucial to ensure the receiver interprets the message accurately. Telephone interviews are often used during the selection process, and students would be advised to practise beforehand, as diction, tone and clarity are paramount.

## Written communication

Written communication can take various form, including CVs, reports and covering letters. The style of writing, presentation and choice of words can all affect the way the message is delivered and received.

## Social media

Twitter, What'sApp, LinkedIn, Facebook and instant messaging can be misinterpreted due to the incorrect use of upper or lower case, the insertion of an emoticon or an abbreviation. Although an accepted means of communication, it is heavily criticised if not used in the right context.

## Effective communication

So how can we communicate effectively? When delivering a message, you need to take into account the context. In what context is the message being delivered? Professional, academic or social. The mode of delivery should reflect the context along with the choice of words.

In addition, to avoid any confusion use the 7 Cs of communication

1 **Clear:** Ensure the aim and purpose of your message is clear from the outset of your written or verbal communication.

2 **Concise:** Less is more when communicating so be brief and targeted.

3 **Concrete:** Be focused in your communication and ensure that you are specific, factual and provide the required level of detail.

4 **Correct:** Ensure that your spelling, facts and grammar are correct. Also ensure that the tone, language and choice of words fit the context.

5 **Coherent:** Reread your message to ensure that it is logical and your ideas flow smoothly.

6 **Complete:** Ensure your communication contains the necessary information required by the receiver to respond.

7 **Courteous:** Ensure that you address the recipient politely and appropriately.

(Modified from Cutlip and Center, 1952)

In summary, when communicating you need to understand the context within which the message is to be delivered, that you choose the right medium for delivery and you choose your words carefully. And then use the 7 Cs of communication to avoid any misinterpretation of your message.

Communication skills can be developed through your academic study or extracurricular activities. Academically your presentation skills and written assignments are all opportunities for you to be assessed on how well you communicate. In addition to the academic environment, opportunities will arise to develop communication skills in different contexts. For example, at networking meetings, engaging with student societies or participating in mock interviews. It is important that you are able to communicate in a wide range of contexts including professional, academic and social.

## Application of IT

Technology is transforming, disrupting and reshaping all industries. No organisation is insulated from the rapid changes taking place within the technology sector, but it's the resounding ripples and waves that affect all industries as well. The dramatic advances in technology are causing industries to question their purpose in the future. An example of this is the retail banking sector.

'There are so many different ways that you can make payments these days; you can pay by email, by Paypal and you can pay by your mobile phone, but all of that relies on the same plumbing and predominately it's the banks that provide that plumbing. Right now it's of value to us but I think we are in danger of just becoming the plumbing.' (Mortimer, 2015)

Industries are not just facing change – they are facing disruption. As a graduate you will be expected to be IT savvy. Question how technology could improve your processes or add value to your role. Continually update your IT skills, undertake short courses to learn about new technologies and new ways of performing tasks.

The application of IT involves the ability to demonstrate basic IT skills, including the familiarity with word processing, spreadsheets, file management and email. These skills can be developed through completing the assessments on your courses: word processing your coursework, using visual aids for presentations. On campus there will be support classes to develop your IT skills. Extracurricular activities can also be used as a means to develop these skills.

IT skills are essential so don't leave university without them. And make sure you keep them up to date. Course providers, such as UDemy, Coursera or General Assembley, provide short courses to ensure your skills remain current.

## Application of numeracy and data analysis

How's your mental maths? Can you analyse data and provide the best course of action? Are you financially literate? When was the last time you calculated an average, percentage or fraction? Well, all of these maths elements can and do feature in selection tests and assessment centres. Numeracy is like Marmite – you either love it or hate it. But either way employers love it.

 **definition**

**Numeracy**
'the manipulation of numbers, general mathematical awareness and its application in practical contexts'

CBI, 2011

Numbers are everywhere and underpin many decisions made in organisations, so as a future graduate you need to understand what numeracy means for your sector. Generally, employers will expect you to have an understanding of mental arithmetic tasks like addition, subtraction, multiplication and division. Graduates will also be expected to analyse quantitative and qualitative data, interpret them and present the data in a visual format. You will also need to understand the financial implications of changes in the marketplace on an organisation, their products and profit margins.

Whether you are an arts, law or tourism graduate you need to have basic numeracy skills. Selection processes can include timed mental maths tests, so it's important to refresh these skills before applying to internships or graduate roles.

Practice tests can be found at the following sites:

SHL Direct: www.cebglobal.com

Talentlens: www.talentlens.co.uk

## Leadership

Are you a future leader? Are you a game changer? Or are you able to take ownership of a situation and bring it to resolution?

Leadership comes in many forms and varying personalities. There are some excellent examples of leadership in the public arena from Barack Obama to Steve Jobs, but on a daily basis many employees within organisations demonstrate leadership skills.

Organisations need leaders on many levels to drive and champion success throughout a business. Leaders are not only at the helm of an organisation, as in order to be sustainable an organisation needs talented individuals who contribute to its continued success. Graduate schemes develop the pipeline of future leaders within the organisation.

How do we define leadership? As stated by the Chartered Institute of Professional Development (CIPD): 'there is no single definition or concept of leadership that satisfies all'.

Leadership is expected from the CEO right down to the most junior employee. Everyone has their part to play in ensuring excellence is maintained. The CIPD defines leadership as:

'the capacity to influence people, by means of personal attributes and/or behaviours to achieve a common goal'.

This is applicable to the CEO, who has to devise the vision and strategy to the graduate, who joins the organisation and works together with the team to achieve a common goal.

 example

What to do and not do to be an effective leader

- Be yourself: There's no 'right' model for a leader, so don't feel you have to be someone else.
- Know your own strengths and weaknesses: As well as knowing where to improve, you can organise teams to complement your own skills.
- Resist the temptation to 'do it yourself': The best leaders encourage their teams to deliver.
- Define what success looks like: Help people to understand what they are aiming for – the more inspirational the better.
- Don't be afraid to admit when you are wrong: People will respect you more, not less.

What to do and not do when you are leading a task or group

- Be clear on the objective and keep reminding people of it to keep on track.
- Find out what the different strengths of your team members are, and make the most of them.
- Make sure everyone gets some recognition, especially afterwards.
- Don't allow those with the loudest voices to dominate the group. Make sure you involve everyone.
- Don't feel it's all down to you: your job is to get the best from the team not to have the best ideas yourself.
- Don't be afraid to make decisions. Consensus can't always be reached.

  John Garnett, Board Advisor, Consultant and former Managing Director

In your graduate application form or the interview you will undoubtedly be asked to provide examples of where you have demonstrated your leadership skills. While at university there are several opportunities for you to develop your skills such as student societies, part-time jobs, volunteering, etc.

Take ownership of a task by developing an action plan of how the goal will be achieved. Employers will be interested in how you approached the task and your learning points. The actual outcome (although a successful one is always good) is immaterial; the way you handle the challenge, plan your time and liaise with others is more important. These will show your ability to lead a team to resolution.

 example

The Duke of Edinburgh's Award and leadership skills

Strong leadership skills are developed while doing a DofE programme. As part of a small team, you will plan, practise and complete an expedition. You will have to do a volunteering activity, no doubt taking yourself out of your comfort zone. This will allow you to gain vital leadership skills, whether by encouraging the rest of your expedition group through a particularly tough time, or leading and guiding your local youth group or sports team. The skills developed will be something that you are able to take through life with you, and that will also become invaluable to future employers.

Peter Westgarth, Chief Executive, The Duke of Edinburgh's Award

## Enterprise

In today's competitive market, regardless of the sector or role that you are recruited into, employers want graduates who are not afraid to disrupt the status quo. The ability to understand and interpret current processes, and how they are interconnected and interrelated, gives rise to opportunities to identify areas for improvement. Being entrepreneurial is not limited to starting your own business; organisations benefit from staff being intrapreneurs, developing new products and processes from within the organisation. This helps to maintain their competitive advantage.

The National Council for Graduate Entrepreneurship (NCGE) states that to add value an entrepreneurial graduate needs to: 'have the entrepreneurial skills that enable them to seize opportunities, solve issues and problems, generate and communicate ideas and make a difference in their communities'.

Students need to seize opportunities where they can be creative and innovative and develop their initiative skills. These can be achieved through involvement with either student societies or small businesses. Both provide opportunities for students to use their initiative to achieve specific goals. In particular, due to small businesses often operating with minimal staff, students can often find that they are exposed to more responsibility within a shorter timescale.

Being entrepreneurial is a must as students need to demonstrate how they will add value to the organisation.

## Emotional intelligence

Businesses continually face challenging, demanding and transforming landscapes, and so workforces need to manage and respond accordingly. Companies increasingly realise that the emotional intelligence (EI) of their employees plays an important role in determining an individual's response to a situation or to other people.

As a result, emotional intelligence has become increasingly important when identifying new talent. The leaders of tomorrow need to develop their ability to remain objective and make decisions based on the facts and data related to the situation.

**brilliant** definition

**Emotional intelligence**
'Emotional intelligence is the ability to perceive emotions, to access and generate emotions so as to assist thought, to understand emotions and emotional knowledge, and to reflectively regulate emotions so as to promote emotional and intellectual growth'

Mayer & Salovey, 1997, p. 87

Daniel Goleman (2014) identified four key components of an individual's emotional intelligence:

- **Self-awareness:** The ability to recognise how their feelings will affect their job performance.

- **Self-management:** The ability to demonstrate self-control and remain calm and clear-headed even during highly pressured situations.

- **Social awareness:** The ability to listen to what is said and more importantly what is unsaid and allow this to guide both your interaction with others and your decision-making.

- **Relationship management:** Employees with high emotional intelligence have the ability to inspire, influence, develop others, challenge the status quo and manage conflict.

These four elements underpin the ability to perform effectively both within a team and when facing challenging situations within the workplace.

 example

## Developing and improving your emotional intelligence

The ability to manage people and relationships is highly regarded by employers, so developing and using your EI can be a great way to show an employer why you stand out in the graduate recruitment market.

Carrying out your own self-evaluation is the first step to developing and improving your EI. You need to look at yourself honestly and identify your strengths and weakness. In addition, you can consider the points and advice in the table below.

| Observe how you react to people | <ul><li>Do you stereotype?</li><li>Do you rush to judge individuals and their actions?</li></ul> | <ul><li>Try to put yourself in their shoes</li><li>Be more open and accepting of others' views and needs</li></ul> |
| --- | --- | --- |
| Examine how you react to stressful situations | <ul><li>Do you become upset if things don't happen the way you want?</li><li>Do you blame others, even when it's not their fault?</li><li>Do you allow your emotions to cloud your decisions and thoughts?</li></ul> | <ul><li>Try to demonstrate the ability to stay calm and in control in stressful situations</li><li>Ensure you keep your emotions in control when things go wrong</li></ul> |
| Consider how your actions will affect others – before you take action | <ul><li>What will be the impact?</li><li>How will others feel?</li><li>Would you want that experience?</li></ul> | <ul><li>Put yourself in their place</li><li>Identify how you can help others deal with the effects</li></ul> |

*Jo Blissett, Career Development Consultant, Career Quest*

When considering the importance of emotional intelligence, you must also consider resilience, the ability to bounce back following an adverse decision.

 **definition**

**Resilience**

'the process of adapting well in the face of adversity, trauma, tragedy, threats or even significant sources of stress'

The American Psychological Association

Having the resolve to continue, whether it be with applications or a challenging situation, is a testament to an individual's character. The graduate market is increasingly competitive in nature, forcing graduates to become more resilient in order to survive. One application is unlikely to result in a positive outcome, and so graduates will receive several rejection letters before securing a graduate position. As a result, resilience is becoming increasingly important to a graduate's success.

There are many opportunities to develop resilience throughout your time at university. For example, a willingness to strive for better grades and to act on feedback from your assignments. In extracurricular activities resilience can be demonstrated by completing challenging tasks such as charity fundraising sky dives, triathlons, marathons, etc.

 example

The Duke of Edinburgh's Award and resilience

Young people are stronger than they think, and the great thing about doing a DofE programme is that it shows them this. Resilience is a work-ready skill, demonstrating that the individual has the capacity to recover quickly from a difficult situation. Learning to put up a tent in all weathers and undertake an expedition in the pouring rain can really test a person. If you can achieve this, many employers will see that you have a trait in you that is gold dust within the workplace.

Peter Westgarth, Chief Executive, The Duke of Edinburgh's Award

 example

### Resilience, opportunities and questions

I recognised my need for resilience upon graduation to avoid accepting my immediate reality. I asked myself what my purpose in life was and where I wanted to be. From there I bullet-pointed my answers and set myself deadlines. I looked for opportunities that would push me to my final destination, as opposed to going into a job that had better financial gain but less opportunity for growth.

I became proactive and sought successful people within my field and was not afraid to ask them questions about their routes to success and what barriers they faced. They said: 'Know your strengths and weaknesses, stand out from the crowd and get comfortable being uncomfortable, as when you're comfortable your success is limited'. I took these words and ran with it and each year from 2010 I have achieved something bigger and better.

After university, my full focus was to be the best version of myself within the sporting industry. I soon realised from assessing my strengths and weaknesses along with personal experiences that I had the drive and determination to start my own business. I set up SLR Fitness (personal training) and made many mistakes but learnt from them. I was also told you should not be fearful of failing in aid of wanting to do something you love or wanting to achieve something as it is all a learning curve.

Remember the most valuable stones (diamonds) come out of really dark places so when you feel all the walls are crashing in, do not stay in that dark place, step out and be that shining diamond.

Here are five tips to develop your resilience:

● Get comfortable being uncomfortable.

● Be persistent and do not take NO for an answer.

● Follow up on everything.

● Be opportunity-focused as opposed to money-focused.

● Be around positive, ambitious individuals in a better position than yourself and ask questions.

Stefan Lloyd, SLR Fitness

 **brilliant** recap

● Developing employability skills, competences and attributes underpin the success of today's graduate.

● In 2015 it is estimated that soft skills contribute £88 billion to the UK economy.

● 97% of UK employers believe that soft skills underpin the success of their business and their importance is valued more than academic results.

● 75% of employers have identified a soft skills gap in today's workforce.

● Self-management is your first trial at being a manager.

● The range of challenges faced by organisations require a multitude of skills and expertise to develop a comprehensive solution.

● Business and customer awareness are essential to understand the challenges and opportunities faced by the organisation.

- Organisations continually face challenges and it is important to identify the key stakeholders and collaborate to provide a solution.

- Communication is an essential skill and will underpin the ability to secure a role within an organisation, and to maintain that role.

- Graduates are the future leaders within an organisation.

- Emotional intelligence is just as important as the technical skills an individual brings to an organisation.

# 2
# TEAM WORK AND LEADERSHIP

## Learning outcomes

By the end of this chapter you should:

- appreciate the importance of team working

- have identified your strengths and weaknesses as a team member and identified any development needs

- be able to identify the roles and behaviours needed to manage group tasks and processes

- understand the importance of clear group objectives

- be aware of the importance of motivation in group work

- be able to identify things that may go wrong in groups and take avoiding action

- be able to make an effective contribution to both formal and informal group discussions

- understand the need to monitor group progress

- understand how to become influential in a group

- be able to demonstrate the contributions that you have made to a group project or endeavour.

# Introduction

The Quality Assurance Agency (QAA, 2015) puts 'People management: to include communications, team building, leadership and motivating others' first in their list of skills of particular relevance to graduates in business and management. Team skills are likely to feature in ads for almost any job you are likely to want, with 'leadership' potential as a close second. These skills are vital for employability and career success. As a student, team skills are equally important. They will help you learn in informal groups, and to make a valuable contribution to group projects. Leadership potential is similarly something that employers are looking for, as a simple search on 'graduate leadership programme' will show. This chapter will help you acquire the skills you need to be an effective team member, and help you maximise your learning in group contexts. It will also look at how you can become more influential in teams and exercise leadership.

Most work in organisations is done in a team context. Many, probably most decisions are taken in meetings. If team members do not work well together a project can fail, or at best produce poor work and demotivate team members. A bad meeting can take decisions that are expensively wrong: at worst they can ruin an organisation. No wonder employers are looking for team skills and see leadership potential as important.

Your course will almost certainly give you opportunities to study the theory of teams and leadership, and to practise team skills in discussion groups, and group assignments. Case study work and projects will almost certainly involve group work, so team-working skills will help you to get better grades, and to learn more effectively. If you are studying by distance learning you may be part of a 'virtual' student group and also need skills specific to virtual team work. These are highly transferable as organisations become more global.

Because team skills are so crucial for both study and employment it is important to grasp the opportunities your course offers for developing them. Also, take advantage of other interactions, whether in your social life or work placements and vacation jobs to practise these skills, and reflect on your team experiences.

## Team Working in Organisations

There are many different sorts of groups which form in organisations. While many use 'team' and 'group' to mean the same thing, much of the academic literature sees teams as a particular subset of groups. In this view teams

- are deliberately formed for a purpose, to perform particular tasks or projects
- have a common goal, which cannot be pursued unless the team members work together.

Teams are essential when inputs from a number of different perspectives or different skills are necessary and where commitment to outcome is important. Teams can be given a considerable degree of autonomy – output may be specified and measured by higher management, but the team left free to decide how best to achieve that output. This way of working offers considerable flexibility, as a team with this freedom can respond to local changes far more rapidly than one waiting for a decision to be taken higher in the organisation. (Decisions taken only after reference up (and up) the chain of command, can be very slow.) Autonomous team working also provides ideal conditions for high levels of motivation, so it is little wonder team working is so widely adopted.

> **Successful team working needs:**
> - clear, shared goals
> - agreed ways of working
> - effective communication
> - support and cooperation between members
> - monitoring of progress.

Even autonomous teams vary widely, as their goals will be different, requiring different members and ways of working. A committee is charged with taking decisions and perhaps seeing that those decisions are implemented. A work group might have the task of producing a particular component or providing a specified service. A project team might be charged with developing an original idea into concrete plans, or with putting those plans into action.

Responsibility within the team will also vary. Some teams may have a specified leader who may or may not also have managerial authority. (While many organisations use 'leader' to mean manager there is a distinction, which will be explored later in this chapter). Other teams may have no obvious leader. Some teams will contain a wide variety of expertise, whereas others may consist of people with very similar skills.

Whatever the team structure and membership, and regardless of whether the task is sharing information and negotiating a decision, gathering information and making plans, or performing a physical task that requires the skills or labour of more than one person, effective working together is essential for success. And while the relative importance of the skills required depends on the situation, the requirements for success are remarkably similar across the spectrum. Success will depend on:

- clarity of goals and acceptance of these among team members
- agreement over ways of working towards these goals
- effective communication between team members
- support and cooperation between team members, rather than competition
- arrangements for monitoring progress and taking corrective action if necessary.

These factors are not, of course, always present. Simply calling a group a 'team' does not guarantee success. 'Team' is an emotionally loaded word, standing for all sorts of positive things. By relabelling groups of people as 'teams' organisations often think that they have solved a problem. If you have already experienced a rocky time in some of the groups you work with in class, you know that the label is not enough. Thought needs to be given to the success factors above, and to ensuring that 'team' members have the understanding and skills needed for this form of working.

## Key factors in team success

Looking at the list above, it is clear that the elements contributing to success can be grouped into three broad classes of factors, as has been done in Figure 2.1 (see later in this chapter). Three sets of skills are important:

- **Managing the task** – clear objectives, monitoring progress towards them and taking corrective action are as important for team working as for managing yourself. The principles are just the same, although applied in a group context.

- **Managing the process** – this is the part that is new. People need to stay committed to the team's goals and motivated to contribute to achieving them. Attention therefore needs to be paid to their support and encouragement. This will be a major topic in this chapter.

- **Communication** – this will be vital for managing both task and process. You have already developed the basic skills of talking and listening (and being assertive where necessary). Their application in a group context is very similar to their use one to one. By practising communication skills in group work, you will become better at communicating in other contexts.

➤ Ch 8

Whatever the type of task a team is addressing, success will depend upon a combination of communication skills (especially talking and listening) and management skills relating to both the task and process. The emphasis will differ depending on the nature of the task, as the following exploration of the different contexts for group working shows.

## Discussion Groups

Because they are a natural extension of the previous chapter, and because almost any group will at times need to have informal discussions about the task, it makes sense to focus first on informal group discussions. You will probably be familiar with these from seminar or study groups.

---

### Activity 2.1

Reflect on a recent group discussion in which you found it satisfactory to take part and another which you have not enjoyed and/or to which you felt you made little contribution. List at least three ways in which the 'good' group differed from the 'bad' group. If thinking of a discussion on your course, try to compare your list with the lists of other people involved in the discussion, If not, sharing lists with others will still be useful, even if you are considering a variety of different discussions.

---

You will probably find that some of your 'bad' experiences have to do with poor task management. Quotes overheard after experiences like this include those in Figure 2.1.

Other 'bad' experiences may have had more to do with poor process management – lack of attention to group needs, perhaps conflict or even aggression between some members. Such meetings produce reactions like those in Figure 2.2.

Informal discussion groups do not necessarily have a 'leader'. All members of the group may be on an equal footing and between them need to ensure that the discussion goes somewhere and that members are involved. But a good chair would have avoided some of the issues reflected in the quotes in Figure 2.1. Informal groups without chairs will only work well if most of the members play their part in contributing to both task needs

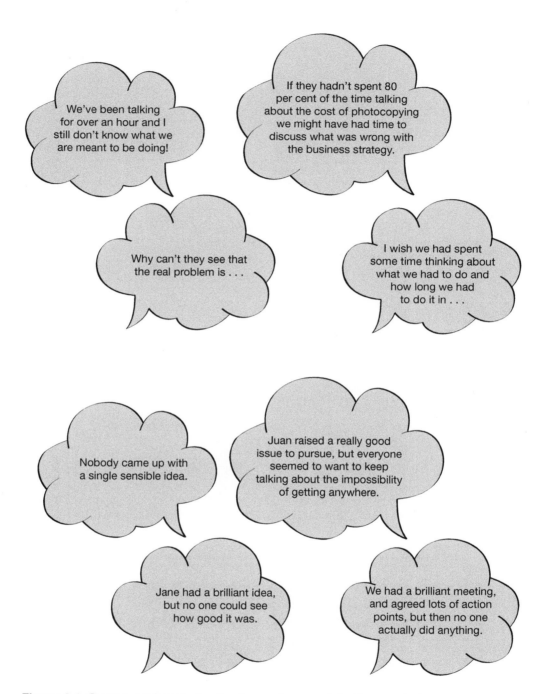

**Figure 2.1** Quotes overheard after 'bad' experiences related to poor task management

and group needs, and avoiding behaviours which get in their way. This means keeping a focus on what the group is trying to do, contributing to this yourself and helping others to make a contribution, valuing other members and their contributions and not letting your own or others' needs unrelated to the task (for attention, dominance or whatever) get

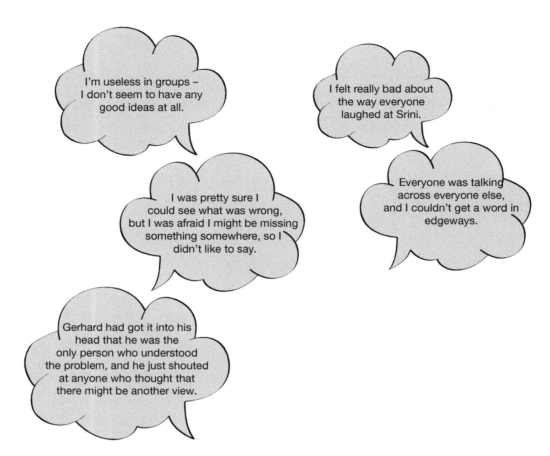

**Figure 2.2** Quotes overheard after 'bad' experiences related to poor process management

in the way of what the group is doing. (Even if there is a chair, and especially if the chair is not particularly skilled, it will help if you behave in this way.)

## Behaviours which help and hinder discussion groups

If you are aware of which behaviours help and which hinder, you will become more aware of your own strengths and weaknesses in this context. The following lists of the most important behaviours in each category may help you reflect on the part you play in group work and to become more effective in future.

## Behaviours serving task needs

- *Clarifying objectives* – unless everyone in the group is clear about what the group is trying to achieve the group cannot be fully effective.
- *Seeking information from group members* – often people are asked to join a group because they know something of particular relevance, or have a particular perspec-

tive. If they are naturally quiet or diffident they may not offer this unless they are specifically asked.

- *Giving relevant information* – this may apply to you, so if you offer any relevant information which you have this will progress the task.

- *Proposing ideas* – these might be ideas about how to address the group task or ideas about possible solutions to a problem under discussion.

- *Building on ideas or proposals contributed by others* – the real advantage in groups is not that members bring lots of ideas but that these ideas can then spark new ones or be developed by others, so that there is a synergy between members' thinking. Acknowledging the person whose idea you are building on is really helpful, as it makes them feel valued rather than inadequate – 'John, that's a really good idea – it would let us do X. But you've got me thinking – if we did Y as well, we could actually achieve this, this and this . . .'

- *Summarising progress so far* – this can be extremely useful in stopping people from covering the same ground over and over, as it helps the group realise what progress has been made. It also helps any note taker.

- *Evaluating progress against objectives* – once progress has been summarised it is easier to see what is left to be done, and plan to achieve it.

- *Time keeping* – most groups usually have a time limit, so it is important to manage the activity to ensure that it is completed within this time.

- *Allocating responsibility for any actions* – all too often a group has wonderful ideas and members go away feeling it was a great meeting, but feel no obligation to actually do anything themselves. Agreed actions are far more likely to be taken if individuals commit, in the meeting, to taking them.

- *Setting up review mechanisms* – if actions will go on for some time after the meeting, some way is needed of reviewing progress and taking corrective action where necessary.

## Behaviours serving group needs

- *Encouraging members to contribute* – this is linked to the task need of eliciting information, but also helps individuals to feel part of the group. (Some members will need more encouragement than others.)

- *Rewarding contributions with praise or agreement* – again, this is helpful in making people feel that they are valued members of the group, thus increasing their commitment to the group's collective activity.

- *Checking understanding* – it is important to be sure that you understand any contribution, but particularly helpful to check that you have understood a point by summarising that understanding in your own words before giving reasons for disagreeing. Many disagreements are rooted in misunderstandings but become heated before this is discovered.

- *Helping to resolve conflicts positively* – in any group, conflicts are inevitable, and by exploring the reasons for conflict a group may uncover crucial information, but this needs to be done in a way that avoids either party feeling rejected.
- *Changing your own position in the light of arguments or information given by others* – many people see hanging on to their original position as a high priority, but this can greatly reduce the ability of a group to make any sort of progress.
- *Helping to control those who talk too much* – there is often someone in a group who just loves to talk. Since this prevents others from contributing, sometimes a way needs to be found of making space for others. Ideally, this needs to be done in a positive way, so that the talker feels appreciated rather than rejected. 'John – I think your point is important, but we really don't have time to go into it in enough depth here, so perhaps some of us could go into it in more depth after the meeting . . .'
- *Praising group progress* towards objectives – if group members feel that they are getting somewhere they will feel motivated to keep working, so 'celebrating' progress in some way can make an important contribution.
- *Dissuading group members from negative behaviours* – again, in a positive way if possible (see below).

## Behaviours interfering with task or group needs

- *Talking too much* – or otherwise focusing attention on your for the sake of it.
- *Reacting emotionally* – while emotions may be an important element in a discussion, and it may be worth saying how you feel about something, contributions driven by anger or other emotions are usually unhelpful.
- *Attacking others' points by ridicule or other unreasoned statement* – attacks (e.g. 'it won't work') tend to be directed at individuals and are different from reasoned disagreement, which is aimed at a point made and which can be extremely valuable.
- *Not listening to others* – this is unhelpful for obvious reasons.
- *Interrupting others* or talking at the same time as them.
- *Introducing a totally different point* in the midst of productive discussion of something else.
- Chatting with others privately during the meeting – a form of not listening.
- *Using humour to excess* – this can distract the group from the task, though a little humour can 'oil the wheels' and contribute to positive handling of conflict.
- *Introducing red herrings* – by this I mean wilful distractions rather than genuinely suggesting something that turns out to be irrelevant.
- *Withdrawing ostentatiously from the group* – for example, by turning away, pushing chair back, crossing arms, determined silence. This can make others in the group feel uncomfortable, and generally reduces effectiveness.

## How do you behave?

The lists above are quite long as they cover much of what helps and hinders group discussion. You will find it difficult at first to keep all the behaviours in mind, but a checklist such as that shown (completed) in Figure 2.3 will help. A blank checklist is available online.

The more aware you are of others' use of these behaviours, the easier it will be to notice – and improve – your own behaviour. A useful first step is to observe discussions without taking part in them. (If you cannot officially act as observer, choose a meeting in which it will not matter if you adopt a low profile and take notes surreptitiously.) Use the checklist as the basis for your observations. At first you may find it easiest to concentrate on one category of behaviour. Two other people might observe the remaining categories. Alternatively, you might observe only one or two people each.

|  | JEFF | SABINE | LING PEI | ASAD | YIANI | CLARK | JO |
|---|---|---|---|---|---|---|---|
| Clarifying objectives |  |  |  |  |  |  | ✓✓✓✓ |
| Giving/seeking info. |  |  |  |  |  | ✓✓✓✓✓ |  |
| Proposing/developing |  |  | ✓✓✓ | ✓✓✓ |  | ✓✓✓✓ |  |
| Summarising | ✓ |  |  |  |  |  | ✓✓✓✓✓ |
| Timekeeping | ✓✓✓ |  |  |  |  |  | ✓ |
| Encouraging/rewarding |  |  |  |  |  |  |  |
| Conflict reduction |  | ✓✓✓✓ |  |  |  |  | ✓✓✓ |
| 'Gatekeeping' |  |  |  |  |  |  | ✓✓✓✓✓ |
| Interrupting/speaking over |  |  | ✓✓✓ ✓✓✓ | ✓✓✓✓✓✓ |  | ✓✓✓✓ |  |
| Attack/defence |  |  | ✓✓ | ✓✓✓ |  |  |  |
| Changing the subject |  |  |  |  | ✓✓ |  |  |
| Excessive humour |  | ✓✓ |  |  |  | ✓✓ |  |
| Withdrawal |  | ✓ |  |  | ✓ |  |  |

**Figure 2.3** Example of a simplified form used in recording behaviours in a group

## Activity 2.2

Use a form such as that provided online to record the sorts of contributions members make to a discussion. Reflect on the extent to which the pattern of ticks which emerges explains the effectiveness or otherwise of the group.

## Activity 2.3

Ask someone else to record *your* contribution to group work and give you feedback on the sorts of behaviours you used most. Reflect together on your effectiveness in the light of this. Such feedback can be a powerful tool in helping you become a more valuable and influential team member. If any of the desirable behaviours seem lacking, practise using them in subsequent meetings. For example, decide that you will try to ensure that even the quietest members are encouraged enough to make a contribution, or make a point of summarising the discussion each time progress seems to have been made so that points are not lost. If you are behaving in a way which interferes with the group, think about why you may be doing this and try to notice (and silently rebuke yourself) each time you do this in future. It should eventually become less frequent. Devise an action plan for becoming more effective.

## Activity 2.4

After a while, perhaps a few months, repeat Activity 2.3 to see whether you have shifted your behaviours in the intended direction. File your comments for future review.

# Formal Meetings

Many managers complain that they spend far too much time in meetings. Formal meetings may seem intimidating until you are used to them. There are rituals to do with approving minutes, making remarks through the chair and identifying 'voting members'. You may feel unwilling to contribute because you feel unsure about the 'rules' or wonder how on earth to take minutes if charged with this task. However, the 'rules' are really only an attempt to avoid some of the things that commonly go wrong in informal discussions. The actual skills involved are much the same, as becomes clear when you understand what the ritual is intended to serve.

## Membership lists

When a meeting is intended to take significant decisions (about costs, policy, progress on an important contract and so on), the informality of a discussion group is not enough.

Cartoon by Neill Cameron, www.neillcomeron.com

It is important that the right people are at the meeting, so a formal membership list will need to be agreed. Otherwise there may be complaints that the decision was improperly taken. Indeed, if key players are not there to contribute their information, bad decisions may be taken.

## Attendance

Since there was a reason for members to be on the list, it is important that they attend. Normally the minutes of the meeting will log those present so that they cannot later disclaim responsibility for decisions. Absentees, who should have given apologies in advance, can also be contacted by anyone who feels the need to 'fill them in' on something which happened. The secretary may also wish to arrange for absentees to send a representative in their place. (This representative would not usually be able to vote and would be minuted as 'in attendance' rather than 'present'.)

## Chair

In an *informal group*, members usually share responsibility for the behaviours necessary to progress the task and manage the process. They are expected to exercise self-discipline and avoid the unhelpful behaviours listed above.

In *formal meetings*, the overall responsibility for all this is vested in the person chairing the meeting. With a skilled chair this can work wonderfully. People are asked to make contributions at relevant points, the discussion is gently 'managed' to ensure that it is kept to the point, progress is summarised at intervals, conflicts are tactfully explored and resolved and, when as much progress has been made as is likely, the point is drawn to a close and the next item on the agenda is taken so that the meeting finishes on time, with all items having been properly covered.

Unfortunately, not all chairs have the skill to achieve this. (They may have been chosen for their seniority rather than their skills.) Provided other group members quietly adopt the necessary behaviours to fill the gap, this does not matter. If they sit back and cheerfully take no responsibility, the meeting can be a disaster.

## Agenda

People need to know in advance what will be discussed so that they can consult with those they represent, gather any necessary information and have thought about the issues involved. An agenda lists the time and place of the meeting and the items to be discussed in the order in which they will be addressed. It should be sent to all members well in advance of the meeting. The chair of the meeting is normally responsible for putting together the agenda and will need to think about how long items are likely to take. Too long an agenda is to be avoided. Items will be given insufficient attention or the meeting may go on beyond the point at which those present are capable of thinking straight. (Most people cannot concentrate fully for more than two hours.) As meetings take some time to warm up, one or two short items at the start of the agenda may be a good idea. But the most important items should follow immediately after this, when people are most alert. Beware the really important item which appears at the very end of a long agenda. This will be one where the chair is hoping to get a decision to go in a particular way and is more likely to achieve this when everyone is exhausted and hungry. It is possible in this case to ask for the item to be taken earlier on the agenda. If you suggest this, giving your reasons, and others present support you, the chair may have to agree.

## Papers

In assembling an agenda it is important to think about how much preparatory information members need beforehand. Small items may not need supporting papers. Their proponents can make a verbal case at the meeting and this will be an adequate basis for discussion. For any complex case, however, where there are reasons for and against a proposal and information which people need to have absorbed before they can discuss it, supporting papers need to be written (the report format discussed earlier is helpful here).

These papers need to be circulated to members sufficiently in advance of the meeting (ideally with the agenda) for them to be able to study their content in detail. If you are asked to write a paper for a meeting, remember that you are trying to make a clear and fair case without giving unnecessary information. Write as succinctly as if you have a word limit. If a paper is too long, it risks not being read properly.

## Preparation

Assuming that the chair and secretary have circulated agenda and papers in good time, you have an obligation to prepare yourself. This means setting aside sufficient time to read papers thoroughly, think about them, discuss them with others who may be involved, gathering all the information you can that might help the meeting, working out what points you would like to make, and how best to make them, given the likely points of view and counter-arguments of others who will be there.

You may not actually make these points, or not in these words, as you will need to respond to the discussion as it develops. Meetings are not best seen as a collection of set speeches. But you will be much more effective if you have worked out what is important for you (and those you represent), and how best to convince others of its importance. This preparation will help you achieve your (task) objectives for the meeting. It will also mean that you appear coherent, focused and well prepared to any senior people there, thus raising your profile (in a good way). Going into a meeting unprepared not only damages your own reputation, but risks wasting the time of everyone present.

## Discussion style

Because the chair is officially responsible for the progress of the meeting, members are normally expected to catch the chair's eye and gain permission to speak. In large meetings this is essential. In smaller ones, provided conduct is reasonably orderly, the chair may let people discuss without this hindrance. (She or he will, intervene only if discussion is becoming disorganised or someone is talking too much, or someone else is contributing nothing on an item on which they would be expected to have useful information to offer.)

The more formal the meeting, the more formal the language that tends to be used in making contributions, but the basics of talking and listening still apply: paying full attention to what others are saying and making sure that you do not undervalue it because of prejudice; 'rewarding' their contributions with agreement; expressing your points clearly; avoiding getting emotional about issues; being sufficiently assertive to make points that have a fair chance of being valid and to make them in a positive enough way that they will be heard and avoiding time wasting of any kind.

## Minutes

Because it is important to know what decisions were reached, and who was involved in reaching them, minutes are usually taken. In addition to listing those present, minutes need to log the basic reasons for a decision, actions agreed and responsibility for progress on these actions. Minutes should be circulated soon after a meeting so that any inaccuracies can be spotted, and the corrected minutes are then approved at the start of the next meeting. As the agreed record of decisions, these minutes are extremely important. There can, in theory, be no ambiguity about what is now agreed policy and it is clear whose responsibility it is to implement it.

The practice, alas, may fall short of this. The person charged with taking the minutes often feels that they need to transcribe every word said, so that the minutes become so long that no one has time to read them. Perhaps because of this, the minutes may be put off as an unimportant or difficult job and appear on the day of the next meeting, by which time no one can really remember what happened and some of those who were supposed to have taken action will have totally forgotten about it. Or the minutes may be circulated late on purpose and record what the chair and secretary wanted to have happened, rather than what really did happen. 'Managing by minutes' can be a very effective tool, if an undemocratic one. Indeed, in an episode of the television comedy *Yes, Minister* it was suggested that the minutes should be written *before* the meeting. If you are taking minutes for the first time, model them on previous minutes. Once you are confident with this, discuss with the chair whether there might be better ways of doing it.

## Action notes

For slightly less formal or more task-oriented meetings, a scaled-down version of minutes may be taken. These will note who was present and log actions agreed and responsibilities for these actions, but no more. Because they are briefer and focus on action, they can be written extremely quickly, even during the meeting, and people can be given a clear statement of their responsibilities the next day.

### Activity 2.5

Review the formal groups to which you belong. (If you don't belong to any, try to join at least one during the next few months so that you can practise these skills.) List them and note against each how effective the formal structure is in progressing the group's objectives. If elements seem to be ritualistic rather than serve their intended purpose, think about ways in which you might be able to contribute to their effectiveness. Draw up a plan for doing this and check your success against this after each meeting you attend.

### Activity 2.6

Find a way of taking at least some responsibility for a meeting. This might be by chairing it (volunteers for this role are often very welcome), acting as secretary or as assistant, joining in agenda-setting discussions and taking some of the responsibility for ensuring that the meeting progresses as desired. Put together an 'exhibit' for your file which describes the purpose of the meeting and the ways in which you contributed to achieving this. An annotated agenda showing which items you suggested and why, any papers you wrote and comments on the interventions you made, together with the minutes and a statement from the chair saying how he or she perceived your contribution, might form a clear demonstration of your ability to function in this context.

### Activity 2.7

Chairing a meeting, at least until you get used to it requires you to think of more things at once than most brains can handle. You will be so involved in task and process that you will have little brain capacity for reflecting on your own performance. If at all possible, the first few times you act as chair ask someone attending the meeting to act as observer for you and to give you feedback afterwards. This can feel very risky but may be encouraging. You may feel that you totally messed things up, but the observer may have noticed a number of things that you did well. If they *do* see weaknesses, surely it

➤

is better to be aware of them and work at improving them. You would not want everyone else to know about them while you remain in blissful ignorance. Such feedback is best given a short while after the meeting, rather than immediately. Chairing is exhausting and frequently traumatic, at least at first, and you are unlikely to be fit for anything, certainly not for constructive feedback, until you have had a recovery period. It can be helpful to write down your own reflections on your performance – what contributed to success and what might, on reflection, have been handled differently – as soon as you feel strong enough and to file these. Comparing your own reactions with feedback from an observer can make future reflection more effective as you will become aware of blind spots, or areas of over- or under-sensitivity.

# Task Groups

Task groups are one of the building blocks of organisations. Teams are formed which contain all the skills needed to progress a specific task. Some task groups have a designated leader. In others, responsibility for the work is shared equally among members. The former is the classic 'supervisor responsible for a group of subordinates' structure. It has the apparent merits of clarity of responsibility and of power. If things go wrong, the supervisor will have to answer to his or her superior. But because the supervisor can, in theory at least, discipline any member of the team not pulling their weight, things should not go wrong in the first place.

There are less apparent, but equally real, drawbacks which parallel issues raised in the discussion of the chairing role above. If 'team' members see all the responsibility as lying with the designated leader they will feel none themselves. Their goal may be to avoid getting into trouble, rather than progressing in the work.

The concept of 'autonomous working groups' (AWGs) was one of the organisational breakthroughs of the 1960s, seen as avoiding many of the problems of assembly lines. AWGs were given collective responsibility for a specified task (in one of the classic experiments Sandberg (2007) describes how small teams working without supervision assembled entire Volvos. With AWGs, supervisors no longer need to coordinate the efforts of individuals, but instead serve as resources available for consultation or are removed altogether. At Volvo all decisions (including the holiday rota) were the responsibility of the group as a whole. These autonomous groups became very committed to the task and produced measurably higher-quality work. Absenteeism was much lower. There were queues of people wanting to work in this fashion.

There were costs, of course. Assembly lines are a very efficient way of operating: tooling up for group assembly was much more expensive; there was more work in progress at any one time; the training of multi-skilled employees was initially costly. But above all, management felt threatened by the autonomy which the workforce had under this arrangement, even though managers had their roles redefined rather than being made redundant. (The original Volvo plant at Kalmar, which pioneered AWGs in the 1970s, and the Uddevalla plant designed around this approach in the early 1990s were both closed by 1995.)

In the harsher 1990s the revolution in information technology meant that neither work groups at the bottom of the organisation nor senior management at the top needed layers of intervening managers to filter information up and down. They could now have direct access to it themselves. Such layers were therefore drastically pruned, or removed altogether, and fairly autonomous work groups came into favour again, variously entitled 'flexible work teams', 'cells' or 'high-performance teams', and have remained a common structure. In professional organisations this has always been a common way of working.

You should have plenty of opportunities to work in task groups while you are a student. Even groups formed to discuss case studies and present conclusions to the class as a whole are task groups as well as discussion groups if some of the work needs to be subdivided between group members. Collective work on an experiment, or on data collection for a topic, offers further possibilities. Project groups of any nature are likely to share many features with semi-autonomous working groups in organisations and offer excellent scope for practising the necessary skills.

Outside university you may find opportunities to develop your team skills through things like raising funds for a good cause, organising a social event or planning an expedition to a remote part of the globe. If you are doing any of these things with other people the general principles underlying success are the same as those for a group discussion. All group members need to understand the group's objectives, communication will be vital both at this and at every subsequent stage, progress needs to be monitored, and so on. Unless a formal leader is chosen, group members will need to find some way of ensuring that these aspects are covered all the time.

Additionally, there will need to be discussion about how to split up the work. What sub-tasks can be progressed independently and how should responsibilities for these be allocated to make best use of the group's resources? If group members can take on tasks which interest them and which they feel play to their strengths the output is likely to be better. This may require a degree of negotiation or even a rearrangement of sub-tasks if some jobs prove much more popular than others. People will need to understand their responsibilities (see comments on action notes in the previous section), will need to use self-management skills to progress their own part of the task (including taking correc-tive action, perhaps in the form of letting people know if there is a problem and seeking help), and will always need to remember to communicate anything which comes up in the course of their work which would be useful for others to know. This is often problematic: as

➤ Ch 8    one's own task assumes great importance it is easy to forget the wider group and its needs.

## Activity 2.8

List the task groups of which you are already a member and use the ideas above as a basis for reviewing their effectiveness. Note whether you are clear about group objec-tives and whether others share your interpretation of these (could you all draw up the same list of what would constitute success and failure?). Similarly, how clear are you about your personal (or subgroup) objectives? Do you know whether or not you are on target? If you know you have done less than you should have, do you know why? Does anyone else know you are behind? Might they be able to help if they did? Do you feel committed to the group and the task? Note down ways in which the group as a whole, and you individually as a member of the group, could be more effective

## Activity 2.9

In the light of the previous activity, try to improve the effectiveness of a group and document the experience as an exhibit. You will need to address the following.

- **Understanding of collective goals** – who set the goals, what constitutes success and what failure, what the constraints are, what the timescales are, how closely group members agree on the goals. (Note that it is important to explore reasons for disagreement: the minority view might be the right one.)

- **Allocation of responsibility for sub-tasks** – what was done to maximise the extent to which these fit people's strengths and preferences, how the group checked that people understood and agreed to their tasks, whether people were clear on interim goals and the timing for these, whether there are arrangements for checking progress and sharing information on an ongoing basis.

- **Support and encouragement** – are there ways of ensuring that people can seek help from others if things go wrong and can 'reward' each other for interim successes? Particularly for long-term projects, such motivational aspects are extremely important.

Your exhibit might include notes of discussions, highlighting your contributions, quotes from others (including your tutor) on the effectiveness of your own efforts, any plans you drew up for group or individual work with progress noted on them, notes of any corrective action or adaptation of plans which was necessary and reasons for this, and of course, if appropriate, the finished product or tutor comments on this.

# Virtual Teams

In global organisations teams are often widely dispersed geographically and need to 'meet' electronically as to meet face to face would be far too expensive and take too much time and energy. Students on distance learning programmes may be similarly dispersed, and teaching and discussions may be mainly or completely online.

## Virtual meetings

Online 'meetings' rely on the same group skills as any other meeting, but some aspects may require more care because of the nature of the medium. You need to understand not only the technical aspects of doing whatever your chosen system allows, but also the ways in which you can improve effectiveness by modifying aspects of your behaviour.

Systems for virtual working range from simple text-based online chat rooms and audio conferences through to simulations of meeting rooms or classrooms allowing most of the features of the face to face situation. There are therefore several dimensions to consider:

- Is the conference synchronous or asynchronous?
- Is the medium text, audio and/or vision?
- Does the system include features to help with managing process?
- What limitations does the system have?

The effectiveness of any virtual 'meeting' will depend on the general task and process skills of participants, the suitability of the channel and system to the task of the meeting, and the degree to which participants have the skills needed to exploit the strengths of the system they are using and minimise its disadvantages. Table 2.1 shows some of the systems you are likely to encounter, and factors to consider when using them. You will almost certainly have experience with using some of these, so can check your own experience against the table.

All the systems listed have the advantage of not needing travel, with its attendant costs, so this is not mentioned on the table. Similarly all real-time systems require people to be free at the same time, which may present diary problems and be difficult in some time zones. In contrast, asynchronous systems allow people to contribute at times that are convenient to them (helpful for a time that spans different time zones). Asynchronous systems also mean you can take time to consider all previous contributions in relation to your own thoughts before responding. The corresponding cost is that asynchronous work needs a period of time, and unless this is strictly limited, the discussion may lose momentum. Asynchronous work is not usually suited to anything needing an urgent response. Again these common features are not shown on the table, but need to be remembered if you are comparing systems.

The extent to which you meet 'virtually' with fellow students will depend on how dispersed you are and the extent to which you are involved in collaborative work. If you live with/are regularly in classes with/have coffee and lunch with others on your course you may not need to do more than occasionally text them. But if this is not the case, consider whether you might find up to four others interested in forming a virtual study group to discuss course ideas in the light of your disparate experiences (aim for as diverse a group as possible) and to offer each other help when someone finds something difficult to understand, but to others it is not at all difficult.

If your university has its own system to allow such interactions, use it. If not, experiment with shared email lists, blogs, Skype, etc. to find what works best for you. The support such a group gives can improve everyone's grade markedly, as well as making study much more fun.

The following guidelines for asynchronous conferencing may be helpful if you choose a text-based asynchronous system. Note, in particular, the need to pay attention to making people feel valued members of the group when you lack the body language (and the beer or coffee) that make people feel welcome and appreciated.

**Table 2.1** Strengths and weaknesses of some commonly used virtual meeting systems.

| System and Features | Strengths | Potential Limitations |
|---|---|---|
| 1. Text-based asynchronous forum (such as university conferencing system, chat room, blog or Facebook group). | Cheap. Can allow discussion to be organised into separate 'threads' for different topics. May suit those with stronger written than spoken English. History of contributions is clear and can be stored. Messages can have documents or other files attached, and can include links to relevant websites. | Text is relatively impoverished as a communication channel – it carries the same risks of misunderstanding etc. as email, so a facilitator/ moderator who can delete unhelpful posts, and more things to better threads, and summarise at intervals is a good idea. (A blog will normally be 'owned' by someone with this role.) |
| 2. Audio conferences via phone system or internet. | Relatively cheap. Real time so can conclude meeting quickly, and participants can 'spark off' each other. Conveys 'paralinguistics' so richer than mere words. | People need to be free at same time. May be hard to know who is speaking. System may cut out all save loudest speaker if people talk at once. |
| 3. Simple video conferences, e.g. via Skype, or Microsoft's Lync. | Can be very cheap or free May allow screen sharing. Allows body language as well as tone of voice and words. | Some systems can be expensive. Low grade video can be a distraction rather than a help. |
| 4. Virtual classrooms – may include a video component but this makes high bandwidth demands. | Designed to replicate key features of a classroom, allowing the tutor to put up slides, write on whiteboard, set instant tests to check understanding, and divide students into breakout rooms for small group work. Students can put up a hand to indicate they want to talk (or in a small group just say something), can move work on a whiteboard back into main forum for plenary, and 'vote' to show views or understanding. Sessions can be recorded for absentees or revision. | The more complex the system, the more the tutor may need to focus on system aspects. A helper can free the tutor to concentrate on the task and process. Students may need time to become comfortable with the mechanics of the system. |
| 5. Virtual meeting systems designed to make people in different locations feel as if they are all in the same room. | Can simulate a shared location so effectively that people really feel as if they are in the same room, and can hold a meeting as easily as if they were genuinely face to face. | Very expensive! May need technical back-up. Usually linked to specific locations, e.g. head offices on different continents. |

## TECHSkills 2.1 Guidelines for asynchronous conferencing

- Meet face to face if at all possible, in order to get to know group members and to start to build trust.
- If you cannot meet, allow some 'social' time in the conference for people to feel comfortable together.
- At the same time, post résumés so that people can check who you are if they forget.
- Include a photo if you can.
- Obtain members' explicit agreement on what is needed to achieve the group task, and how it will be most effective to operate (times of logging on, deadlines for contributions and so on).
- Break tasks down into constituent parts with deadlines, and be absolutely clear who is responsible for doing what.
- Ensure that someone accepts responsibility for reminding people of incipient deadlines.
- Be particularly careful to give feedback in a constructive and supportive way – and pay attention to making people feel their contributions are valued.
- Summarise discussion at regular intervals and check on progress.

It can help to set aside some short periods when people will all try to log on at once and respond quickly to each other – this can be a useful antidote to the more disconnected and 'measured' asynchronous communication.

## Working collaboratively on a shared document

You may find virtual meetings extremely useful as a study group, or when working on a group project. They can help you agree on how to progress the project, allocate tasks and share reports on progress. Once the work is done, you may need to produce a shared report. You can do this via email, sharing and commenting on drafts, or by attaching drafts in an online text-based forum, with the message explaining why a draft is as it is, what needs still to be done, and/or explaining edits to a previous draft.

## TECHSkills 2.2 Working with google docs

You will probably have seen, or worked on, a Google file in your study. These correspond broadly to the standard applications from the Microsoft Office package. Google Sheets works like Excel, Google Docs like Word and Google Slides like PowerPoint. Their key advantages are:

➤

- Access any time, any place – it doesn't matter if you're on campus or at home, or at a friend's house – you can always access your documents. This comes in particularly handy when you need to deliver a presentation in class, or print something – no need to remember to save a copy on a USB stick, an internet connection is all you need to bring a document up on any screen.

- Automatic saving of changes – so you don't have to worry about losing your work.

- Multiple collaborators/viewers – you can work on the same document with a number of people, including editing it at the same time. This great feature allows you to collaborate in real time, which is key for time-sensitive projects. You can also give 'view only' or 'comment only' access to others, e.g. your lecturer or even potential employers, without worrying that they edit your version.

- You can upload standard files (like .doc) into Google Docs and create an editable version (likewise for the other apps) – and you can download a version that can be opened in standard programmes. Note, however, that you should always check such files for formatting – some features are specific to the applications the files originated in, hence you may need to update fonts, effects or sizing to suit your needs.

- Best of all – so far, access to Google apps is free – so you can be sure that anyone working on those with you is operating within copyright.

(written by Natalia Jaszczuk)

An alternative approach is to set up a wiki. In a forum or blog messages cannot usually be edited (apart from being deleted by the moderator). A wiki uses software that makes it very easy for collaborative working, as all participants can add to, or amend a document that has been posted. It also allows a series of pages which have been so authored to be linked. This allows for rapid production of a document by a group – 'Wiki' comes from the Hawaiian word for fast. Your university will probably provide you with wiki facilities.

A wiki system means people can write and/or change parts of the document until everyone is happy. The best known user of such software is Wikipedia. The collaborative authorship is what makes academics wary of using Wikipedia as a main source. But its collaborative nature can give it a richness that is valuable when you are starting to explore a topic, provided you use it critically, and as a signpost to more reliable sources.

## Challenges of Online Collaboration

Despite the availability of a wide range of software for online collaboration, some aspects still present particular challenges. It may be harder for members to be clear on, and committed to, the team objectives, yet this is as important as with face-to-face teams, as is the need to continue to feel involved. You cannot make someone feel better with a smile or tone of voice if using a text-based system.

If you are conferencing in real time while sharing screens, you will need to work hard at ensuring that 'airtime' is shared fairly. Gatekeeping is essential, and even if you do not have a formal chair you will almost certainly need to designate someone to manage the turn-taking element. In an asynchronous conference this is less of a problem, but it is easy for people to feel 'distanced' and withdraw, so particular attention needs to be paid to process and making people feel involved.

When working remotely the early stages of teambuilding may need particular attention. Clarifying objectives, deciding on the roles members will play and agreeing ways of working may take more effort as it is less easy to thrash out complex issues and explore areas of disagreement remotely. Nor is it easy to develop the sense of membership and mutual support essential for effective team working.

It helps if virtual teams can go through these early and crucial stages face to face. Once members feel they 'know' each other it is much easier to sustain subsequent progress while working remotely. If this is not possible, care needs to be paid to achieving this online. Familiarity with remote working also makes things easier. If you get the chance to work in this way during your course you should use the opportunity to develop your remote team-working skills as they may increase your employability.

# Developing Effective Groups

Some of the classic research on groups is still helpful if you are trying to put together an effective team, regardless of the nature of the task. In case you have not covered this research in a social psychology course, some commonly used frameworks are outlined here. These relate to selection of group members, to the stages which groups go through when they first form and to two main hazards of an established group: groupthink and scapegoating. If you are aware of these aspects of group working, it will increase your chances of being a member of an effective group.

## Assembling an effective group

You may well have found that your 'bad' group experiences listed at the start of the chapter arose at least partly because the group seemed 'wrong' in some way. It may have been too big or too small to do the task effectively. Some key skills or perspectives may have been lacking. Perhaps the group got on *too* well and developed its own view of the world which was out of kilter with that of other groups working on a wider task. Or perhaps the group got off to a bad start and people dropped out because it wasn't working. You need to understand some of the features common to groups in order to comprehend and avoid such hazards.

## Group size

The optimum size of group will depend on the task. If a large number of perspectives or skills need to be included, or a great deal of work is needed within a short timescale, then obviously a large group will be needed. But the larger the discussion group, the less the scope for individual contributions, and the larger the task group, the greater the task of coordination. Larger groups can also present logistical problems as members find it difficult to identify times when they are all free. As a general rule of thumb, if you can do the job with between four and eight people, then stick with a group of this size.

## Expertise

Linked to the point above is the need to ensure that the group includes the necessary range of expertise. If you are choosing a group to work with on a project, this can be an important point. Again, you may feel most comfortable with like-minded people, but the task may be better done if you deliberately choose to work with a more varied group, with a wider range of backgrounds and knowledge.

## Motivation

In forming groups, it is important to maximise the extent to which people *want* to do the task. At work they may not have much choice, but even then there will be issues that seem of burning importance to some and insignificant to others. Where possible, the more commitment you have to a task at the outset, the better the group is likely to perform. If you are choosing a group to work with on an assessed project, it is important to try to find others who have similar goals to your own. If you want to get top marks, you will be very unhappy in a group where no one else cares about doing more than scraping a pass. If you want merely to pass, you may feel out of place in a group of people aiming for a first.

## Individual behavioural differences

When you looked at the behaviours that were shown in a group and who was using those behaviours, you may well have found some quite clear patterns. Some people often behaved in certain ways and seldom, if ever, in others. You might, for example, be very good at proposing ideas, but never get involved with making sure that they are implemented. Someone else might be quite the reverse, or do these activities some-times but spend much more time on, say, clarifying objectives and checking progress. Although if you are aware of the behaviours needed you can make a conscious effort to fill any gaps, you are likely to have natural preferences and to be able to behave in these ways without effort.

Noting this variation, Belbin (1981) suggested that, for a group to be fully successful, a number of roles were needed. He was working with groups doing real tasks in organi-sations, so although there are clear links with the behaviours seen in group discussions, you will also notice some differences. He originally suggested that eight roles could be identified, as Box 2.1 shows. Later he added a ninth role, that of *specialist*.

## Box 2.1 Belbin's team roles

- Chair, who acts as coordinator, working primarily through others. The role calls for discipline and balance.
- Plant, who comes up with original ideas, is imaginative and usually very intelligent, but can be careless of detail and resent criticism.
- Shaper, who stimulates others to act.
- Monitor–evaluator, who assesses ideas or proposals.
- Resource investigator, who brings in resources and ideas from outside. While usually extroverted and relaxed, this person is not usually original. Nor is she or he a driver, relying on the team to take up and develop his or her contributions.
- Team worker, who works on process, holding the team together.
- Company worker, who is strong on practical organisation, administration and turning ideas into manageable tasks.
- Completer–finisher, who does the essential (if unpopular) work of checking details and chasing when deadlines approach.

It is fairly clear that for most tasks to be progressed all these roles will be needed. You will probably be able to think of people who seem to be particularly good at some and less good at others. You may even have a clear idea of your own tendencies. (If not, Belbin includes a questionnaire that, by asking you about your approaches to and feelings about certain situations, enables you to identify your perceived preferred roles. Your tutor may have access to the questionnaire, or you can obtain it from the Belbin website, although you need to pay to get it scored. Other free team role tests are available online, some using more recent frameworks of roles.

If you have the luxury of choosing members of a group according to their preferred Belbin (or other) team roles, then there is considerable evidence to suggest that it is worth doing this. But the fact that you cannot is no excuse for poor performance. Regardless of preferred behaviours, the roles are necessary and the group will have to find ways of ensuring that there is attention to process and that details *are* checked, even if this means, say, that one or two people who do not score highly on 'finisher' or 'team worker' have to make a conscious effort to take these responsibilities.

## Myers–Briggs typing

Belbin's is but one of a large number of approaches to classifying people. One typology which is widely used by organisations for selection and/or team formation is the Myers–Briggs Type Indicator (MBTI). This is based on thinking by Jung, a contemporary of Freud, and uses a fairly complex questionnaire. Your tutor may be able to administer this so that you can locate yourself on the four dimensions shown in Box 2.2, and thus identify your 'type'. Again, a variety of online testing options are available if you want to pursue this, or you can be tested by a qualified Myers–Briggs tester.

## Box 2.2  Myers–Briggs dimensions

- **E or I:** Extravert vs Introvert – this assesses whether you are externally or internally driven. In the first case, as an 'E' you will react to things and people, acting before you think. In the second, as an 'I' you will be more internally focused, more reflective.

- **S or N:** Sensing vs iNtuition – this looks at what you pay attention to. If you are an 'S' this will be your normal five senses, you will focus on the 'real', take a pragmatic approach. If an 'N' you will use your 'sixth' sense, and be more future-oriented, more of a theorist.

- **T or F:** Thinking vs Feeling – this reflects the way you tend to decide or judge. If at the 'T' end, you will reason from principles, using a logical system. If an 'F' you will use heart rather than head, subjectively emphasising values, preferring compassion to justice.

- **J or P:** Judgement vs Perception – this looks at the way you live and work. A 'J' will adopt the planned approach, organised, controlled and with clear goals. A 'P' will be more spontaneous, preferring to 'go with the flow'.

Since the dimensions are independent, this gives sixteen different types, each of which has distinct characteristics. You will hear people proudly declaiming their 'MBTI type'. Many organisations have found this information useful in helping people to understand why they are finding it difficult to work together. For example, if you are an ISTJ person, you might find an ENFP person to be hopelessly disorganised, whereas they might find you hopelessly unimaginative and unadventurous. MBTI types can also be used to help assemble a suitable team for a particular purpose – you would not want all Js on a project requiring high creativity – though you might need one on the team to increase the chances of an output.

## Activity 2.10

If you have not been 'typed', estimate where you might lie on each dimension. Now think of two people with whom you find it difficult to work in a group. Where do you think they might lie? Can you attribute some of this difficulty to their being different 'types' from you? If so, try to think about the strengths their type might contribute and see whether it helps you to work together more effectively in future.

If you have not done the questionnaire, or if you would like to gain further information, it is possible to find many questionnaires online that will give you an indication (of varying reliability) of your characteristics and their impact on team behaviour. You might like to explore the possibilities and compare your results on one or more of these with the results of other group members.

List the task groups of which you are already a member and use the ideas above as a basis for reviewing their effectiveness.

## Group life cycles

Often when groups first work together they are far from effective. Sometimes (perhaps if there are no team workers and lots of plants) arguments can become very heated and destructive. Some members may withdraw from the group altogether, either physically if membership is voluntary or mentally if they have to be there but hate every minute of it. There may be disagreements about objectives and about how the group is to work, two or three people all wanting to be 'in charge' of the group, some people behaving in ways that others find unacceptable. Tuckman (1965) found that groups commonly go through a sequence of stages in becoming effective. Knowing that this is normal may make the stages easier to bear and enable you to find ways of minimising any negative effects.

The stages nicely rhyme (this may in part account for the continued use of this framework):

- **Forming** – this is when individuals are trying to establish their identity within the group and find out what the 'rules' are. Behaviour is often tentative at this stage and extreme politeness may prevail, with no one saying what they really mean. A leadership pattern may start to emerge.

- **Storming** – the politeness vanishes and all positions established earlier are challenged. Personal agendas emerge and there may be fierce status battles. This can be an uncomfortable time in a group: sometimes the group may disintegrate totally. But if the conflict is constructive it may generate greater cohesion, a realistic commitment to objectives and trust between members.

- **Norming** – out of the storm, more enduring norms emerge for how the group will operate, and what is acceptable behaviour within the group is established.

- **Performing** – provided that the necessary roles are being filled, the group can now really start to perform well.

Some people suggest that it is important to recognise a fifth stage. For groups that have worked closely together there can be unhappiness, even distress, when the group stops working together. Indeed, some groups keep going long after they have achieved their original goals. It is therefore helpful to talk about a stage of:

- **Adjourning** – here the process of group dissolution needs to be handled with care so that members can move on to other things.

# Managing Diversity and Conflict

A major advantage of teams is that they can draw on a range of expertise and different sets of assumptions and perspectives. But to exploit this advantage you need to be prepared to work constructively with people whose world view is very different from yours. This diversity can stem from 'type', but also from cultural and other differences. In diverse groups, conflicts will sometimes arise, and you need also to have the skills to manage these.

Workforces (and students) are increasingly diverse. Many organisations now operate around the globe. Many workforces even within a single location draw upon an ethnically diverse workforce. You are likely to work with people from a wide range of backgrounds during your career. Furthermore, different professions have different 'cultures' too – different values and different ways of working. Yet many work teams are interdisciplinary, as are most customer groups. An ability to work effectively in diverse groups is a crucial management skill.

Most people are fairly tribal, and easily adopt an 'us' and 'them' position: 'We are OK, they are not.' This is the comfortable view as it preserves familiar ways of thinking and doing. It is probably barely conscious. I was once assessing teaching quality in the Midlands and commented afterwards that it seemed odd to see students working in such unmixed subgroups. The four West Indian boys worked together. The three West Indian girls, the five Asians and the three slightly older white women formed the other three groups. The lecturer seemed surprised I'd mentioned it. 'But they always do that,' she said.

Yet this micro-segregation was a hugely wasted learning opportunity. Each of these different groups was bringing different viewpoints, assumptions, values and experiences to the task. But because these were not being exchanged and debated, there was no learning about how others see the world. None of the students was finding out what was important to other people, or realising how their own perspectives might be limited. Nor were they learning how to manage the inevitable differences of opinion. Given concerns about global warming, it is a great pity not to exploit the opportunity to understand other people's ways of thinking without impacting upon your carbon footprint.

Working in mixed groups takes more effort. It becomes even more vital to check understanding at every stage than it is with a homogeneous group. Words may mean slightly different things within different cultures. Some cultures are less assertive than others: their 'agreement' may be mere politeness. Some cultures express themselves very directly, in ways that may seem almost offensive to others but are just the 'normal' way of saying things to those concerned. Some cultures treat deadlines differently from others.

If you get the opportunity to work in groups from a range of backgrounds, seize it. The potential for learning about others, and about yourself, is great. But to realise this potential you will probably need to make 'understanding each other's viewpoints and backgrounds' an explicit team objective, and to check progress on this regularly. You will also need to pay particular attention to setting 'group rules' – agreed ways of operating. These may need to include procedures for ensuring that less assertive members contribute at regular intervals, and regular checks on how people are *feeling* about how other members respond to their contributions. (Many of the indications of potential for learning will be at the implicit 'feeling' level.) You will also need to accept and examine explicit conflict.

When conflict *does* arise you need to handle it as a phenomenon to be explored rather than as a personal threat. Be assertive, not aggressive. In particular, aim to explore the situation rather than judge right and wrong. What exactly is the *nature* of the disagreement? Are people perceiving *facts* differently, disagreeing about *ways of working*, operating with conflicting *values* or bringing different sets of *assumptions* to the situation? If the latter, are these assumptions based on different experiences, perhaps in different contexts? By exploring questions such as these you may as a team come to a much more comprehensive understanding of the task and its context.

It may also be useful to explore why people feel so strongly about a point on which they disagree. This is a potential minefield, so you need to tread carefully. Think honestly about your own feelings first. Do you feel threatened? Undervalued? Are cherished values being called into question? Do you carry 'baggage' in the form of ingrained negative attitudes about certain groups of people? Where possible, check your feelings against the facts. For example, 'You are always saying my contributions are rubbish,' might not match the perception of others in the group. Could you have an observer sit outside a discussion and check how your contributions are actually received?

By exploring such issues for yourself you may come to a much clearer understanding of your own attitudes. By exploring the issues – carefully – with others, you may come to see both how they perceive you, and the strengths and weaknesses of their, and your own, ways of thinking.

Feelings are dangerous territory. But an ability to appreciate how others are feeling, and how they are *likely* to feel if you say or do something, is an important management skill, and a key component in 'emotional intelligence', described shortly. You can go a long way towards increasing your interpersonal sensitivity by treating conflict within groups as a learning experience. Use your talking listening and assertiveness skills, focus on the behaviour not the person, refuse to 'give up' until an issue is dealt with, and accept that your view may not always be the only, or even the best one. Check your progress at regular intervals as a group, and try to capture what the various members feel they have learned.

➤ **Ch 8**

## Developing Your Leadership Skills

A favourite interview question is 'Describe a time when you showed leadership.' While many organisations use 'management' and 'leadership' to mean the same thing, it can be helpful to think of management as exercising authority (given by the organisation), and leadership as exercising influence which does not derive from position, formal power and/or authority.

As part of a team carrying out a project, or working in a group on a case study, you are unlikely to have a formally designated leader. If you use the opportunity to exercise your (non-authority derived) influence, you will be demonstrating your leadership skills. Developing confidence in taking the lead on such occasions, and knowing how to increase the chances that others will want to follow your lead, will help you show leadership in work and other contexts.

A vast amount has been written on leadership (check out how many items Amazon. com currently lists on 'leadership'), but there is still a lack of agreement over a definition of leadership, and how it differs – if it does – from management. The distinction in terms of authority versus other influence is now fairly common in the academic literature. This sees management as exercising influence from position, aimed at achieving conformity and control. Leadership, in contrast, is seen as influencing by other means and has to do with inspiring people to change.

The emphasis on 'leadership skills' for people in positions of authority is therefore interesting. If it is more than mere fashion, it suggests a growing awareness of the importance of internal motivation rather than 'sticks and carrots' – a form of motivation consistent with a team-based organisational structure.

So what skills does leadership demand? Goleman (1998) claims that his research 'clearly shows that emotional intelligence (EI) is the *sine qua non* of leadership'. (Note that he is clearly taking 'leaders' to mean senior managers, here.) He identifies five components of EI at work:

- **Self-awareness** – the ability to recognise your own emotions and drives and their impact on others, to be honest with oneself and others.

- **Self-regulation** – the ability to control impulses and moods, to suspend judgement, to think before acting.

- **Self-motivation** – a passion for the work itself, and energy and enthusiasm to pursue goals.

- **Empathy** – the ability to treat people according to their emotional reactions (rather than your own).

- **Social skills** – proficiency in managing relationships and building networks.

➤ **Ch 3**

If you are working through the activities in this book you should be developing most of these components. Reflective learning, as outlined in Chapter 3, should be increasing your self-awareness, and if you are including reflection on feelings, will also impact upon self-regulation. Your work on planning and on motivation will help with self-motivation. So, too, will ongoing emphasis on the need for clarity of objectives. This chapter and the previous one, together with the feedback you manage to gather on your own impact, will help with developing social skills.

If you have the emotional sensitivity Goleman describes, you will be well on the way to being able to influence people by making them *want* to follow your lead. I would argue that understanding their motivation is also important for this, and being able to make them feel good about the group task. (The process-oriented group behaviours are a big help here, while being able to listen, both attentively and actively, will help greatly in one-to-one situations.)

➤ **Ch 8**

A number of writers on leadership emphasise 'authenticity' as a key component. This is a combination of the self-awareness that Goleman lists, and the willingness to be honest with other group members about your own feelings, possible inadequacies and mistakes. If you are working in a group, this kind of honesty can help to build trust with other group members. If you are all honest about your shortcomings and your worries about being able to do a task well enough or to meet deadlines, the group will be much better placed to exercise control in the sense of planning to cope with the problem so that objectives are met despite any deviation from the original plan.

Other dimensions to leadership concern the task and the environment. As a student, using the task behaviours listed earlier will help you to exercise an influence on a group. At work it will help to be the one who can see what is needed to meet changes in the wider organisation, or its competitive or wider environment. Part 4 of this book addresses many of the relevant conceptual skills, though you will be developing these throughout your degree course.

## Activity 2.11

Consider the extent to which you currently influence a team of which you are a member. What are your 'leadership strengths'? List those factors which you think are helping you to exercise leadership – perhaps you are good at making others feel part of the team and wanting to contribute to the task, or good at organising meetings. Make an action plan to become even more effective through these strengths. Look at any possible reasons for your influence being less than it might be. (Feedback from fellow team members can be really useful here.) Make an action plan to develop your skills in these areas too.

## Activity 2.12

Look for an area where you can demonstrate leadership. Ideally, this should be something which you already feel passionate about, whether a hobby or a charity. Aim during your degree to have devised a project within this area, got together a group to work on it, and acted as explicit leader. Log the experience in your learning journal and reflect on it as a basis for further learning. Write up a version of it that could form the basis of answers to 'give an example of when you have exercised leadership' on an application form or in an interview.

# Potential Hazards of Team Work

Much of this chapter has looked at how to make teams effective. Can a team be *too* cohesive? If the group *process* is going well, and teams become really close, then there are three related things that can go wrong with the *task*. All are variants of the hazard hinted at earlier: the team becomes the main focus, and the wider task vanishes from awareness.

## Dominance of sub-objectives

If sub-objectives predominate, the team may end up in competition with other teams working towards the same wider objective. If the team becomes too committed to its own task and to 'winning' in some way (for example, getting the highest production output), it may forget that it is part of a wider endeavour, and competition (rather than necessary collaboration) may get in the way of achieving the overall objective.

## Groupthink

Where 'groupthink' exists the group develops such a good feeling about itself, with members reinforcing each other's good opinion, that all indications that anything is wrong are disregarded. Any member brave enough to suggest that there is a problem will be made to feel a traitor to the group. This phenomenon is common in organisations. You will often find a board of a company refusing to believe that the signs of major problems are more than temporary blips, even though it is blindingly obvious to everyone outside this group that there is a significant disaster looming. You may find the same thing in project groups, where members get on very well together and are sure that they are doing brilliantly despite evidence to the contrary. If they know what 'groupthink' is, you may be able to make progress by asking if they think it is happening. But the tendency to deny it is a strong one.

## Scapegoating

If things do go wrong, and this is finally so obvious that the group has to accept it, its members may still try to preserve their positive feelings about the group by finding one individual to accept all the blame. A group that realises that its presentation on a case study was the worst in the class may blame something outside the group – the tutor for giving unclear instructions, or a task that was harder than that given to other groups, or a single member of the group (perhaps the one who was trying to alert them to problems earlier).

There are two negative consequences of scapegoating. First, the scapegoat, if she or he is a group member, may be unhappy and lose self-confidence. Second, the group will not learn what went wrong if it does not accept responsibility for there having been a problem. This is common in work situations. A single person will be sacked when a problem arises. Yet often it is the system that is at fault and many people in that position would have behaved in the same way. Indeed, they will go on to behave in that way in future if the real cause of problems is not investigated.

## Guidelines for effective team working

- Select members with appropriate skills, knowledge, and, if possible, a mix of preferred team roles and types.
- If working remotely, try to have an early face-to-face meeting.
- Ensure that all members understand and accept the objectives.
- Pay attention to both task and process.

- Accept that feelings may run high during early storming, and when working in a mixed group.
- Explore the reasons for disagreements and conflict.
- Value all contributions.
- Review both task progress and group process at regular intervals.
- Reward success.

## SUMMARY

This chapter has argued the following:

- Team-working skills are essential in employment, aid learning, and can be developed in many ways while you are a student.

- All teams need to manage both task and process, and good communication is essential.

- To work effectively in a team, you need to apply your personal management and communication skills in a group context and understand the requirements for effective teams.

- To be effective in a formal group, you need to understand the role of agendas, minutes and a formal chair. This understanding is also relevant to informal groups.

- In establishing a group, group members should be chosen to cover the necessary range of expertise and of roles. Sometimes it will be necessary to agree ways of dealing with missing expertise or handling non-preferred roles.

- A new group can feel uncomfortable, but later performance will actually benefit from early conflict, provided that this is firmly faced and prevented from being damaging.

- Virtual teams are increasingly common in global organisations. Group process may need particular attention when meeting virtually.

- A 'mixed' group can produce better task outcomes and help you increase your interpersonal sensitivity.

- It can sometimes be helpful to designate a group leader, or to allocate responsibility for different aspects of leadership to team members.

- Leadership skills are increasingly valued by employers, and team working gives you an opportunity to develop your skills.

- Key tasks for leaders include identifying requirements, task management and process management, particularly making individuals feel valued and motivated. Relevant skills include 'emotional intelligence' and conceptual skills for problem identification and clarification.

- Groups are at risk of becoming too cohesive and inward looking losing track of the wider goal, 'scapegoating' and/or showing 'groupthink' when things go wrong. Team working is a rich and varied area of activity, with many dimensions. You will need to observe others and yourself in groups and ask others to observe you and give feedback if you are to develop your skills.

## Further information

Belbin, R.M. (2010) *Team Roles at Work, 2nd edn*, Routledge.

Harvard Business Review (2014) *Running Meetings*, HBR Press.

Maginn, M. (2004) *Making Teams Work*, McGraw-Hill.

West, M.A. (2012) *Effective Teamwork*, Blackwell.

# 3
# LEARNING, REFLECTIVE PRACTICE AND PROFESSIONAL DEVELOPMENT

## Learning outcomes

By the end of this chapter you should:

- have a better idea of what 'learning' means

- appreciate the difference between knowledge, concepts, skills and competence

- understand what is meant by learning style and recognise your own preferred style

- have started to develop less preferred styles

- be starting to develop your reflective learning skills, both individually and collaboratively

- understand the role of feedback in the development of both practical and conceptual skills

- have explored the learning opportunities offered by your degree programme, identified any gaps and be starting to plan to fill these

- be developing a systematic approach to evidencing skills relevant to employment.

# Introction

Good grades – and a good career – come from knowing what and how to learn. In today's rapidly changing business world, employers are often looking for evidence of the ability to learn fast. This ability will contribute to success in interviews and rapid progress thereafter. Membership of a professional institution will depend on the ability to demonstrate ongoing professional development. This chapter will help you to understand the learning process, recognise your own preferred learning style and develop your learning skills, particularly your ability to use reflection as a means of learning. It will help you to start a learning diary as an aid to reflection, and to organise a portfolio of evidence of learning, particularly from experience. A better understanding of the learning process, and of the role of reflection within this will help you gain better grades and maximise the learning potential of any situation you meet at work.

We all learn from the moment we are born, but are often not aware of the process. As you work through this chapter you will become more aware of how you learn, and can start to apply your developing self-management skills to improve your learning both on your course and outside it. Managers or leaders who know how they learn, and who go on learning, are far more effective than those who lack this awareness.

## Learning Theory

Children are voracious learners, eager to master walking and talking and countless other skills, including how to influence people, and get their own way. Outside of school, children are seldom aware that they are learning, and indeed you still may not have thought much about what helps and hinders your own learning. Indeed, what exactly *is* learning?

### Activity 3.1

Write a brief definition of learning as you understand it. Discuss this with some other people if possible. Unless you have all just done a course on 'learning', which included an approved definition, you may be surprised at the range of possible ways of understanding the term.

_____

_____

_____

Traditionally, learning was seen as acquiring knowledge. There are still countries where 'education', even at university level, consists of giving students information and then testing that they can repeat it. The underlying metaphor is of 'jug and mug', with the 'knowledge' being poured from the jug (lecturer) to the mug (you). Yet, in many situations academic knowledge is not enough. You may *know* that to ride a bicycle you sit on the saddle and use your feet to turn the pedals and your hands to steer via the handlebars. But this knowledge would not stop you falling off the first time you tried to ride. Being able to *do* things is also important. Beyond both, there is the ability to *understand* and interpret situations and respond effectively, even if the situation is different from any you have yet encountered.

It is this learning of *conceptual* skills that is most exciting. And for this, the passive mug metaphor is singularly inappropriate. Learning conceptual skills is necessarily an *active* and continuous process, not a one-off operation performed on a passive recipient. Some years ago, Krishnamurti expressed this convincingly when arguing for a form of psychological learning which goes beyond the accumulation of knowledge or the acquisition of skills. For example, he says:

Learning is one thing and acquiring knowledge is another. Learning is a continuous process, not a process of addition. Most of us gather knowledge as memory, as idea, store it up as experience ... we act from knowledge, technological knowledge, knowledge as experience, knowledge as tradition, knowledge that one has derived through one's particular idiosyncratic tendencies. In that process there is no learning. Learning is never accumulative; it is a constant movement. You learn as you are going along.

(Krishnamurti, 1995, meditation for 12 January)

Refer to your definition of learning above. Did it include *skills* as well as *knowledge*? Was there any reference to understanding, or to a conceptual dimension? Did it refer to accumulating knowledge or skills? One workable definition of the sort of learning that this book addresses, though it has an accumulative dimension that could be seen to conflict with the view quoted above, is:

Learning is a purposeful activity aimed at acquisition of skills, knowledge and changed ways of thinking intended to improve effectiveness in future situations.

This begs many questions about what constitutes effectiveness and which situations are relevant, but it teases out a number of dimensions that it will be useful to explore. It covers the three aspects of knowledge, skills and thinking. It also highlights the need to *use* what is learned and implies that others will only know that you *have* learned by observing your more effective behaviour. (You might, subjectively, know that you have learned

## Activity 3.2

Rewrite your definition taking the above ideas into account. There is no need to use exactly the words above. Try to find a way of defining learning that feels right to you, as a reflection of what you now think learning is. Then think of three recent instances when you have felt you learned something of significance and check that each would be learning according to your definition. Note your thoughts below:

_____

_____

_____

something because you are aware of increased understanding, but others will need you to translate this into something – words or action – that they can observe.)

## Competence and vocational qualifications

In the UK, and some other countries, the early 1980s there was a move towards emphasising the importance, in a work context, of what you can *do*, rather than merely what you *know*. This led to a profound change in the approach to vocational and professional training and qualifications, and the construction of a set of National Vocational Qualifications (NVQs, or SVQs in Scotland) each based on a set of occupational standards against which to assess competence. This prompted the specification of observable learning outcomes for educational and training modules (and book chapters). Organisations frequently develop their own standards, or competence frameworks for use in recruitment and development of staff. Professional institutes usually base their assessment of candidates for membership on a set of standards.

Assessment against such sets of standards often requires candidates to present a portfolio of evidence demonstrating their competence against each standard. The use of portfolios has now spread far beyond the NVQ realm. Universities are highly likely to expect you to compile such a portfolio, and will probably offer a centralised system for storing its contents. It is also now fairly common for people further in their careers to develop a portfolio to 'showcase' their work or experience online for potential clients and employers. Throughout this book you will be asked to file the results of activities directed towards developing (and demonstrating) your skills. This will result in part of a portfolio you can draw upon whether to seek a competence-based qualification, to impress potential employers or professional institute, or as a requirement of your university and key part of your learning process. Understanding the portfolio-building process, and developing the skills involved, will contribute to both your learning and your employability. There will be more on developing a portfolio at the end of this chapter.

## What are you learning now?

It is worth exploring ideas about learning in more depth. Consider your own current learning. What more do you need to learn than the 'facts' about your chosen subject? How are you becoming potentially more *effective*? The first chapter suggested some things that the government and employers think you should be learning – key skills to do with communication, working with others, using numbers, using IT, problem solving and, of course, 'learning to learn' in the applied sense of improving your own learning and performance in any situation. If you have never thought about the wider learning that your student experience offers, it is worth taking time for a brief audit of this. By the end of the book you should have a clearer understanding of the range of possible transferable skills and be able to update and expand your audit. Do not, therefore, spend too long on the following exercise. Regard it as a rough first draft.

If you are not used to thinking of such a wide range of learning and have not reflected on your own learning before, you will almost certainly have found this difficult. Don't worry – it will have raised questions in your mind that you will be able to answer later and highlighted areas that you need to think more about.

## Activity 3.3

Think about the modules you are studying this year. What broad areas of specialist knowledge do they address? What skills specific to your subject will you also be developing? Which of the above key skills can you develop within your studies? (For example, you can practise communication skills in class discussions – face to face or online, in negotiating extensions to deadlines with your tutor and in writing assignments. You can practise team skills when working with others on activities from this book, or on group projects.)

List the things that you think you are currently learning. Leave space beneath each to write other things, and file this for future use. If there are key skills which you are *not* earning; for example, if you have managed to avoid touching a computer, or if there is no group work, log these on a separate list. Log also anything which you think you are *supposed* to be learning but for some reason are not.

## Kolb's theory

Even for specialist knowledge, an employer would probably be interested in your ability to *use*, rather than merely recite, what you know. Application – that is, using the knowledge to do something *better* – is crucial but often difficult. Using conceptual frameworks to *understand* a situation better is hardest of all. Yet, it is crucial to the sort of learning you need from your studies.

Employers expect graduates to be able to understand problematic situations in order to respond appropriately. What used to work may no longer work when things change. To adapt to a new situation you need to understand what you were doing in the old one, and why it worked there.

Organisational life is complex, and conceptual frameworks, that is, mental models, help you to make sense of it. Some of these frameworks or sets of assumptions you will already be using, probably without being aware of them. Kolb recognised the importance of these unconscious 'theories' and of the role of conscious reflection in their development or change (Kolb *et al.*, 1984). He suggested a model of how ideas and experience are integrated. In this, learning is seen as circular rather than a one-off. You do something, reflect on your experience, try to conceptualise it and then test these concepts through action, which generates more experience. Figure 3.1 shows a simplified version of this process.

Behind the model is the assumption that assumptions, beliefs and often unconscious theories drive our action. Key points to note from this simple model are first that learning is shown as an *active* process. Action generates 'experience' of the results of action, which provides food for reflection. This reflection involves trying to make sense of the experience in the light of existing ideas and understanding. 'Theorising' involves changing your beliefs/ideas/assumptions/unconscious theories in order to make better sense of the experience. You then test your new theories through action, applying them in another

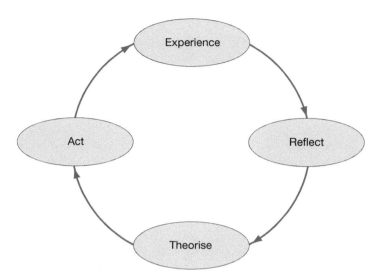

**Figure 3.1** Learning as a continuous process (adapted from Kolb)

context and seeing whether experience of the results of your action is as expected. By going round the loop again and again as you have new experiences, you can continue to develop your understanding.

If parts of the process are missing, learning will not take place. You could do something ineffectively for years if you never stop to think about how you might do it better. Experience without reflection will teach you nothing. A friend works for an appallingly bad manager. For decades the manager has never questioned the ways in which he operates. Indeed, he is completely unaware of the 'theories' or assumptions on which his behaviour is based. As far as he is concerned, the way he thinks is the only possible way: anyone who disagrees with him has to be stupid or perverse.

One belief is that a subordinate should account to his manager for every moment. Yet, the job is one which requires thinking, networking and other 'invisible' activities for success. The 'control is all' assumption of this boss is making it impossible for my friend to perform. He and the rest of the team are currently actively seeking other jobs, purely because of this ineffective boss and his faulty assumptions.

Theory unlinked to past experience and untested in new contexts is equally unlikely to contribute to competence development. (In the 1980s most of those on MBA programmes were recent graduates. They tended to be avoided like the plague by most employers.) This is why work experience is a crucial part of an undergraduate business studies degree.

# Learning Styles

If learning is to be effective – and it is vital for your studies and for your subsequent career that it is – then feedback and reflection on experience are essential. You need to work to ensure that you get feedback on what you do, and on how you think, and to constantly reflect on your practice and the experience that results. But although this much is true for everyone, people vary in the way they learn, and it is essential to understand your own learning style. There are many different approaches to classifying learning styles. For example, Drucker (1999) suggested that some people learn best by listening, some by reading, some by writing and some by doing.

Another suggestion is that people vary in their dominant sense (see, for example, Andreas and Faulkner's 1996 book on neuro-linguistic programming, or NLP). Some will talk in terms of 'I hear what you are saying,' 'Tell me what …,' 'That sounds as if …' For these people, the auditory sense is strongest, and they will presumably learn by listening. Others say things like 'Show me …,' 'I see what you mean …,' or 'It looks as if …' For them, vision is strongest, so they presumably would learn best by watching, or perhaps reading. Yet others will say, 'It feels as if …,' 'I can't quite grasp …,' or 'You need to touch on …' For them, the kinaesthetic sense is important, and presumably they would be the ones who would learn in a 'hands on', or 'doing' fashion.

Educators often talk of VARK (visual, auditory, read/write and kinaesthetic) learning preferences although there seems little evidence that designing learning for particular preferences (even if practicable) is effective. However, considering your own preferences and adapting your approach to learning may help. The idea is certainly interesting, and you can assess your style online.

## Activity 3.4

Observe one or two friends talking for a while, noting whether they use 'seeing', 'hearing' or 'doing' words most. Once you have identified their dominant sense, ask them how they feel they learn best. If possible, then ask them to observe you and identify your own sense dominance. If not, observe yourself – it will be easier once you have sensitised yourself by watching them. Think about the implications of this for your own learning and note them in your file.

Kolb devised a complex set of learning styles based on his model, but again there is little evidence that this is helpful. Honey and Mumford (1986), faced by managers who found Kolb's styles model difficult, suggested a simpler way of classifying people in terms of the stages in the Kolb cycle. Although all of the stages are necessary for learning, they suggest that people tend to be happier with some stages of the loop than others. They identified four different *learning styles* which reflect these preferences and developed an inventory to help people to identify their own. There are strengths and weaknesses associated with each style. You can get a 'quick and dirty' approximation of your own preferred style from the following. If you are really interested in your own style you should obtain the full inventory. (Your institution may have rights to use this.)

## Activists

If you chose statement 1 in Activity 3.5 you may tend towards activism. If so, you are probably open-minded and love new experiences, get bored easily, are highly sociable,

Think about each of the following statements. Check the one that is most characteristic of your own reaction to a learning situation.
1. I'm game to try it – let's get started.
2. I need some time to think about this.
3. What are the basic assumptions?
4. What is the use of this?

love group decisions and bring welcome energy to a task. You are probably not very good at things which require consolidation, or indeed anything which requires sustained effort – even sitting through a lecture may be difficult. Producing a dissertation or other sustained piece of work will be extremely hard for you. You will scorn caution and tend to jump into things without enough thought. Other group members may feel you don't give them a chance in discussions and you may miss opportunities to learn from other people's experience.

## Reflectors

If you chose statement 2 you may be a reflector, preferring to think about all possible angles before reaching a decision, taking a low profile in discussions, cautious and unwilling to leap to premature conclusions. You will thrive on dissertations, provided you do not spend far too long on planning, leaving no time for data collection and writing. You will be a great asset as an observer of others and provide useful feedback, but may not take opportunities to get feedback yourself.

## Theorists

If you chose statement 3 you may be a theorist, approaching problems logically, step by step, analysing and synthesising, establishing basic assumptions, insisting on a rational approach. You probably hate uncertainty and will have trouble with the chapter on creativity, while loving complex problems which have a clear structure. You will hate having to work with problems where you do not have all the information you need, or where some of the factors can be assessed only subjectively. You may find it infuriating to work with people with a strongly activist style. You will love the more theoretical aspects of your courses, but when you come to apply them in a real situation you may be somewhat at a loss.

## Pragmatists

If you chose statement 4 you will love new ideas *provided* you can put them into practice. You will hate open-ended discussion and love problems and the search for a better way of doing things. Theoretical aspects of your courses may leave you cold, but you will really enjoy any skills development as long as there is adequate feedback on performance. You will prefer learning from case study discussions to sitting through lectures and, if you are a part-time student, will benefit greatly from the chance to apply what you are learning to your job. You may tend to leap to practical solutions to problems without thinking about either the conceptual underpinning of what you are doing or whether a more creative approach might be possible.

Any simple classification of something as complex as learning will be an over-simplification. And the self-assessment questions above are crude. If you want a more accurate picture you need to work through the full inventory. But the strengths and weaknesses identified above suggest that if you have a strong tendency to one learning style then you need to be aware of its associated risks and plan ways of coping with these. Furthermore, it is worth seeing whether you can become a more effective learner by developing some of the strengths of your non-preferred styles so that you can go through the whole cycle. Your years as a student offer you an ideal opportunity to do this. The following exercise is designed to help. You will need to do the suggested activities over a period of time, in parallel with other work.

## Activity 3.6

Decide which styles you need to develop. Choose at least six of the following activities and make an action plan for carrying them out. Monitor your progress at regular intervals. Describe your experience of each in your file. This could constitute a useful demonstration of your ability to learn.

### To develop activism

- Do something completely out of character at least once a week (for example, talk to strangers, wear something outrageous, go to a new place).

- Force yourself to fragment your day, switching deliberately from one activity to another.

- Force yourself to take a more prominent role in discussions. Determine to say something in the first ten minutes. Volunteer to take the chair or make the next presentation.

- Practise thinking aloud. Next time you are thinking about a problem, bounce ideas off a friend, trying to get into the habit of speaking without thinking first.

### To develop reflection

- In discussions, practise observing what other people are saying and doing and thinking about why they might be saying, doing or thinking this. (This will be useful in Chapter 4.)

- Spend some time each evening reflecting on what you have done during the day and what you have learned from it. These notes could be kept in your file.

- Aim to submit a perfect essay/assignment next time. Do several drafts, and think carefully about their relative strengths and weaknesses.

- Select a topic you have covered in your course that really interests you. Try to find out as much as possible about it and write a short paper summarising this. (If you have the opportunity to speak about your findings, this will link to work on presentation.)
- Before taking any decision, force yourself to draw up as wide as possible a list of pros and cons.

### To become more of a theorist
- Spend at least 30 minutes a day reading something really difficult about one of your subjects, trying to analyse and evaluate the arguments involved.
- If you hit a problem, whether in your studies or elsewhere, try to identify all the causal factors involved, and work out how they were related and what might have averted the problem.
- Before taking any action, ensure that you are absolutely clear about what you are trying to achieve. Having clarified your objectives, see what you can do to increase your chances of success.
- Listen to what people are saying in discussions, trying to identify any dubious assumptions or faulty links in their arguments.
- Practise asking a series of probing questions, persisting until you get an answer that is clear and logical.

### To become more of a pragmatist
- When you discuss a problem, make sure that, before stopping, you have agreed what needs to be done, and who will do it, in order to make things better.
- Do the practical exercises in this book!
- Ensure that you get feedback on the skills you are practising in the exercises.
- Tackle some practical problem (for example, mending clothes or appliances, choosing and booking a holiday, cooking a meal for friends).
- You will find that working through this book will help you to develop all four styles to some extent, provided you do all the activities suggested.

# The Role of Reflection in Learning

The activities you have done in this chapter should have introduced you to a range of reflective activities, and started you on the road to developing a reflective learning style as part of a 'full-circle' approach to learning. Reflection is now seen as crucial to professional development, and is receiving increasing emphasis in undergraduate studies in professionally relevant subjects. It is therefore worth looking in more detail at what reflection actually is, and the role it plays in learning. This will help you to use the process to full effect both for your own development and to meet course requirements for evidence of reflection as part of your assessment. This section looks at how reflection 'works' to strengthen learning, and at why it is important to develop a lifelong habit of reflection. It also covers some of the main reflective tools.

## Deep or surface learning?

Much of the argument for reflection rests upon the idea of 'levels' or 'depths' of learning. You might, for example, learn five key theories of motivation, their authors and the text-book diagrams in order to regurgitate them for an examination. This is the surface level of learning – it is unlikely that you would then be able to go into a situation where staff seems to be demotivated, find out why and do something to improve the situation in the light of this analysis. Being able simply to reproduce material from the textbook seldom helps you sort out real-life problems. To do this you would require rather more understanding than is implied by mere reproduction, and a deeper level of learning.

Suppose that you get really excited about the idea of motivation. You search for, and read, a range of relevant articles, comparing what different authors said. You assess the relative merits of the different theories you encounter, and their weaknesses, perhaps with a view to writing a new paper. You achieve a much deeper level of learning than the simple ability to reproduce material.

In an educational context, Entwistle (1996) suggests that a *surface approach* is directed merely towards meeting course requirements, often when there is a feeling of being under pressure and/or worried about the work. Study is done without regard to its purpose, beyond that of passing the course. The material is approached as a series of unrelated 'bits'; there is an emphasis on routine *memorisation*, without making sense of the ideas presented.

A *deep learning approach* is driven by the desire to *understand* the ideas, and is associated with an active interest in the subject matter. Thus you try to relate each new idea you come across to your previous knowledge and to any relevant experience. You look for patterns and any underlying metaphors. You look carefully and critically at the author's evidence and logic. Material approached like this is far more likely to be remembered. And if ideas are related not just to other ideas but to relevant experience, they are far more likely to lead to improved practice. A deep learning approach is thus particularly important for any study of vocational relevance. Trying to apply ideas in a work context without fully understanding them often leads to expensive misapplication, and worsens problems rather than improving the situation as intended.

You might think that if you adopt a deep approach you will inevitably get better marks than by taking a surface approach. Usually you will. And you are more likely to be able to remember what you have learned after the course and be able to incorporate it into your practice as a manager. But it is possible to get so carried away by passion for a subject that you forget the course requirements altogether and actually do worse. It is therefore suggested that a third type of approach, the *strategic approach* is important. This is directed at doing as well as possible on a course, always alert to course requirements and the need to use time and effort to best effect in meeting them, balancing deep and surface learning in order to achieve this. Much of this book is devoted to enabling you to do just that.

Ideally, assignments will be designed so that the best marks will be gained by the sort of learning most likely to help your future career.

Rather than making a simple 'surface–deep' distinction, Moon (1999, p. 128) suggests a series of levels of learning with increasing changes to the way you perceive and think about the world. The division between surface and deep would occur around level 3. Moon indicates how your tutor or lecturer would detect this in your work. Note the presence of 'reflective' at the two deepest levels (4 and 5).

1. Noticing – represented as 'Memorised representation'.
2. Making sense – represented as 'Reproduction of ideas, ideas not well linked'.
3. Making meaning – represented as 'Meaningful, well integrated, ideas linked'.
4. Working with meaning – represented as 'Meaningful, reflective, well-structured'.
5. Transformative learning – represented as 'Meaningful, reflective, restructured by learner, idiosyncratic or creative'.

Although this book is trying to improve your ability to be an effective strategic learner, and to get the best grades possible, I firmly believe that it is deep learning which is of importance for your career after you graduate. The emphasis in many of the activities will therefore be to deepen your course learning towards the 'working with meaning' level. This is where you are really engaging with ideas and questioning – and perhaps improving – the mental models with which you make sense of the world. Moon describes this as 'a process of "cognitive house-keeping", thinking over things until they make a better meaning, or exploring or organising the understanding towards a particular purpose or in order that it can be represented in a particular manner'.

Both Entwistle and Moon were considering education in general, rather than vocationally relevant education, and so did not particularly concern themselves with application of ideas to work contexts. While the deeper levels of understanding they identify are important, you need to go beyond making sense of the ideas themselves, and into the area of using the ideas to make sense of work situations. Your course will give you practice in using the ideas to analyse case studies. You can gain further invaluable experience by reflecting on your own work experience and that of others willing to talk to you about their jobs and organisations and issues they have faced.

Consider the difference between being able to recite five different motivation theories (including Maslow's hierarchy of needs, and expectancy theory) and being able to improve the motivation of a disgruntled team in the light of this knowledge. To do the latter you might need to find out what rewards were important to team members, to check their understanding of objectives and their beliefs about their ability to achieve objectives and the likely rewards if they did. You might also, if you had developed a habit of reflective learning, ask yourself what you were doing or not doing as their manager that was contributing to the lack of motivation, and what thinking (beliefs, assumptions, unconscious theories) was driving unhelpful aspects of your behaviour, and therefore might need to change.

Deeper, more reflective learning is far more exciting than surface learning. And if you can make the connection between ideas and real situations it will have an even more profound impact upon your ability to go on learning from your experiences throughout your life. Many professional organisations now require evidence of such ongoing reflective learning and practice as a condition for continued membership. If you already have a habit of 'reflective practice' you will need no convincing of its worth. But you may be relatively new to such learning, or yet to experience it. (There is a suggestion that the ability to learn in this way does not develop until around the age of 20.) If so, it is worth paying attention to developing the necessary skills through reflective practice.

## The reflective process

You will remember that Kolb *et al.* (1984) suggested that for learning to take place experience needs to be followed by reflection, and then conceptualising, or theory building. Thus you move from action in the real world, to a process of detached observation taking place somewhere inside your head. Clearly, this is not surface learning. But the nature of this process was relatively unspecified, and there are still differences of opinion as to how best to reflect. It is something many students struggle with. If you are finding the Kolb cycle a bit too abstract, you may prefer to use a simpler cycle. This was shown to me by one of the best management teachers I have ever met, Dr Reg Butterfield. It has three stages in the cycle: Wot? So Wot? Wot next? This is as 'simple' as can be, and with the misspellings and cartoon faces, totally memorable. At its centre is the essence of the whole process, the 'So wot?' 'So what' is the key question in almost any analysis, followed by the equally important issue of what to do in light of your analysis?

What follows works for me and for many of my own students. It is offered for those of you who do not quite know where to start. If your own course has already given you tools, ignore what follows.

> **The basic elements for successful reflection include:**
> - time to reflect
> - something to reflect upon
> - medium for capturing reflection
> - skills in reflection
> - honesty
> - feedback.

Successful reflection depends first and foremost on making time to reflect. Time management will be dealt with shortly, and once you are convinced of the value of reflection, making time for it will become a priority.

So what to reflect upon? Kolb suggests 'experience'. Dewey (1910), the source of many of Kolb's ideas, suggests reflecting whenever something surprises or perplexes you. Perhaps you cannot understand why someone is upset at something you said, or why a team is falling apart or an assignment gets a lower score than expected. Perhaps a theory you are taught does not seem to fit your view of the world at all. The perplexity is a signal that some of your assumptions or theories about some aspect of the situation need re-examining. Reflection on practice is also useful if things went as expected, but you would like them to go better.

For example, you might be working on a group project. After a meeting you might ask yourself what went well, and why, to make sure that it goes at least as well next time. You might also ask if there was anything that might have gone better. How did you feel during the meeting? Was this how you expected to feel? Why? How did your own behaviour influence others in the group and contribute to the progress you made? Were there ways in which you might have been a more effective team member? What might you do differently next time? Any of these questions might prompt useful learning.

You might reflect, individually or better still as a group, upon how well the team as a whole is progressing and ask whether there are ways in which this might be improved. Your reflections on your own and others' behaviour in the light of theory – perhaps motivation theory or what you have learned about effective group working – might also help you to realise the significance of parts of that theory that you had not appreciated before. It might make you aware of shortcomings in a particular theory in terms of its ability to cast light on your experience. You might reflect on the content of the project work in the light of theory you have been taught which is potentially relevant to the project itself, and whether you might make fuller use of that theory or seek other theories.

Some of your reflection might be prompted by reading or lectures. After the event you can usefully deepen your learning (and make it far more likely that you will remember the material) by thinking about how what you have read or heard relates to what you already know. Does it contradict other theories or support them? Does it suggest different interpretations of data on which they are based? Does it relate to your own experience, or to things you have read about business in the newspaper? What light does it shine upon things that you didn't fully understand before? Does it make you realise the importance of something that you had previously disregarded? Does it make you doubt something that you had previously assumed might be true?

Much of this more abstract reflection on the relation between different ideas and on the extent to which they are based on firm evidence relates to the *critical thinking* that you will see listed as a key learning outcome of most university-level study. This will be discussed further in the context of critical reading and writing answers to assignments, which demonstrate critical thinking skills.

Perhaps most important of all, since your primary objective during your course is to *learn*, is to reflect upon the learning process itself. For any experience, whether reading, lecture, other course work or work experience, ask yourself questions such as:

- How did that go?
- How did I feel about the experience?
- What did I learn from it? What did I fail to learn?
- How might I have learned more effectively?
- What will I do differently in future to help me learn better?

Thus reflection is about asking yourself (or yourselves if doing this in a group) a whole lot of different questions and thinking hard about the answers. It is about being prepared to think about how your own thinking is affecting your actions. It is about realising how your thinking is affecting what you are observing in a situation. You are more likely to be able to 'think about your own thinking' if you are working with other people: this way you can find out that others see things differently from you, and then start exploring both the reasons for, and the implications of, these differences.

## The role of feelings in reflection

You may have been surprised to see the 'How did I feel' question above, but exploring your feelings is an important part of reflection. Often, your feelings will highlight areas of concern that you have yet to put into words and signal profitable areas for reflection. Suppose, after a job interview, you ask yourself 'How did I feel?' and get the answer, 'Somewhat uncomfortable from the very beginning.' Identifying the source of this discomfort may help you learn a lot. Ask yourself questions like: When did it start? Was it before I even walked into the room? Such reflection might show that you felt unprepared for the interview, with obvious implications for future action. Or perhaps you weren't sure about whether this was a company you wanted to work for – maybe you have concerns about the ethics of their product or way of working. This might affect your choice of companies to apply to in future. Perhaps you felt 'unworthy' of the job? If so, and assuming you were honest on your application and they decided to interview you, does this suggest that perhaps you undervalue yourself? Or did the discomfort start with a particular question that you were asked early on? If so, what was the question and why did it make you feel uncomfortable? I could continue, but you should see by now where exploring feelings can lead you.

Feelings can also be important when you are thinking about things you have read or which someone has said. They tend to be driven by your non-conscious, non-rational brain, which has far more processing capacity than the conscious part. Discomfort here may mean that there is a mismatch that you have yet to access consciously. It may be that assumptions which form a central part of your way of looking at the world are being challenged. It is very easy, and feels comfortable, to dismiss such challenges as rubbish. Our very identity stems from the set of assumptions, values and beliefs about ourselves which act as a filter through which we see and interpret what happens to us. We tend to be very protective of our identities. It can be unsettling, even painful, to have them challenged. But it is through such challenges that 'cognitive housekeeping' – or even an extension to our cognitive house – is achieved.

One of my most profoundly disturbing experiences as a very young trainer in the civil service occurred during an interviewing course I ran for people working in the equivalent of HR. I went through some of the relevant theory and guidelines for effective interviewing, and then had the course members roleplay interviews. Nothing very innovative, but a large number of the participants, most of whom had been interviewing for decades, burst into tears. I had not said anything about their performance; however, reflecting on the roleplays in the light of the material we had covered had made them realise that for years they had been really bad at interviewing. Part of their identity was 'expert interviewer', and this identity was now threatened.

There are three morals to this story. First, the interviewers needed to change their way of thinking not only about what they did but also about themselves, as a step on the way to doing it better. Second, it took honesty with themselves to bring about this change. In order to protect themselves they could have decided that the material I was teaching was wrong or that any feedback they received was useless. Honesty in answering reflective questions is an essential component in learning from reflecting – it is all too easy to rationalise away any need to change. The third message is that such change can be seriously painful, and support may be needed. I was totally unprepared and unqualified to give such support, and failed the group quite badly. You are probably much younger than they were, but you still need to tread carefully when exploring your own assumptions, particularly about yourself, or when working as part of a group which is reflecting.

## Activity 3.7

Think about something you have read or experienced, or perhaps received feedback on, which occasioned some discomfort. Think about your feelings in more depth and try to explore why you felt like that. Note any learning points from this exercise.

## The value of group reflection

There have been several references to reflecting in a group. For group reflection to be effective, group members need to trust each other, all need to understand the principles of reflective dialogue, and the group needs to agree to abide by these. (You may find it helpful to read the chapter on group working before attempting collaborative reflection.)

Effective group reflection has many advantages over reflecting individually. The aim of reflection is to question not only what happened and how your behaviour affected this, but also to consider the extent to which the thinking which prompted the behaviour needs to change. Since much of the time we behave in a way that seems 'obvious', rather than consciously thinking about what to do, it may be hard to find out what your underlying thinking was. Discussing what happened, or your views on what should happen, with other people provides you with a starting point. By identifying differences of views, and digging into the thinking that generates such differences, you can become more aware of your own 'invisible' theories about how the world works, or what is important. You may find others have noticed different aspects of the situation because of their different unconscious theories or values.

Collaborative reflection need not be carried out face to face. It is possible to work together online, whether synchronously or asynchronously. However, this requires even more attention to showing respect for others and their views. When working online, your body language and tone of voice cannot convey your intent, and people may therefore not feel as valued and respected as you intended. If you are new to online dialogue of this kind, you may find TECHSkills 3.1 helpful.

**Collaborative reflection works only if you observe the following rules for effective reflective dialogue:**

- Agree that the purpose of your dialogue is to compare and contrast your different ways of perceiving and of conceptualising the situation
- Value each other's views as much as you value your own
- Seek to identify reasons for differences rather than debate which is 'correct'
- Use these differences to become more aware of your own invisible 'thinking tools'
- Be willing, once these are uncovered, to change them if you can see ways in which they may now be unhelpful.

# TECHSkills 3.1 Netiquette for virtual collaborative reflection

When working online the same factors apply as when reflecting together face to face: you may find it helpful to read Chapters 2 and 4 on talking and listening, and group work, alongside this file note.

Virtual collaborative reflection offers obvious practical advantages. If you are working asynchronously you avoid the need to find a time when all involved are free. If working synchronously you still avoid difficulties of location. But the cost is the reduced informational capacity of all save the most sophisticated teleconferencing systems.

When you are working face to face, your words carry only part of your 'message'. Body language and tone of voice carry far more. Without these additional channels, your choice of words becomes far, far more important. While you can use 'emoticons' such as smiley faces they do not have the same impact as a real smile.

'Netiquette' (internet etiquette) refers to a set of rules for online interaction that is designed to help with the challenges of working online. Check whether your university has such a set of rules, and if so, study and observe them. If not, start from first principles and remember that reflective dialogue can feel potentially threatening. It is therefore essential to check that anything you post is (very) carefully considered. It helps to:

- Take part! You may want to hold back because you feel your views are less valuable than others, or because your upbringing has suggested that it is wrong to put your views forward, or because of laziness. Whatever the reason, your learning and the learning of others in the group, will suffer if you do not take part

- Greet people at the start of your message, whether as a group ('Hi, everyone') or individuals

- Offer your view as a view, nothing more ('I saw this as….')

- Appreciate others' views before adding your perspective ('That's really interesting, Shen, I hadn't seen it at all like this – I'd assumed that … You've made me wonder whether…')

- Never say anything that suggests someone's view is worthless. They may never dare venture an opinion again!

- Limit your contributions. Too much can be as bad as too little. When you post a message you are asking people to devote time to reading it. Make sure that you have thought enough about your message to be reasonably confident that is worth their time. Note: this point only applies to those who are posting much more than the average. If you are culturally or congenitally reluctant to post any messages at all, ignore it – you probably seriously underestimate the value of your potential contribution!

- Check you have understood a point before disagreeing – it is very easy to assume someone intends something just because they have used a word that provokes a strong reaction, or you assume, from your knowledge of them that they 'would say that, wouldn't they?' Such assumptions are often wrong!

- Read – and re-read – anything you write before sending. Ask yourself: What am I assuming about the people who read this? Are my assumptions justified? Will they know/understand what I mean? Is there any way at all in which they could take offence to this?

In addition to observing any rules, you need to be constantly aware of your choice of words, and their potential impact on others.

## Tools for Reflection

You should by now be clear that the main item in your toolkit is a good list of questions. A number of such questions are given in the box above. A slightly longer set is available online, but this is still far from comprehensive. You need to select those questions that work for you, in the contexts in which you are reflecting, adding any which are missing from the list and which you feel are important.

Reflection is essentially a dialogue based around these questions – and honest answers to them – so you need a medium within which this dialogue can take place. I have referred already to the need to create a personal development file as an aid to capturing, evidencing and managing your learning. You should by now have a number of responses to activities that are worthy of filing, so it is time to think about how best to organise this file.

Before doing so, it is worth exploring some of the terms that are used to refer to another important category of tools for reflection, namely, different forms and formats that may be helpful. Key among these are learning logs, learning diaries and journals, development records and plans, audio diaries and blogs.

As is often the case, definitions for many of the terms used vary and are not universally agreed. However, some distinctions are worth noting. The first is between a simple record and writing with more reflective content. The second concerns the extent to which you move on from your reflection to planning further learning.

### Simple recording

A learning log might be a simple record of what you learned and when. You could, for example, note key learning points from each lecture and each occasion when you did some course-related reading. A simple format would suffice. The following is one example.

| Event and date | Reason for doing | What I learned |
|---|---|---|
| 2.11 Read first part of course introduction | Required reading | Key management roles, current management challenges (ICTs, globalisation etc.), Kolb's learning cycle |
| 14.11 Attended first tutorial | Get better idea of course (and tutor) requirements | Need to make explicit reference to key concepts in assignments, need to submit on time, word-limit penalties, importance of avoiding plagiarism, value of online discussion |

Such a factual record can be useful both to sustain motivation and for quick reference after. Professional institutes may require a similarly basic record of continuing professional development. Thus the Chartered Institute of Personnel and Development (CIPD) requires members to keep a record of their development and suggests the following continuing professional development (CPD) recording format – though it allows any reasonable format to be used. (I've included an extract from my own record to show how this might reasonably be used.)

| Key dates: | What did you do? | Why? | What did you learn from this? |
|---|---|---|---|
| 5th May | Attended London seminar run by BIOSS on their consultancy model | Wanted to see whether this model would be appropriate for inclusion in new course 'The HR Professional' | How Jaques' ideas on levels have been developed into a full consultancy model – this would be a useful example of theory-driven consultancy |

Such records are normally stored on your computer and/or shared storage area. This makes it easy to update records, and to submit them electronically when required. Cloud storage, or use of space on your university server, allows you to access them from anywhere, and to allow access to tutors or others who might need to see them.

## Learning journals – a reflective record

Learning logs and development records have their uses but are directed towards demonstrating that learning has taken place (or at least, towards claiming that it has). They do little to encourage more in-depth reflection.

If you want to create a forum for a reflective dialogue – with yourself or with others –then less structure may be helpful. This is where the idea of a learning journal comes in. Reflection on an event or experience is usually best carried out as soon as is convenient afterwards. You are more likely to do this if you use something you always have with you and are comfortable with. Phone, tablet or a small notebook are popular options. Some like to make an audio record, others like to include diagrams with words. If you do use a notebook then you will usually want to transfer notes to your main file. While this can seem extra work, it can also be an opportunity for further reflection. You may also sometimes find that a little distance allows you to be a little more honest with yourself about things that went badly or are challenging your identity. In my own example, above, on the train on the way home I noted in my little book (I was still a paper person at the time):

 This felt really weird – why? Think it was mainly time travel element. Last time I was in this room was 30 years ago – when I worked for the DE just around the corner and was doing my MPhil research on Jaques and his levels. Comforting that some ideas endure, though they seem to have developed it quite a lot. The 'flow' idea from Csikszentmihaly really resonates with my own experience of being over- and under-stretched. Someone mentioned this the other day as relevant to some other research. Wonder if/how it relates to coaching. Need to get his book and read more about it. If we want to demonstrate some HR consultancy underpinned by sound theory this would be a really good example to pursue. Need to contact BIOSS to see if they would be willing to provide a case study.

Part of the 'reflective conversation' needs to take place over a period of time, as your thoughts develop and also as you are able to distance yourself from the original event and your reactions to it, so revisit your reflections from time to time and see if there are additional thoughts you would like to add. (If resolutely paper-based, leave blank spaces in your notebook for such additions.)

Your reflections on learning form what is normally referred to as a learning journal. In contrast to a daily diary entry, a journal is driven by events – you record anything significant fairly soon after it happens, but significant things might not happen every day. Crucially, your learning journal incorporates a strong element of reflection, and captures this in a way that is easy to revisit and extend. Many students find it easiest to keep their learning journal in the form of a blog, and indeed many universities will offer space for personal blogs for staff and students. Such a blog can be private, or a vehicle for collaborative reflective dialogue.

## Activity 3.8

 Construct a journal entry on your learning from this chapter thus far. Choose your medium. Label your entry 'work on Chapter 3', date it, and write a fairly free-form entry. Possible questions to address, if you are unsure how to start, are:

- What is the most interesting thing I have read in this chapter and why was it interesting?
- What are the three main things I have learned from it?

- What, if anything, that I previously thought was true now seems as if it may be wrong?
- What was new or surprising in the chapter?
- Was there anything missing that I expected to find? Can I find this some other way?
- What am I still unsure about?
- What did I dislike about this chapter and why?
- Was there anything that particularly interested me? Can I find out more about this?
- What do I intend doing differently as a result of reading this chapter?
- What do I need to do to make it more likely that I will carry out this intention?

The questions in Activity 3.8 suggest a journal based purely on words. However, reflection is likely to be far richer if you extend your recording to include diagrams such as mind maps or rich pictures. One of the key elements in reflection is looking at relationships between things, and diagrams are normally far better for this than are words. If you are doing comparisons between different ideas say, you may also find it useful to use a table. The golden rule is to use what works for you and what works for the particular sort of thinking which the learning event requires.

## Managing Your Learning

Understanding your own learning preferences and seeking to expand the range of learning styles which you can use will improve your ability to learn. Making time for reflection even – or perhaps especially – if your preferred style is more active will also help you learn in a way that will increase your employability. But perhaps most importantly, you need to *manage* your learning, using the self-management skills and the classic control model introduced in the previous chapter. It is this approach, with its emphasis on identifying learning needs, setting targets and monitoring progress which is likely to do most to improve your ability to learn – as well as practice your management skills. Key steps in managing anything, including your learning are:

- identify objectives
- develop an action plan to achieve objectives
- implement the plan
- monitor progress and make any changes necessary to keep on target.

Targets need to be CSMART objectives (challenging, as well as the other criteria) which are fairly short term (achievable within three months), but which contribute to your achieving longer-term personal or career objectives. They should be based on an accurate assessment of strengths and weaknesses (and adequate evidence), should be agreed with your tutor, supervisor or other appropriate person, and regularly reviewed. These agreed targets need to be the starting point for an action plan which includes target dates for achieving each objective. Interim review dates will help you monitor progress, and you may need to revise the plan if progress slips. If you do, it is worth noting the reasons for any changes.

## Formats for planning

Simple planning chart which can be used to manage your studies as a whole. But your learning journal may throw up things which are more complex than 'read X', or 'complete assignment Y', which such a chart easily accommodates. A slightly more complex format which sought to capture the 'wot next' in the Butterfield version of a learning cycle would add a 'what next' column for further action.

A separate action plan might then be required for items in this column. Once you have tried a very basic format you might develop your own framework, in the light of course requirements and suggestions and your reflections from experience with the basic model.

The following example uses a format derived from that suggested by the Chartered Institute of Personnel and Development for demonstrating continuing professional development – a condition for remaining a member. It has four columns:

| What do I want to learn? | What will I do to achieve this? | What resources and support will I need? | What will be my success criteria? |
|---|---|---|---|
| How to reflect more effectively | Experiment with the formats provided in this chapter to see what works for me. Discuss with tutor whether I could get some feedback | Notebook. Time. Input from others in my learning set. Feedback | To have actually kept journal for a month and submitted it for feedback. To feel I'm learning more effectively. To have used output from reflection to drive further learning via plan. Feedback from tutor to say this approach is acceptable as evidence |

If using your plan as part of a portfolio exhibit giving evidence of your ability to manage your learning, you would need to include a commentary describing and justifying all the aspects outlined above; for example, your chosen priorities and learning activities, and the support you sought and obtained.

# Learning Opportunities and How to Exploit Them

This chapter has considered learning as a continuous process of changing your thinking and ways of making sense of situations, rather than a series of one-off additions to a stock of relatively static knowledge. Whether you think in terms of the control loop or the Kolb cycle, learning from experience involves a process of sensing results of actions and modifying thinking and/or behaviour as a result. Feedback is thus a crucial component. Almost any situation will offer the scope for such feedback, and therefore the potential for learning, provided you want to learn. This means accepting that you are not yet perfect and all-knowing! While this may sound obvious, it can be quite difficult in practice as Chapter 8 makes clear. It is much more comfortable to see yourself as competent and doing an excellent job, and to blame other people or outside factors if things go wrong, than to accept the responsibility yourself.

➤ **Ch 8**

People who are protecting their view of themselves in this way will see any feedback which suggests scope for improvement as a slur on their competence, rather than a valuable piece of information. They are likely to reject the feedback with a 'Yes, but ...' reply instead of thanks. Just stop for a minute to check whether you have not already decided that while this may be true of others, you would never act in this way yourself. Learning from experience, from reflection or from feedback takes a degree of self-confidence, together with the belief that you do not have to be perfect to be a valuable person. Many of the books currently available on leadership stress the importance of self-awareness to effective leadership, and an honest self-appraisal as a route to this. (Justified) self-confidence is another key element in leadership.

If lack of confidence is making you avoid reflection, self-appraisal, and unfamiliar situations, your learning opportunities will be limited – new challenges normally offer far greater learning opportunities than the steady state. Welcoming the new is an important aspect of creativity and of leadership. More prosaically, if you actively seek new situations, you are likely to progress faster in any job than the person who stays with the safe, familiar, 'official' role. This is because taking on a challenge is likely to develop new skills, understanding and confidence. Of course, you need to understand your strengths and weaknesses. You will lose respect if you push to be allowed to do something way beyond your capacities. Instead, offer to do small extra jobs when someone senior to you is busy, or to cover for a colleague who is sick. Take on a challenging, but realistic, project. Such things will be noticed by those who can influence your progress, as well as provide material for your CV.

If you have always 'played safe' you can usefully work at improving both your confidence and your motivation to learn. As a student you are in a relatively safe and supportive learning environment. You can take 'risks' very safely. So use the opportunity to experiment with non-preferred learning styles and to practise things you feel unsure about. If you are shy, force yourself to make contributions to group discussions and to make as many presentations as possible. If you hate IT, try to use as many of the bells and whistles on your computer as you can. Sign up for an optional course that you think you will find really difficult. Your confidence will be boosted by trying – and succeeding at – a challenging task. Your desire to learn will also grow.

## Work experience

Explore the opportunities for gaining work experience as soon as possible if your experience is limited. Practising your transferable skills in a range of different contexts will help you develop them to a higher level. Potential employers will also be impressed. If your course offers the option of a placement year, start thinking about it *now*. If you are already committed to such a year, start thinking about the sort of placement that would offer the greatest learning opportunities. Think about how you can increase your chances of gaining such a position. If your course does not offer this kind of year, think instead about how to put your vacations to best use.

By the end of this book you should have a clearer idea of what skills areas are most relevant to you, and be much better at finding learning opportunities. But there is no need to wait until then. Each chapter offers you the chance to reflect on your learning needs and suggests approaches to meeting these. Indeed, the activities you have already done should have started this process.

## Activity 3.9

Revisit the work you did in Activity 3.1 and the list of transferable skills outlined. See whether you can add to your file note any learning opportunities that you missed – any situation where you can exercise a relevant skill, either practical or conceptual, and obtain feedback. (You should by now be more aware of possible opportunities.) Now think about whether there are things you are not currently learning but could be, if you sought the opportunity. The learning style exercises should have provided a starting point for thought.

Learning opportunities might come from adding a feedback and/or reflection dimension to things that you are currently doing, from taking a course that you had perhaps rejected as 'too difficult', or from taking advantage of opportunities outside your course during both term and vacations. Link this to the previous activity, to see whether you can progress your plans at all by taking a broader view of learning opportunities. You should be starting to get into a mindset of continually asking: 'What can I learn and how best can I learn it?'

## Activity 3.10

Think about the past two weeks. What feedback did you receive on things you did? Did you consider it all carefully? Did you reflect on its implications? How might you have gained more feedback? What things did you fail to do that might have allowed you to learn? Did you take any decisions that would stop you from taking advantage of future potential learning opportunities?

If possible, discuss your thoughts with two or three other people, and plan to do three things differently in the next two weeks to make learning more effective. Review progress and note down your reflections at the end of that period.

# Organising Your File

I have talked a lot now about the need to capture your plans, your reflections and your learning file. Indeed, you may be starting to feel that the activities directed at developing a file are just too time consuming. Relax – it doesn't take as long as you might think. And the potential benefits are enormous, even if you are not required to submit your file for assessment. Remember, you are trying to change some of the ways you think and some of the ways you do things so as to contribute substantially to your future success as a manager and leader.

Any change takes time and energy until it is embedded in your normal way of working. In the previous chapter you needed considerable energy to improve your time management. It takes similar energy levels to develop the habits of reflective practice, to seek learning opportunities and to plan actions that will maximise your learning. But as with time management, the benefits far outweigh the 'cost' in terms of effort.

Think back to what you learned about motivation, and apply this to motivating yourself.

- You need a clear goal, and one that will be rewarding to achieve. Remember, you are aiming to manage your learning in order to get a better degree than you otherwise would, and to prepare yourself for a really rewarding career – what you do now will affect much of the rest of your life.

- You need to believe that you *can* do it. It is fairly easy to get started if you use one of the suggested formats for planning and recording your learning. Although the initial time may be a scarce resource, the process is designed to make your learning more effective in future, so should save time overall. You will also be accumulating potential 'exhibits' for use in job applications or for an online showcase.

- You need to set yourself manageable milestones and to reward their attainment. Social rewards are powerful – you might like to work with someone on this. (Providing such rewards is the business of a whole industry of life coaches, but working with a fellow student who is trying to do the same thing allows you to practise 'co-coaching', and give feedback and mutual support.)

You also need to continually reassess your strengths, weaknesses and development needs. It is particularly important to appreciate and value your strengths – from these come both your confidence and your 'competitive advantage' in a group or organisation. As you learn, you will probably become far more realistic in your assessments. To quote Drucker (1999), again:

 Most people think they know what they are good at. They are usually wrong. More often, people know what they are not good at – and even then more people are wrong than right. The only way to discover your strengths is through feedback analysis.

Drucker goes on to explain that this involves writing down expected outcomes of all key actions and decisions and revisiting them a year or so later, comparing what really happened with the expectation and learning from the discrepancies. You could usefully revisit your SWOT at shorter intervals. It is worth making diary notes to ensure that you do revisit these aspects.

What is important is that you work out a file structure that works for you, and that you use it, and develop it further so as to maximise your learning, and create a history of your personal and professional growth during (and after) your time as a student that will showcase your talents and your work to potential employers or clients. Once you are motivated to plan and monitor your actions, and reflect and capture your reflections and learning, you can start to think about how you can usefully organise your file. Remember, the possible purposes for your file include:

- Helping you capture your learning to date so that you can see your progress
- Helping you manage your ongoing learning
- Keeping your reflections in one place, thus helping you to reflect more effectively
- Acting as a source of materials that showcase your learning and experience to tutors and potential employers and clients.

To achieve this you need at very least a clear contents list, sections relating to each of these purposes, and a means of cross referencing items as many may fit within more than one section.

Paper may be great for immediate reflections and notes, but a paper file is not easy to manage once it gets to bigger. Modifying, updating and sharing documents is not easy, nor is including photos, or audio or video recordings. Working electronically has obvious advantages. It is perfectly possible to keep your development file on your computer (with a good system for backing up, as it will become an extremely valuable set of documents). But most find that keeping your file somewhere that you – and others – can access wherever you are has many advantages. Free cloud storage is (currently) available from providers such as Google and Dropbox, or you can use your university's facilities,

---

## TECHSkills 3.2  Virtual learning environments and ePortfolios

Universities use virtual learning environments (VLEs), sometimes called learning management systems. Such systems allow the university to communicate easily with students. Administrative information, timetables, assignment briefs, lecture notes, library links and other resources can be provided via the VLE. Staff can monitor student activities like assignment submissions and course registrations. VLEs also allow communication between students through chat rooms, wikis and blogs. Most also offer students an area to store their own learning materials, such as marked assignments, project outputs, reflective learning journals and other evidence of learning. When such materials are organised along the lines suggested for your learning file, they are often referred to as an ePortfolio.

➤

Different levels of access can be granted: some areas of the VLE can be private while some allow access to tutors, some to study group or module members, others may be open to everyone in the university. For students, a VLE makes it easy to share work and ideas with other students because of common formats and frameworks. You will be able to include not only text, but photos, video and audio files. It is easy to link to documents from different 'areas'. Backing up becomes the university's responsibility. Storage is free.

On the potential down side, access will normally be limited to university members, so sharing with friends on similar courses elsewhere will need some other system. More importantly, while you will probably be able to use your area for a year or three after graduating, you will need to remember to export your portfolio to some other system before your access is withdrawn.

### Providers of ePortfolios outside of university

There are also new players in the market that offer ePortfolios independently of the VLEs. As they are stored outside of the university systems and access is usually more flexible – i.e. you are able to restrict access to particular documents only to yourself, to your peers, to your lecturer, to the whole institution, but crucially, also to the wider world.

This could allow you to share your portfolio with a potential employer, and even build a website that you could link to, for example, from LinkedIn. Importantly, they may also allow you to keep the portfolio live after you graduate – this way, the work comes with you, wherever you go.

An important caution, though, is that in making a portfolio publicly available on the web you are in effect 'publishing' it, so need to observe copyright law. Plagiarism in anything you publish is illegal, and the penalties more severe than those for plagiarism in your coursework. Similarly, there are libel laws you might potentially break if you say something unjustifiably negative about someone else.

## Activity 3.11

Ask around in your Career Centre, or ask a Student Support representative to tell you about portfolio options available at your university. Then, conduct research online into external portfolio providers and see if any offer you a good storage solution as well as allows you to share the portfolio externally.

# SUMMARY

This chapter has argued the following:

- Learning, in the sense of developing knowledge, skills and ways of thinking that will make you more effective both as a student and in your subsequent working life is clearly crucial in a world that is highly competitive and rapidly changing.

- Learning is usefully seen as a continuous process dependent on feedback. Seeking situations in which such feedback can be obtained, and using it, will increase learning.

- Learning to make sense of complex situations (as is expected of graduates) involves using existing theory, and building and testing new models in the light of experience.

- People tend to have preferred learning styles which emphasise some aspects of learning at the expense of others. Developing less preferred styles can make learning more effective.

- Reflection is a crucial element in learning, and a habit of reflective practice is essential for any professional.

- Reflection involves a dialogue, with yourself and/or others, in which you question your experiences and responses to them with a view to developing the way in which you think about them and your future practice.

- Learning will be most effective if it is managed, with learning needs identified and action plans drawn up for what needs to be done for the necessary learning to take place. These plans need to be implemented and progress reviewed, with adjustments made if need be.

- Explicit plans need to be supplemented by a constant alertness to the learning opportunities and a willingness to take some risks in order to learn.

- Organising relevant materials (plans, reflections, etc.) into some form of personal development file or ePortfolio is essential.

# Further information

Andreas, S. and Faulkner, C. (1996) *NLP: The New Technology of Achievement*, Nicholas Brealey. This provides a range of exercises designed to increase your motivation and accelerate your learning.

Bassot, B. (2013) *The Reflective Journal,* Palgrave Macmillan.

Honey, P. and Mumford, A. (1986) *The Manual of Learning Styles*, Peter Honey.

Krishnamurti, J. (1995) *The Book of Life*, HarperCollins. This is a useful introduction to Krishnamurti's thinking, containing extracts from his writings during the period 1933–68. It addresses 'learning for life' in a very different way from the present book, but this different perspective can sometimes sharpen your awareness of existing assumptions and preconceptions.

Moon, J.A. (1999) *Reflection in Learning and Professional Development*, RoutledgeFalmer.

**www.cipd.co.uk** for examples of CPD logs.

https://www.youtube.com/watch?v=6B3tujXlbdk introduction to ePortfolios.

http://vark-learn.com/the-vark-questionnaire/ to assess your VARK preference.

https://books.google.co.uk/books?id=K-4cBQAAQBAJ&pg=PA5&lpg=PA5&dq=netiquette+ for+online+dialogue&source=bl&ots=NipPONeloh&sig=KKiTFcQ6bBi1s3f5v0DFo3eJchY&hl= en&sa=X&ei=J_8OVbqaBo3qOOnhgMgD&ved=0CC8Q6AEwBDgK#v=onepage&q=netiquette for further guidance on netiquette.

http://www.pebblepad.co.uk/cs_documentation/PP_V2_Getting%20Started.pdf for a description of how to use one of the popular VLE systems and links to examples.

# 4
# PRESENTING TO AN AUDIENCE

## Learning outcomes

By the end of this chapter you should:

- be alert to the things that can go wrong with presentations

- have assessed your own strengths and weaknesses in this area

- be able to structure a presentation in a way that is appropriate to your audience

- be developing your delivery technique

- be using appropriate software and other visual aids to good effect

- be confident in handling questions from your audience

- be able to control nervousness.

# Introduction

Most managers will need to give talks or make presentations as part of their job, and such presentations are often an opportunity to raise your profile in an organisation. Your presentation skills may be tested at a job interview. Becoming better at making presentations can therefore make you more employable, and accelerate your career, as well as being useful to you as a student. Many people are terrified of public speaking at first, yet, with practice, most come to enjoy it, though usually with an element of nervousness. This chapter looks at the necessary skills and suggests ways in which you can improve your skills as a presenter. You may not become brilliant at it – such people are rare – but you can become good enough to get high marks on your course and impress potential employers.

The final face-to-face communication skill you need is that of making a presentation to a group. Poor presentations can be an ordeal for speaker and audience; good ones can be a delight for both. Furthermore, both good and bad presentations are *remembered*. Whether you are presenting your research results to a group of potential collaborators, talking to a group of senior managers in your own organisation, making a pitch to a potential major client or giving an after-dinner speech for a professional association, it is important to make a good impression. You may pay an invisible price for years to come if you do not. On the other hand, if you do well, unexpected opportunities may come your way in the future. You will also have an immediate feeling of power and euphoria from having had your audience exactly where you want them.

This chapter addresses the problem of nervousness and the skills that you need to make a good presentation. Again, these overlap with skills already covered. Being clear about your objectives, understanding your listeners' (albeit now in the plural) needs, expressing yourself appropriately and clearly and checking understanding will be as important as in one-to-one talking or in making a contribution to a group discussion. But additionally, you need to know how to ensure that your audience can see and hear you, to gain and hold their attention and to use visual aids to good effect. The bulk of the chapter looks at presenting formally to a captive audience. However, there is a short section on presenting more informally via a poster display with a passing audience.

➤ Ch 8

## The Risks in Presentation

Presentations, like written papers or reports, showcase you to a wider audience so it is important to do all you can to avoid the risks of anything going wrong. Because you are operating in real time, the risks of this may be greater than for a written report. If something is difficult to express in writing, you can keep trying until you get it right. If your reader finds that concentration has lapsed, they can go and make a cup of tea, then try reading again from where they 'switched off'. In a live presentation, neither presenter nor audience has a second chance.

There is normally less interchange between speaker and listeners in a formal presentation than in one-to-one or group discussion. Keeping the audience awake, interested and involved is therefore a considerable challenge. You probably know all too well how easy it is to stop concentrating in a lecture and have found sitting still and being 'talked at' a fairly stressful experience. Unfortunately, the older you get, the harder it becomes to be a member of an audience.

As in other areas, the best way to become more aware of what is required is to look at what other people do less than well. You can then look at how those who are more competent do the same thing. Once you are more alert to the different dimensions required, you will be better able to reflect on, and develop, your own skills.

## Activity 4.1

Think of an unsatisfactory presentation that you have attended recently (lectures are fair game here, as well as presentations by fellow students). List all the factors which contributed to your dissatisfaction. Now think of an experience of a good presentation. List any additional features which distinguished this. (You can go on to do this again at the next presentation you attend.)

**Good features:** _____

_____

**Bad features:** _____

_____

If your experience is anything like mine, your list of bad practice might include occasions when the speaker did some or even all of the following:

- read a prepared speech in 'written' rather than 'spoken' English
- mumbled, whispered, went too fast or was otherwise inaudible
- used illegible visual aids – perhaps with far too much text in the smallest font
- faced away from you, perhaps while writing on the board or flipchart
- used a hypnotic monotone making sleep irresistible, probably with no visual aids at all
- distributed handouts during the presentation, so that you read these rather than listened
- was muddled incomprehensible, or said nothing you did not already know
- 'lost the thread' by responding at length to barely relevant questions
- went on long beyond the scheduled end
- got into an argument with a single member of the audience.

The remainder of the chapter addresses these common faults as well as covering features which may well have appeared on your list of 'good' points.

## Activity 4.2

Did you mention presentation skills as a strength in your SWOT? If not, use the following questionnaire to assess your skill level (score 5 if the statement is completely true, 4 if mostly true, 3 if it is neither true nor untrue, 2 if it is not very true, and 1 if it is totally untrue)

I have lots of experience in giving presentations                                            _____

The presentations I give are usually very well received                              _____

I always think carefully about what I need to communicate, and how best to
do it to any particular audience                                                                     _____

I am good at thinking of how to use visual aids to reinforce my message    _____

I am confident in using PowerPoint to produce effective overheads            _____

I think it is really important to watch the audience, and modify a presentation
if it does not seem to be working                                                                  _____

**Total**                                                                                                          _____

If your score is 25 or above you should not need this chapter – assuming your assessment of your skills is accurate. Below this, you might think about developing an action plan to improve aspects of your skills.

# Structure

A clear structure is perhaps even more important in a presentation than a written report. It is very easy for your audience to lose the thread of what you are saying and very hard for them to find it again if they do. They cannot go back and read the difficult bit again. So the classic advice of 'Say what you are going to say, say it, then tell them what you have said' still holds good.

> **Good presentations:**
> - have a clear structure
> - are clearly signposted
> - are clearly delivered
> - use varied visual aids
> - interest the audience throughout
> - do not overrun.

## Introduction

At the beginning you need to settle your audience, so say who you are, what you are aiming to achieve, how long you will be talking and how you plan to operate. Do you want to save all questions except those for clarification to the end, for example, or are you happy to take questions at any point? Will you be handing out copies of your overhead transparencies (OHTs) at the end or do people need to take notes? Once the ground rules have been established, you then need to outline the main points that you will be covering during your presentation. If you can say something that catches your audience's attention at the outset and makes them *want* to hear what follows, then the presentation is likely to go well.

## Main presentation

As with a written report, you need to make clear what situation or topic you are addressing and use evidence to support the arguments you are making. Because of the difficulty of following a spoken argument, you need to make your structure absolutely clear and give your audience as much help as possible on this: 'What I have established thus far is . . . (brief summary). The next point I want to make is . . .' If you give such pointers at regular intervals, perhaps with slides or other visual aids to reinforce them, your audience will find it easier to maintain concentration and to stay with your argument.

## Conclusion

This is the 'tell them what you have said' section. You need to summarise the points you have made, again using visual aids to reinforce them if possible. If you are making a proposal, then it is worth emphasising the main points of this again. It is also good practice to thank the audience for their patience and to invite questions or discussion.

# Delivery Technique

If you do come across good presenters, study them carefully to see if there are ways in which you could improve your own performance. Even if you are not exposed to skilled practitioners, the following guidelines will give you a good foundation.

## Relate to your audience

How well do you relate to a speaker who seems to be talking to a point on the back wall, in a monotone? Try to sound human in your introduction. Look at people. Say things in the way that they are most likely to understand. Check with them that you are on the right lines: 'Was that point clear?' 'Can you all see this slide?' 'Am I going too fast?'

## Make it easy for people to hear

Speak clearly, not too fast, and vary your tone. Use short sentences and straightforward language, avoiding unnecessary jargon. Use 'spoken language' not 'written language'. If you have ever heard someone (literally) read a paper they have written, you will probably be all too aware of the difference. If not, try reading part of a journal article out loud, and then rephrase it using words you would normally use in talking. Avoid turning your back on your audience (whiteboards are a real hazard here) or being hidden by equipment.

## Try to be interesting

Vary your pace and use a variety of visual aids if there are appropriate ones; showing something as simple as showing a pile of books on a subject can reinforce the point that there has been a lot written on it. Occasional humour can be useful, but don't overdo it (unless you are making an after-dinner speech, when a high proportion of jokes seem to be the norm). Above all, make the relevance of what you are saying clear. It may be less obvious to your audience why something is significant than it is to you: you need to *work* at making sure that they see it too.

## Beware of becoming bogged down in detail

It is far harder to absorb detail from a spoken presentation than from a written report. Indeed, detail is likely to obscure the main point. Try to give only as much detail as you need to make your point. If a fine detail is crucial, it is probably better to give this as a handout. (If you are doing this at the end, let people know so that they do not take unnecessary notes.)

## Avoid giving handouts while you speak

If you give out handouts while you are talking it distracts people, and you will lose your audience; everyone will be reading rather than listening. It doesn't matter how often you say of a handout 'don't read this now' – the temptation to look at it immediately seems universally irresistible. If you distribute handouts before you start, early arrivals will have something to do while they wait. It will also be clear to them how many additional notes (if any) they need to take. Handouts distributed at the end can be a good way of concluding, but you need to tell people at the outset that you are going to do this; otherwise they can feel annoyed if they have taken careful notes which the handout makes superfluous.

## Keep your notes brief

Particularly if you are new to giving presentations, it is tempting to write out – and then read – the whole thing. Such a script can be reassuring as you know that if you dry up you can simply read the rest. But resort to reading only as an emergency measure. And if you do write out a full-text version, write briefer notes from which, barring the onset of total panic, you will actually speak.

These notes should indicate the key points to be made, in order. Hard copy notes are ideally made on index cards, numbered and joined with a treasury tag or similar in case you drop them. (Trying to reorder a hopeless jumble of cards while facing an audience can be deeply embarrassing.) Alternatively use a phone or small tablet – this is better than staring at a laptop. Indicate in your notes each point at which you need to use a visual aid. And cross-refer to your transcript so that you can easily switch to that if necessary. (After a few presentations, when you have never used the full notes, you will probably feel confident enough to dispense with them.)

It may seem obvious to use your slides as notes. But what will help your audience grasp and remember key points from your presentation is likely to be very different from what will help you remember what to say next. Slides should serve the first purpose!

## Watch your audience

You need feedback on your delivery as you go along, so that you can adjust accordingly. People may not tell you in words, but their body language will speak volumes. If a glaze of incomprehension is stealing over your audience you may need to slow down and explain more, or perhaps check understanding by asking a question. If eyelids are drooping, you may be going too slowly already or have underestimated the prior knowledge of people there. Or you may need to vary your delivery more. If people are tense, tapping feet or fingers with restrained force, you are seriously getting on their nerves. You need to find out why. Unless you are fairly sure what you are doing wrong, *ask* what the problem is – and adapt your presentation in the light of the answers.

## Be honest

Trying to fool people seldom works. If there is a weakness in your case, admit it rather than hoping that no one will notice. If they do notice, they will not think well of you for seemingly failing to spot the weakness yourself. But if you admit to it and have formed a good relationship with your audience, they may help you to strengthen the point. Similarly, pretending to know something when in fact you don't may make you look foolish. But admitting your ignorance may allow someone in the audience who does know to contribute their knowledge – to everyone's advantage.

## Manage your time

Inexperienced presenters are often surprised at how little it is possible to communicate in a specified time. This is because they do not allow for speech being slower than reading, for questions of clarification, for introductions, for interim summaries or for use of visual aids. Do a 'dry run' in front of a friend to judge how long a presentation will take and adjust it if your guess is wrong. Aim to undershoot slightly. It is generally better to risk allowing slightly too long for questions than to run out of time, and to stop before you have said everything necessary.

# Effective Visual Aids

Communication will be far more effective in either writing or speaking if you use images to reinforce your words. Visual aids have already been mentioned several times: this should have indicated that they are essential in formal presentations of any length or complexity. Such aids have three main functions: they can help the audience *understand* a point; they can help the audience *remember* a point and they can keep your audience *awake.* To make good use of visual aids, you need to think about how each of your points could be reinforced by an action, an object or a picture, and then how best to achieve this reinforcement. The best visual aid to use will depend on both the point you are making and the audience to whom you are making it.

Some things can be conveyed far more effectively by means other than words alone. Relationships are more clearly shown in diagrams, whereas trends are clearly demonstrated in graphs. Video clips can provide powerful and memorable examples. Other chapters cover representing data visually and diagramming other aspects of a situation. You can incorporate such visuals into your presentation as you would in a written report. The same principles apply, though within the restrictions of what can be seen from a distance. Revise these principles if you are in doubt. But although you will probably use visual aids similar to those suitable for a report for most of your points, your scope in a spoken presentation is potentially far wider.

Video clips of products, processes, people or places can be hugely effective. Concrete objects can also make a lasting impression. To take an example, when running open events to attract potential Open University students, I needed to explain how distance learning works, especially for a subject like management. *Showing* the audience a course pack, with written units, and print-outs of course assignments covered in teaching comments from the tutor, together with extracts from teaching videos or a video of a seminar (or recording of an online event) conveyed far more about the course than would a mere spoken description.

I have seen speakers hold up broken items to make a point about quality, or a new product to make a different point. Cognitive psychologist Stephen Pinker held up a comb to make a point about the innate distastefulness of using a comb to stir coffee. Such images make a lasting impression – though the point they demonstrated is not always clearly remembered. If the image is too strong, then it may overshadow the point (what *was* the significance of the comb-related distaste?). Even for points which might be adequately made in words, an appropriate visual aid might help people remember the point.

It is also important to incorporate variety to keep people awake and interested. For any presentation longer than, say, half an hour, it is worth using a range of visual aids for this reason alone. You can mix PowerPoint or Prezi slides with diagrams you draw on a board or flipchart at an appropriate point (do this quickly and avoid talking while drawing), and add photos and video clips to enliven your presentation. Because visual aids can be so powerful it is important to make sure that any you use will reinforce rather than distract from your message.

If your talk is short, you do not need to work so hard at keeping people's attention, and too much variety in visual aids can be counterproductive. It is better to reserve them for points that are best made visually, plus those which you really wish to emphasise.

## TECHSkills 4.1 Choosing and using presentation software

It is now normal to use presentation software: PowerPoint is perhaps the most widely used, as it comes as part of Microsoft Office, but there are several other popular options. PowerPoint is basically designed to deliver a series of slides, stored on your own device, downloaded onto a data stick for portability, or stored a cloud for access from anywhere with internet access. Similar tools include Apple's Keynote, and for those with a Gmail or Google account, the web driven Google Drive slides, which since they exist on the Google cloud can be shared with 'friends'.

A popular alternative for those who find PowerPoint or comparable systems too linear is Prezi. Instead of a series of discrete slides, Prezi allows you to assemble your presentation on something akin to a giant board, constructing frames at different places and then zooming in and out from the big picture to individual frames as you give your presentation. The 'track' of the focus is pre-programmed, so you decide on the order the frames will appear beforehand, just as you decide on the order of your slides in PowerPoint, but what the audience sees is much more dynamic and visually interesting that a series of discrete PowerPoint slides.

Prezi provides a much wider range of templates, too, and makes it easy to use frames for pictures, video clips or other non-textual material to add variety, and to resize, move or rotate frames. The ability to see the 'big picture' is the visual equivalent of the summary in a report, and zooming out at intervals enable the structure of the presentation to be clear. A basic version of Prezi is (at the time of writing) free and there are many free tutorials online (see online resources for suggestions). This basic version should be adequate for your use until presentations become a key part of your job, at which point their hope is that you will purchase the more advanced system, which offers far more features.

If you want something even more different from PowerPoint, PowToon is another popular system. This allows you to create animated presentations, and if you love graphics you may enjoy playing with it.

As well as software that helps you directly create the visual aspect of your presentation, there are programmes such as SlideDog, which help you create the equivalent of a playlist of videos, documents or other things you might want to use in a presentation, and then link them to Prezi or other presentation software.

In recent years the range of options has increased hugely, and your choice of presentation software becomes correspondingly harder. What is best for you will depend on answers to a number of questions:

- What packages do you already have? (For example, PowerPoint comes as part of Microsoft Office, and your university might provide other options.)
- Do you want to be able to access slides or the whole presentation remotely?

➤

- How important is it to create a good impression with your visual aids?
- How much time (and money) do you want to spend on acquiring new software and the skills to use it? (Though as noted, there are often free basic versions available usually offering only a limited number of features, and therefore perhaps less learning time.)

You will find online reviews of the main presentation software packages, and may like to check some of these out (see online resources for a suggestion). Check who is writing the review. If it written by the company selling one of the packages being reviewed you might expect a degree of bias!

Whatever presentation software and other visual aids you are using, it is important to consider how to use these to engage your audience and convey your message in a way they will understand, be convinced by and remember. Your aim is to communicate, and your visual aids are a tool for this, not something to be considered in isolation.

Resist using the features of your system just because you can. While it is important to know what the system can do, you need to choose those features which will best serve your objectives for the presentation. Only use features that are impressive in their own right rather than there to make your message more powerful if your main aim is to show your technical competence rather than to communicate a more substantive message.

If using PowerPoint or a similar system you need to be careful it does not constrain your presentation to an endless series of bullet points. As Naughton (2003) pointed out, Power-Point was conceived in a software sales environment, so it tends to turn everything into a sales pitch. There was a version of the Gettysburg address doing the email rounds a while ago that demonstrated this limitation (see **www.norvig.com/Gettysburg** for some light relief on this topic, or explore versions fitting the actual speech to the slides or critiquing PowerPoint, which you can easily find online).

Tufte, a Yale professor and expert on visual communication argues that PowerPoint's ready-made templates tend to weaken verbal and spatial reasoning and corrupt statistical analysis. He attributes the Columbia space shuttle disaster to a slide that led Nasa to overlook the destructive potential of the crucial loose tile (see 'PowerPoint does rocket science', on Tuft's website **www.edwardtufte.com**). His analysis may also add to your understanding of the idea of argument mapping outlined.

## General requirements for visual aids

There is often a temptation to cram too much onto a slide. The amount of effective information people can absorb from any one screen is surprisingly small. Before finalising your visual aids, check that they will be visible to the normal eye from the same distance as the back of the room in which you will make your presentation. A good rule of thumb is to aim at no more than four points per slide.

Colour can either enhance or hinder clarity. Think about how you use it. I have seen tasteful but totally useless slides in shades of blue on blue, the words invisible from more than three paces. Use both colour and light/dark contrast to enhance legibility and emphasise key points. And be careful about fancy backgrounds and too much animation of slides: they may look good in themselves but they can distract, and obscure your message.

For 'transient' presentations, for example on group work, where all you are seeking is to convey your thought processes to fellow students, it is fine to use flip charts. But it is still important that you manage the amount of information per chart, and ensure that charts will be legible from the farthest seat. (Avoid using red pen, or any light colour, as these are not easily visible at a distance.) You can prepare flipchart sheets in the same way as slides and ask a fellow student to be responsible for displaying the right one on cue. (Trying to talk and manage a flipchart is possible but not easy. It helps considerably to split the responsibility.)

## Activity 4.3

You can easily assemble an exhibit for your portfolio that addresses both your ability to use images and your ability to read and respond to materials. Take as the basis for this a presentation you make in class, perhaps summarising something you have studied. The exhibit should include the notes for your talk and copies of the images used, together with a description of how you selected the content and images, any feedback on their effectiveness from tutor and other students, and your reflections on what you would do differently next time.

# Handling Questions

Sometimes questions are helpful, but I have seen them wreck a presentation completely. Until you are fairly experienced, it is safer to take substantive questions at the end. Make it clear at the outset that during your presentation you will deal only with requests for clarification and that there will be time for questions at the end.

Otherwise, you risk being completely sidetracked from your main argument or disconcerted by challenges to what you are saying before you have completed your case. If you want to postpone a question, either take a note of it so that you do not forget or, better still, ask the questioner to ask it again at the end. This means that your brain is not distracted by trying to remember the question while giving the talk.

When you do accept a question, your listening skills will be important. It is hard to listen carefully when you are nervous, particularly if someone is asking a complex question with many, perhaps not closely related parts. If this happens, jot down the key parts of the question, otherwise it is easy to answer the first part and forget all the rest. If you are at all uncertain what the question means, clarify this with the questioner. You may feel that it makes you look stupid if you don't understand. But if the questioner is far from clear it is sensible to pick up on this. You may tie yourself in knots if you try to answer a question that you have only partially understood: this does not look all that impressive either.

If a question challenges what you have said, resist the temptation to become either defensive or aggressive. Take their view seriously, looking for ways to develop your position in the light of it, unless you are convinced that the questioner really has missed or misunderstood your point or is misinformed. If the point has been missed by the questioner, others may have missed it too, so it is worth trying to repeat it in a slightly different way. If you cannot quickly satisfy the questioner, suggest that you discuss it after the presentation is finished. This avoids getting into an argument that will be of little interest to most of the audience.

People ask questions for many reasons. In work presentations, there will be some who are trying to make an impression on the audience, perhaps with a view to establishing themselves as a rival expert or advertising their own business. Or they may simply like being the centre of attention. Where questions are clearly being asked in the questioner's personal interest, it is simplest to thank them for raising their point, agree with as much of the point as you can, perhaps suggest a discussion outside the meeting and move on to the next question.

If questions reveal a genuine weakness in your presentation, it is usually better to accept this and ask for suggestions from the questioner and the audience for ways around the difficulty. You may find that someone can suggest a way forward. If, however, the difficulty seems to you to be much less significant than the questioner is suggesting, you will need to make sure that the audience does not end up devaluing the bulk of what you have said.

## Virtual Presentations and Podcasts

Virtual presentations are becoming increasingly common for reasons similar to those driving growth in virtual meetings. Again they may be take place in real time, with scope for some at least of the scattered audience to email or phone in questions. Such presentations are often recorded to allow access by people not available at the time of the podcast, or there may be no live version, only a recording. Such presentations may be 'broadcast' through a conferencing system or made available (via Dropbox or Google Drive) for people to access on demand.

If you are studying online using a 'virtual classroom' you may be asked to make presentations on group work within this system. If not, you may well need to make virtual presentations at some point in your career, so can usefully think about any modifications that may be needed. If you are presenting privately, the general principles above may be enough, although it is worth using any 'voting' or other option to check understanding as you go along.

If you are 'broadcasting' your presentation on a public platform you will need to think about copyright implications. Video clips, music, quotations and images copied from elsewhere are all likely to be subject to copyright legislation, so should not be used without permission. You can find some music which is not copyrighted, but need to hunt for it. Podcasting is an excellent form of advertising if you eventually choose to set up your own business. A wealth of podcasting tips are available online should you wish to develop your skills in this direction.

# Poster Presentations

Thus far the chapter has addressed formal presentations to a (normally) seated audience. At conferences it is common to supplement the formal presentation programme with less formal poster presentations. A large space will be made available, and each presenter will be allocated wall space for a poster. The audience will wander round the room, looking at the various displays and stopping to discuss those of particular interest with the 'presenter', who will be standing by the poster ready to answer questions.

This allows participants to access a much greater number of presenters than would otherwise be the case, and is often used to allow students to present their research. If you are doing a dissertation you may have the opportunity to take part in a poster session within the university or at a larger conference. This sort of presentation is also sometimes used in organisational contexts, at meetings between members of different project groups, so it is worth extending your presentation skills to include this format. In either case the poster presentation tends to be aimed primarily at peers and/or colleagues.

Poster presentations present different communication challenges to the presenter. The 'talking' part tends to be less intimidating: you are talking to people individually or in very small groups. On the other hand, these conversations are equivalent to the 'questions' part of a formal presentation, which is in many respects the most challenging part as much of the control passes to the questioner.

The real challenge for most, however, is in poster design. Typically you will have a space 1 metre high, and 1.5–1.75 metres wide. This space has to work hard for you. As with any communication, your first task is to clarify your objectives. What do you want the poster to achieve? Clearly this will depend on what you are presenting upon and the context in which you are presenting. Are you simply aiming to inform as many participants as possible? If so, what are the key points you are trying to get across? Are you trying to sell yourself or your research, and if so, to whom? Are you aiming to engage colleagues in conversation? If so, what would you particularly like to talk with them about? Are you seeking like-minded people from other universities with whom to network? If so, what would be most likely to interest such people? This is not an exhaustive list. It merely indicates the sort of objectives you might have. You need to be absolutely clear of your objectives on each occasion.

> **Posters aim to:**
> - attract
> - inform
> - start conversations
> - advertise your work
> - summarise achievements.

Clarity is paramount because 1.5 square metres is not very big, and anything within this space has to be visible from around 1.5 metres away. So every word needs to count, and you need to use pictures (or graphs or whatever) as much as possible. Aim to 'show' rather than 'tell'. A good rule of thumb is 20 per cent text, 40 per cent graphics and 40 per cent space. Do not underestimate the importance of this white space, on slides, as well as in posters. It is what gives the other 60% its impact.

Given overall space limitations, and the need to include a lot of white space, you need to think very carefully about what to include. Useful questions to answer include.

- What are your (very few) key points?
- How can you convey these graphically?
- How can you lay these out on a poster so that they will communicate to someone walking past at a distance of up to 2 metres?

Remember, you may be in competition with dozens of other posters, and participants will not look in any detail at more than a small proportion of these. You will not have time to talk to everybody even if you attract them. So, how can you ensure that you engage those people with whom you are likely to have the most profitable conversations, prime them to ask the most useful questions, and leave a favourable impression both of you personally and of the work that you have done?

If you Google 'poster presentations' you will find a wealth of information on how to lay out posters for maximum impact. The essential messages are:

- You need to say who you are, where you come from and the topic covered by your poster – IN VERY LARGE WRITING.
- You need to have a clear 'path' through the poster so that people can follow the narrative easily.
- You cannot afford to waste a single word – 'Findings' or 'methodology' do not convey information by themselves. Something like '80% misunderstand age legislation' carries a message. Think newspaper headlines here. Write large, and with bar charts or other simple graphics to support them.
- You need a way of continuing the exchange when you have 'engaged' someone's interest. At the very least show your email address clearly on the poster. But it is even better to have a handout expanding on key points, with your email address on it. Safest of all, particularly if your key aim is to network, is to have people write *their* email address (or write it for them) and email a more substantial document – the text behind the headlines – a couple of days later, with a note saying how much you enjoyed talking to them.

Figure 4.1 shows two possible layouts for poster presentations for a standard research presentation. You may be able to be far more creative – but do remember the need for clarity from 2 metres distance. Messy and cluttered do not, on the whole, attract.

## Controlling Your Nerves

It is natural to be nervous when standing up in front of a group of people, whether for a formal presentation or a poster display. The adrenaline it generates can give your performance an excitement that it would otherwise lack, so do not aim to become totally blasé about it. But excess nerves can be a liability, drying your throat and making you physically and verbally clumsy. If you think that you are worrying more than is reasonable, there are several things that can help considerably: get as much practice as you can; concentrate on exposing yourself to similar situations; practise deliberate relaxation and prepare for each specific presentation.

Sheila Cameron
The Open University

LEADERSHIP: THE ANSWER TO
EVERYTHING?

Introduction
xxxxxxxxxxxx
xxxxxxxxxxxx
xxxxxxxxxxxx
xxxxxxxxxxxx
xxxxxxxxxxxx
xxxxxxxxxxxx

Title C
xxxxxxxxxxxx
xxxxxxxxxxxx
xxxxxxxxxxxx
xxxxxxxxxxxx
xxxxxxxxxxxx
xxxxxxxxxxxx

Title A
xxxxxxxxxxxx
xxxxxxxxxxxx
xxxxxxxxxxxx
xxxxxxxxxxxx
xxxxxxxxxxxx
xxxxxxxxxxxx

Title B
xxxxxxxxxxxxxxxxxxxxxxxxxxx
xxxxxxxxxxxxxxxxxxxxxxxxxxx
xxxxxxxxxxxxxxxxxxxxxxxxxxx
xxxxxxxxxxxxxxxxxxxxxxxxxxx
xxxxxxxxxxxxxxxxxxxxxxxxxxx
xxxxxxxxxxxxxxxxxxxxxxxxxxx

Conclusion
xxxxxxxxxxxx
xxxxxxxxxxxx
xxxxxxxxxxxx
xxxxxxxxxxxx
xxxxxxxxxxxx
xxxxxxxxxxxx

Sheila Cameron
The Open University

LEADERSHIP: THE ANSWER TO
EVERYTHING?

Context
xxxxxxxxxxxxxx
xxxxxxxxxxxxxx
xxxxxxxxxxxxxx
xxxxxxxxxxxxxx
xxxxxxxxxxxxxx

2
xxxxxxxxxxxxxx
xxxxxxxxxxxxxx
xxxxxxxxxxxxxx
xxxxxxxxxxxxxx
xxxxxxxxxxxxxx
xxxxxxxxxxxxxx
xxxxxxxxxxxxxx
xxxxxxxxxxxxxx

4
xxxxxxxxxxxxxx
xxxxxxxxxxxxxx
xxxxxxxxxxxxxx
xxxxxxxxxxxxxx
xxxxxxxxxxxxxx
xxxxxxxxxxxxxx
xxxxxxxxxxxxxx
xxxxxxxxxxxxxx
xxxxxxxxxxxxxx

1
xxxxxxxxxxxxxx
xxxxxxxxxxxxxx
xxxxxxxxxxxxxx
xxxxxxxxxxxxxx
xxxxxxxxxxxxxx
xxxxxxxxxxxxxx

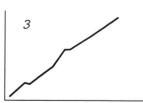

5
xxxxxxxxxxxxxx
xxxxxxxxxxxxxx

**Figure 4.1** Possible layouts for poster presentations

> **Increase your confidence in presenting by:**
> - frequent practice
> - relaxation techniques
> - thorough preparation.

If you *are* over-nervous, you probably avoid situations where you need to talk in front of people. But the best way to reduce nervousness is to seek out such situations and force yourself to talk. Find the least threatening situations first – talking to a small group of students before addressing the whole class, getting used to the class before giving a paper at a conference would be good ways to start. But *do* it. Each time you will feel less nervous.

This is one form of practice which 'desensitises' you to the general trauma of the situation. Another form is to have one or more 'practice runs' of a specific presentation. This will mean that you are confident about the structure of the talk, have practised some of the phrases you will use, know where to use your OHTs or other visual aids and have checked how long it takes, so that you are not worried about having too much or too little material.

Relaxation techniques, discussed as part of stress management, can help reduce this sort of stress too, though you need to be familiar with the techniques for best effect. If you have not yet practised them, a short period of deep breathing will help. And a *small* alcoholic drink can sometimes be useful.

But your best weapon against nerves is the knowledge that you have done everything possible to prepare for the event. If you have carefully researched your subject and audience, your talk (or poster) is well structured and your notes are well organised, your visual aids are well chosen and you have at your fingertips supporting evidence and examples, you have little to fear. Dry runs, described above, can be part of your preparation. Remember, a presentation is a challenge, but it can be exciting and rewarding, and can provoke interesting discussion on a subject dear to your heart. Preparation is so important that more detail is given below.

Even if you have prepared, you may well experience an initial onrush of nerves when you stand up to make a formal presentation. To get you over this, make sure that you have your introductory remarks written out in full, preferably learned by heart. Take a sip of water and a deep breath, go over your introduction and by then you will have calmed down enough to enjoy yourself.

## Preparation

Preparation is the key to successful presentation and you cannot afford to cut corners if you want to do well. You need to have thought carefully about what to communicate, how to structure it and how to add impact to your arguments by examples and visual aids. For important presentations, you will want to rehearse your arguments several times. Much of this can be done piecemeal, for example while exercising or in a waiting room, *sotto voce*. But you will need one full-scale, real-time rehearsal to check timing, use of aids and flow of arguments – or responses to a poster and likely questions. Ideally, find colleagues or friends to act as an audience and ask them to give you feedback afterwards. If this is impossible, then, for a formal presentation, tape yourself and replay the tape after a decent interval, listening critically and noting points where you need to change something. For a poster, come back to it a few days later and try to pretend that you know nothing about the topic.

If you are giving a presentation at work, to clients or potential customers, or a paper at a conference, your preparation needs to extend to ensuring that the location is set up as you want it, temperature is appropriate and equipment working properly. You do not want to be struggling to get your laptop to talk to the data projection system in front of your audience! So arrive early and make all the necessary checks.

Preparation for your *next* presentation should be informed by feedback from the last, so it is important to capture as much feedback as possible. Make a note of your immediate reactions in the light of audience response. Do this as soon as possible after the event, noting in your learning journal your feelings and points for future action. If possible, have a friend in the audience charged with giving you their reactions and suggestions. You may even be able to design and distribute a short questionnaire for the audience to complete on leaving. If the presentation is one of a series, this can be extremely useful in helping you to adjust future events to meet audience needs more effectively. If you are likely to have the chance to participate in more than one poster display, feedback may have the same benefits. If you are preparing an exhibit on your presentation skills, it will

➤ **Ch 8**  be important to include all such feedback.

## SUMMARY

This chapter has argued the following:

- Presentation skills are an important part of communication in the work context and may indeed be tested during selection procedures.

- During your studies you will have many opportunities to develop these skills and they may even influence some of your marks.

- Successful presentation depends on adequate preparation. You need to be clear on your objectives and those of your audience, and structure is even more important here than with written communications.

- Good visual aids help audience concentration, comprehension and retention. A range of presentation software is available, but it is important to use it to reinforce your message rather than to flaunt your technical skills.

- Audibility, visibility and ability to pace your delivery to suit your audience and your content are essential.

- Questions can be an asset or a disruption. Substantive ones are probably best taken at the end.

- Poster displays present major challenges of distilling the core message into words and graphics visible from 1.5 to 2 metres away.

- Extreme nervousness can be disabling but lower levels can help. Practice, relaxation and preparation will help you to reduce excessive nerves.

# Further information

Bradbury, A. (2010) *Successful Presentation Skills*, 4th edn, Kogan Page.

Conradi, M. and Hall, R. (2001) *That Presentation Sensation*, Financial Times Prentice Hall.

Kermode, R. (2013) Speak So Your Audience Will Listen, Pendle Publishing.

Leech, T. (2013) *Say It Like Shakespeare*, 2nd edn, Presentations Press. This gives an interestingly different slant on presenting.
http://guides.nyu.edu/posters – there are many useful websites but try this one.

Customshow (2015) for a review of alternatives to PowerPoint at http://www.customshow.com/best-powerpoint-alternatives-presentation-programs/ for another 2015 comparison of alternatives to PowerPoint and explanation of how SlideDog works – but better still, look for a range of up-to-date alternatives to this (assuming you are reading the book a year or two after publication).
https://www.youtube.com/playlist?list=PL09A34EF19596B7BB for a series of tutorials on using Prezi.

# 5
# IMPRESSING ASSESSORS

# Learning outcomes

By the end of this chapter you should:

- understand what is involved in the activity of assessing

- appreciate the perspective of those doing the assessment

- be better able to use feedback on assessment to do better in future assignments

- be aware of some of the common causes of student failure

- appreciate the importance of taking action immediately there is a threat to success

- be better able to interpret assessment questions correctly

- be better able to plan a structured answer

- be better able to use analytical and critical reasoning skills in your answers

- compile a portfolio demonstrating your competence.

# Introduction

As a student you want the highest marks possible. In a job interview you will want to be judged the best candidate. At work, your promotion prospects will depend on how your seniors assess you. In each case, two things will influence the resulting judgement. The first is your knowledge/skills/performance, or whatever else is being assessed. The second – and equally important – is how well you communicate this to your assessors. While the main focus of this chapter is improving your marks while a student, you will find that much of what you learn will be relevant throughout your career.

The general ability to communicate in writing is essential to gaining good marks. Some skills are more specific to assessment. One is the ability to understand precisely what is being asked and answer *that question*. Another, for most university assignments, will be to demonstrate your conceptual skills. Tutors will be looking for the ability to analyse a situation in the light of both its context and the theory which you have learned. They will often want you to construct a balanced and well-reasoned argument for action on the basis of your analysis. Job interviews may be seeking similar analytical and reasoning skills, and the ability to communicate your thinking.

This chapter looks at interpreting questions and planning the content and structure of a good answer. It looks at meeting assignment requirements in the context of essays, reports, written exams, portfolio assessment and viva voce examinations. It also discusses some forms of assessment you may encounter once working, such as annual performance appraisal and seeking professional accreditation.

## The Aims of Assessment

For any communication it is essential to understand your *receiver*. What are their objectives? What criteria are they using? Why are particular assessment methods being used? When marking essays or exams, I am assessing how well the student has met a specific set of requirements. Try to put yourself into the shoes (or head) of the person doing the assessing.

### Activity 5.1

Select one of the modules you are currently studying. If you were the lecturer, what do you think you would be trying to achieve when you set and marked assignments? Write down what you think your objectives would be and, if possible, discuss them with one or two fellow students on that course. Discuss, too, how sure you would be about your judgements when marking and what might make them more, or less, reliable.

What follows is based on many years of setting and marking assignments and exams, chairing exam boards, and acting as an external examiner for other institutions. Despite this experience I cannot guarantee to speak for all examiners everywhere. You need to check what I say against the views of your own assessors.

My main objective is fairly simple: I want to check that students have learned enough from the course to be able to move on to subsequent courses without difficulty. I am also concerned to 'maintain standards': students who pass our courses should not reflect badly on the institution or qualification because of their ignorance or lack of competence after graduation. If students who are incompetent, or seem to know little gain a qualification, employers and other universities will cease to value our degree. This would be a disaster for other students, who have worked hard and performed well to gain their degree.

By 'learning' I do not mean merely the ability to regurgitate what has been taught. Examinees need to use ideas and techniques appropriately in a given context in order to come to a better understanding of the situation and, usually, of how to respond to it. My final objective is to distinguish between those who have barely learned enough and those who have a high level of mastery of the subject.

➤ **Ch 3**

Another objective of assessment is to help learning to take place. The act of writing an assignment can lead to a deeper understanding of the material covered and the ways in which it can be used. (It also helps to develop skills in written communication.) Examinations will exert pressure on students to learn the material so that they retain it and can draw on it when necessary long after the course has finished.

Assessment is difficult, as I am painfully aware. Assessing this deeper form of learning in subjects such as business and management is inevitably subjective. It is easy to test whether someone can correctly define a particular concept, or remembers the author of a particular theory. It is fairly easy to see whether a person can use a particular formula correctly. It is much harder to judge whether someone can use relevant concepts appropriately, even creatively, in a particular situation.

Unless a lengthy case study is used, the context will be described so briefly that it will probably be fairly obvious which concept to use. Word or time limits will work against answers that go into depth. It is easy to be over-impressed by clear writing (rather than particularly clear thinking) and by a high level of word-processing skills. (This is why it is important to develop these skills.) It is even easier to underrate an assignment that looks rushed and scrappy. It may be impossible to make any judgement about the knowledge of someone who totally misinterprets a question.

Much of what follows is intended to help you avoid these difficulties, or even to exploit them to your advantage.

## Why Students Fail

Failure is seldom due to intellectual inadequacy. Some people may have to work harder than others, but almost all those selected for a place on a course should have the ability to pass. Some, however, will lack the ability to manage their learning. A very small number have problems, such as illness or difficulties in their private life, which puts success at risk. Figure 5.1 is a composite multiple cause diagram for the most common causes of failure, showing how factors can interact.

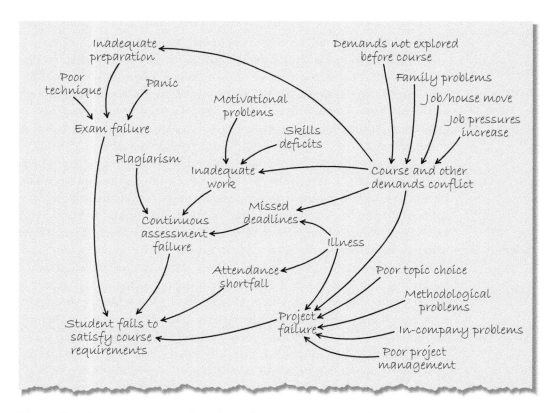

**Figure 5.1** Common causes of student failure (a composite multiple cause diagram)

## Activity 5.2

Think about factors which you feel might threaten your own success. If you cannot find them on Figure 5.1, add them at appropriate points. Highlight all the factors which you think are particularly relevant to you.

The factors shown, and probably those you have added as well, fall into three categories: some factors are beyond your control, some you might be able to do something about with the aid of this book or other assistance, and for some factors you already know the remedy.

## Coping with factors beyond your control

Sometimes your success is put at risk by factors beyond your control. You might fall seriously ill, or all your revision notes might be in your car when it is stolen. If so, you need to take steps to minimise the effect of the disaster. An essential first step will be to let the system know. Tell your personal tutor, or someone else in authority. They can help you work out how best to cope with the situation, whether by asking for special consideration, extensions to deadlines, or changing your study plans. They can also help you make sure that any relevant forms are filled in, and evidence of your problems provided. Most institutions are prepared to make considerable allowances for students who meet with misfortune of one kind or another. But they are not psychic, so need to be told of your problems, often in the correct way, by a specified deadline, and with particular evidence. Such disasters are rare, so there is no point worrying about them in advance. Just remember the need to take urgent action and seek help if you are unlucky enough to experience such a problem.

## Things you can control

Many students experience problems which should have been within their control but somehow got beyond them. The commonest cause is poor time management. If, in the self-assessment activity above, you highlighted this as a threat, and you have not yet developed the skills covered, you need to work on them urgently before you fall irremediably behind. You will note from Figure 5.1 that dissertation failure forms a major causal strand. If your course requires a dissertation, and your time management is already giving you problems this may be a serious risk factor. Start improving your time management skills so that they are well established before you start your dissertation. You will also need to pay careful attention on managing projects. You also, of course, need to avoid plagiarism.

If 'potentially controllable' factors get beyond control, it is again imperative that you seek help from your supervisor, personal tutor or other member of staff. It is far better to alert them to a possible problem and, with their help, to avert it, than to persist in denying that things could go wrong until the situation is beyond remedy. Sticking your head in the sand may feel good at the time, but sooner or later you will feel very much worse.

## Activity 5.3

Should things look like getting out of control, see it as an opportunity! Set a specific objective for averting disaster, develop an objectives tree and then develop an action plan for achieving your objective. If you also document the circumstances, the help you seek, remedial actions taken and the outcomes, you will have the basis of an excellent 'exhibit' for the part of your portfolio devoted to 'managing your own learning'.

## Motivational problems

Time problems are one major cause of failure, whether generated by circumstances beyond your control or poor management on your part. Motivational problems are another. Indeed, the two may be closely interlinked: either can cause the other. Expectancy theory suggests that poor motivation is likely if you feel that:

➤ Ch 3

- no matter how hard you try, your grades do not improve – effort does not produce performance – whether because of poor study skills (if so revisit Chapter 3), or poor assessment technique

- performance does not produce rewards (perhaps your long-term objectives have changed or there are too few shorter-term rewards).

A further possible reason, not covered by the model, is that:

- you are depressed generally and have little motivation for anything. (If so, try the normal remedies of sleep, healthy food, exercise/yoga and talking to friends. If these don't help within a week or two, or you cannot find the motivation even for these steps, seek medical help.)

The main sources of motivational 'recharging' are your teachers, your friends on the course, and yourself. If these fail you then you may need to seek professional help. Institutions vary greatly in the support they offer students, but most will assign students to some sort of personal counsellor or academic advisor, with a back-up counselling service for more serious cases. If you experience motivational, or indeed any sort of problems, you should not hesitate to take advantage of whatever help is available. This will not be held against you, or affect your grades in any way other than positively (as your advisor can argue for your circumstances to be taken into consideration when your final marks are decided).

> **Motivational resources:**
> - your teachers
> - friends
> - fellow students
> - your academic advisor
> - yourself.

## Improving Your Assessment Technique

Success in assessment requires skills in learning, critical thinking, number, reasoning and writing, plus some techniques specific to the academic context. These are covered in the remainder of the chapter. If you work hard and understand the subject matter but your marks do not seem to reflect this, study what follows carefully. Remember that most assessment in business and management is closer to an art than a science. Your assessors are *making inferences from* what you write in response to a specific question. There is a technique of responding in such a way that they will infer that you are competent. This technique will also help you in interviews and when you get a request for a report on a topic of interest to management. It is therefore well worth developing.

➤ **Ch 3**

### Interpreting questions

A key factor in good exam technique is the art of question interpretation. A common cause of exam failure is that a student appears to have answered a question that bears little resemblance to that which was asked. Perhaps the question, following a description of a particular organisational scenario in, shall we say, Case Study and Co., was:

Analyse the motivational problems in the customer billing department of Case Study and Co. and suggest action which the organisation might take to reduce labour turnover.

## Activity 5.4

Jot down possible headings and subheadings for an answer to the above.

_____

_____

_____

When a question similar to this was set, many students lost marks through poor 'question interpretation' skills. Some seemed to have read the question as 'Tell me everything you know about motivation' and regurgitated all they could remember of the lecture on the subject. Others read it as 'What symptoms are there of low motivation in the above description?' and repeated all the bits of the scenario, in only slightly different words, that relate to motivation. Some realised that they had to *analyse* the situation, but got so carried away by this that they forgot all about the need to offer suggestions for remedial action. Some made lots of assertions as to what would improve the situation without giving any underlying reasoning or evidence. (An approach to case-study-based assessment is given.) Check that your headings in Activity 5.4 avoided these traps.

Any misinterpretation of a question can cause huge loss of marks. This is *much* more common in exams because of the pressure you are under. If feedback on your assignments suggests that you sometimes miss parts of a question, or misinterpret them, you need to address this as soon as possible, and well in advance of any exam.

Make absolutely sure that you now understand where you missed something, and why, whenever you received such feedback. This is probably the most critical thing for you to address of all those covered in the book because it can seriously reduce your grades and even mean failure. It will also cause you to waste a huge amount of time and effort in directions that not only gain you few marks but also contribute little to the learning your tutor intended.

Refer to the helpfile at the end of this chapter if you meet terms you are not sure about, or even to check that you are correctly interpreting those you think you understand. If you encounter a term which is not on the list, or have doubts about the meaning of one which is but seems curious in the context, check its intended meaning with the person setting the assignment. If you are unsure about the meaning of a term used in an examination, avoid that question if you can. If you have to answer that question, say at the outset how you are defining the problematic word. Your markers may accept your interpretation and mark you in the light of that meaning. If you are not explicit in this way, they may merely think that you have not answered the question very well.

## Deconstructing Questions and Planning Answers

Answering exactly the question asked demands more than merely being sure of the meaning of the words used. It is important to identify all the separate parts of the question and plan an outline answer covering all of these before planning the answer in more detail.

For simple questions this is not a problem. But questions are often complex and you may need to practise teasing apart the separate 'building blocks' of which they are composed. A couple of examples follow of questions that might be asked about the content of this book. Spend some time on Activity 5.5 and look at real questions drawn from your own course.

## Activity 5.5

Before reading on, highlight the key words in the following question and jot down possible headings and subheadings in an answer.

*Discuss the adequacy of the control model as a framework for understanding poor student performance. Suggest three steps which you might take to improve your own performance, drawing on this or other appropriate theory.*

_____

_____

_____

There are two clear parts to the question: the evaluation of the control model and the suggested steps for improvement. Within each there are implicit sub-parts. To evaluate the control model you need to establish what it is – it would be almost essential to include a diagram here, but you would need to describe it in words as well. You would also have to establish what you meant by 'poor performance'. Note that there are different ways in which performance can fail to meet required standards – Figure 5.1 would be a good starting point.

Once you have established these two bases, you can start to examine the extent to which the control model helps with the different causes of poor performance. You would probably argue that for some sorts of poor performance the model could add considerably to your understanding of the shortfall, as some part of the control loop (establishing standards, perhaps, or monitoring performance against these standards) is usually at fault when this sort of shortfall occurs. But for other causes of poor performance (poor motivation, say, or serious illness), the control loop might be of limited or no usefulness. Again you would need to say *why*.

The second part of the question requires you to draw on the first, but also to link it to your own situation. Thus you could start by identifying the three ways in which your own performance could most be improved. Perhaps you are poor at managing your time. You tend to hand work in late after a rushed last-minute effort and your 'clear writing' skills are poor. Note that while your example has to be plausible, you will not be judged on its 'truth'. In an exam it would make sense to pick something that allowed you to show fairly easily that you could apply the ideas, rather than agonising over what were your real performance problems.

You could then show what the control loop would suggest – perhaps the need for interim deadlines to address the time management issue. Then you could refer back to the first part of your answer to establish that some of your shortfall could not be understood in control loop terms and briefly establish some other theory – showing the breadth of your knowledge – which might help. Suppose that you wanted to say that part of the problem was that you couldn't be bothered to practise good time management or work hard at written work. This could be understood in terms of expectancy theory – because you lacked the ability to write well, you knew that effort would not translate into performance anyway. Therefore to improve your performance you would need to work on your writing skills and strengthen this link in the motivational chain.

Given that you are asked only for three suggestions, you might be able to make these based on strengthening various parts of the control loop. But if you had been asked for more, then drawing on at least one other theory would have been advisable. Note that for each suggestion you would need to make it clear how it addressed an underlying reason suggested by the model or theory. Thus to address the second part of the question merely by saying: 'The three steps I would take are to work harder, hand in my work on time and try to be neater', would probably gain you no marks at all.

Figure 5.2 shows a mind map for a possible answer to the question in Activity 5.5.

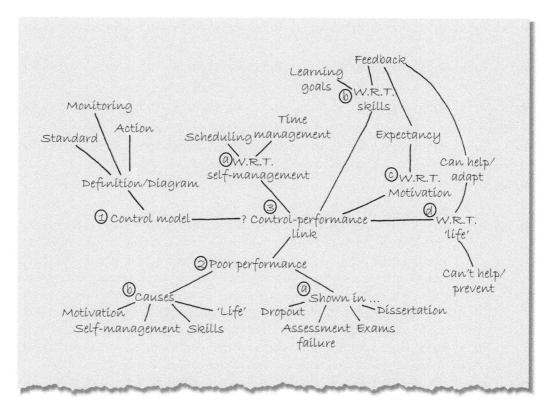

**Figure 5.2** Mind map based on 'deconstruction' of a question about student performance and control

Let's take a second example, albeit more briefly. Think briefly about how you would approach this before reading the analysis which follows.

'Organisations today are likely to recruit graduates primarily because of the knowledge that they have gained during their degree studies.' To what extent do you agree with this statement?

This question is asking you to demonstrate your understanding of relevant factors in organisations today and link these to employer views about graduates as potential employees. It is also checking your understanding of the whole idea of transferable skills, even though these are not mentioned. Any student who restricted their answer to knowledge, and made no mention of skills, would probably fail.

The other implicit instruction is to give a *reasoned* conclusion for agreeing or disagreeing with the question, so you are also being tested on your ability to argue from evidence. In building your argument you might want to think about the principles of argument mapping introduced. Most assessments will expect you to look at arguments for and against whatever conclusion is being presented in a balanced way, taking all the evidence into consideration.

Many assignments will require *analysis*. Some will require you to analyse a case. All the issues discussed in this chapter are relevant to this, but you will also need to understand how to work with cases.

## Activity 5.6

Collect samples of assignment and exam questions from your own course(s) – lecturers should be able to provide these if you do not already have them. Working with one or two other people if possible, first highlight the 'instruction' words (explain, compare, etc.), then try to break the questions down into their constituent parts.

## Planning an answer

Once you are absolutely clear what the question is asking for, you need to start planning your answer. You were starting to do this in the activities above, but there is more to do than think of the obvious headings suggested by the question. Essay planning is ideally a fairly leisurely process: your ideas need time to develop and cohere. In an exam, time is seriously limited. But in either case, planning is an essential stage. Indeed, all the stages of the control loop – setting or clarifying objectives, planning to meet them, marshalling resources, checking progress against schedule and objectives and taking corrective action if necessary – are vital for both essays and exam answers.

Note that you need to control time as well as material. Part of your planning therefore has to involve a work schedule, and an essential part of your control will be directed towards ensuring that you keep to this schedule. If possible, spread both your planning and writing over several days to allow a 'fallow' time between first and final draft of both plan and assignment. During this gap you may find that your subconscious develops your ideas considerably without effort on your part. You will also find it easier to spot logical inconsistencies and poor English if you edit your essay after a decent interval, rather than on completion.

Planning your time for exams is equally important. If you finish early, use any spare time to re-read earlier answers checking they do answer the question, and adding anything else that improves them.

There are two popular approaches to planning the content of an essay or report. The first is to collect together all the possibly relevant things you might wish to cover and then to organise these into some kind of structure. The other is to develop the structure first and then search for the appropriate material to flesh it out. Sometimes it may be worth adopting a mixed approach, starting with either a rough structure or reading a few relevant materials and then moving to the other approach, which may then prompt developments or additions to the first, and so on. If you are already completely happy with how you go about planning (and your grades are as high as you want), stick with what works. Otherwise, experiment with each approach first, before trying the mixed one.

> **Assignment planning involves:**
> - noting deadline
> - clarifying question requirements
> - identifying resources needed
> - scheduling activities to:
>   - acquire resources
>   - extract information
>   - plan assignment structure
>   - write it
>   - review what you have written
> - monitoring progress.

In either case, remember the importance of selecting your material carefully with a view to relevance and currency, keeping careful notes as you read, and making sure that you keep a record of the full reference of anything you are at all likely to use, as an integral part of your notes. (References are of little use if you cannot marry them up with the relevant notes.)

In an exam you will normally need to keep any 'collecting of materials' to the minimum. Some students find it helpful to jot down single words or short phrases to 'capture' everything they can remember that may be relevant to an answer before it is driven out of their heads by the first thing they start to write. But such notes need to be written very quickly so as not to use time that might be better devoted to analysing the question, planning the structure of your answer and *writing* it.

## Mind maps for planning

Whichever approach you adopt, you will find that mind maps (used in the deconstruction example above) can be invaluable. If you have collected notes on a number of relevant books and articles, you can use a mind map to organise the content of these. If you are starting with structure you can represent this as a mind map. In either case, once you have your main 'branches' and 'twigs' established, all that remains is to order the branches in the best way and then for each branch to order the twigs. This gives you the outline of your essay plan. If structure came first, you will then need to search for relevant sources. You may find that these cast new light on the subject. If so, you may need to do some reordering or alter the groupings. If your structure was developed from notes, you may be ready to start writing once you have ordered the branches on your map.

In an exam, a mind map can be a useful way to establish, very quickly, the structure of your answer. While you write, use it as a reference point against which to check your progress. It is a good idea to number the branches in the order you intend to cover them. Sometimes it can be useful to cross off branches when they have been completed. (If you prefer to generate mind maps for essays on a computer, affordable, or sometimes free, software is readily available.)

Your resulting essay plan, however derived, needs to be as brief as possible – a list of section headings or a diagram (with order indicated) is usually enough. Remember to include an introduction and conclusions and, if relevant, recommendations, as well as the structure of the main section. Writing a good answer is much easier if all you have to do is work your way through the stages you have set out for yourself. It is easy to check your plan against the question, to ensure that all the parts you have deconstructed are covered. It is easy to see whether the order you have planned is logical and likely to flow well. It is easy to check your answer, at intervals, against the plan. Writing without a plan and subsequently trying to check your full answer for flow and completeness is far more difficult. You should still, for safety's sake, perform a direct check of answer against question at some mid-point and again at the end, to ensure that you answer the question, the whole question and nothing but the question! If you keep this requirement in mind while you perform both the check via plan and the direct check, you should end up with a good, clear, relevant answer.

## Test Exercise 5.1

Draw a mind map and brief essay plan based on the 'reasons for graduate recruitment' question used to exemplify deconstruction of a question.

## Rough drafts

Are you prone to procrastination, or more severe 'writer's block'? Do you find it hard to put pen to paper or finger to key? If so, you may find it liberating to write a deliberately rough first draft. Resistance to writing often stems from a fear of not being able to do it well enough, or dread at the sheer size of the task. This latter is a particular problem with long essays or reports. Setting yourself to write something that may be total rubbish removes this fear.

So set yourself an interim task of completing a quick, *very* rough draft well in advance of the deadline. This has several advantages:

- The draft will clarify your thoughts greatly, highlighting points where your structure or arguments are weak, or evidence is lacking.

- It will give you raw material to work with. You can then craft this into something far better than you could ever have produced at a first draft.

- It will stir your subconscious into action, as mentioned.
- If you come down with flu or suffer some other disaster, you will have something which you can hand in with an explanatory note if asking for an extended deadline is not a good option.

Once you have a draft it is usually fairly painless to turn it into something good. It can even be enjoyable – but only if you are prepared to treat the draft as an interim stage in your thoughts and do not become attached to it. Read it in 'critical bystander' mode and discard or seriously modify those parts which do not work. If you are unhappy with the quality of your writing, rather than the quality of your thought.

---

## Box 5.1  Checklist for final drafts

When you have polished your draft into something that you are reasonably happy with, it is still worth performing a final check. Ask yourself:

- Does the introduction serve to orient the reader adequately?
- Is there a logical flow through the essay?
- Are argument chains clear?
- Is the language clear and appropriate?
- Have you covered all the parts of the question?
- Is the proportion of your answer devoted to each part reasonable, given the way the question was phrased?
- Have you provided enough evidence and clear arguments to convince your reader of each of the points you wanted to make?
- Have you made use of diagrams or graphs where these really help make your points?
- Have you used relevant concepts from the course to develop your answer wherever possible?
- Is there any material which could be deleted as less than fully relevant or necessary?
- Does your conclusion flow naturally from the points you have made earlier?
- Are you (just) within the word limit?
- Is your reference list complete in that all the sources you cited in your answer are included?

---

You may also find it helpful to ask a friend on a related course to read the essay and tell you of any points that she or he is unhappy about. (If you swap essays with someone on the same course for this purpose, you may find it very difficult not to swap good ideas too, so that your essays come to resemble each other more closely than is safe. Remember, cheating and plagiarism will attract severe penalties.)

## Learning from feedback

Feedback from a friend before submitting can be extremely helpful in pointing out areas that lack clarity. Feedback from your tutor can be even more helpful. Universities (and tutors) vary in the amount and specificity of feedback given, but you need to make sure that you understand what would have improved your mark, and how you can do better next time.

There will always be a tendency to become defensive when faced with a low mark or what may seem harsh criticism. Defensive reactions include refusing to read any comments, or brushing them off as 'rubbish'. It is important to treat all criticism as relating to your *work*, rather than as something personal. Try to see it as a gift from your tutor, who may have spent time thinking about how to explain where you went wrong. Where the tutor has said you went right, think about how to build on the strength identified in future assignments.

There is more on both giving and receiving feedback in the next chapter, where the focus is on spoken feedback. The following guidelines relate particularly to written feed-
➤ **Ch 8**   back, but apply also to any verbal feedback you receive on your assignments.

### Guidelines for dealing with feedback

- Take a deep breath and relax.
- Read feedback carefully, checking that you can see why the tutor said what she or he did.
- If having read the comments you don't understand why your mark was not higher, or cannot see how the comments will help you to do better next time, ask your tutor for help in understanding them.
- Reflect on your work in the light of comments and make notes of any actions you need to take (such as allowing more time, reading questions more carefully, making clearer use of concepts, or using chapters from this book to help with basic maths or whatever weakness has been identified).
- Plan actions, carry out, and monitor.
- Re-read comments before your next assignment to make sure that work will not attract similar comments!

## Doing Well in Examinations

Once you are good at writing essays to a plan, with a clear structure, and ensuring that you answer all of the questions, you are halfway to doing well in examinations. 'All' you need do beyond that is to manage your time so that you prepare adequately. Part of that preparation

> **Causes of exam failure include:**
>
> - inadequate preparation
> - poor time management
> - answering too few questions
> - missing out parts of questions
> - misinterpreting the question
> - not using course ideas.

may be to practise relaxation techniques so that you control any tendency to panic in the exam. You also need to manage your time carefully during the exam itself. Answer the correct number of questions, giving each part of each question an appropriate amount of attention. The basic principles involved are those already covered in the context of managing your learning and written communication. What follows is merely a brief outline of the key points as they relate to the specific context of examinations.

## Exam preparation

In one sense, you are preparing for the exam from the moment you begin to study a course. Think about what you are learning, aim for 'deep learning' and take notes in a form that will be useful for revision and half your work is already done. However, at some point prior to the exam you will need to focus more specifically on revision and on developing a strategy for gaining good marks. As with much of what is suggested in this book, the action needed is straightforward. But it does require careful planning and good time management. You will probably find the following stages helpful for managing your preparation.

➤ **Ch 3**

### Identify requirements

As with all management, you need to clarify your objectives, in this case by becoming as clear as possible about what will be required of you. Analysing past papers is one of the best means of doing this, unless it is a new course or the exam has changed recently. Look for the type of questions asked and the most popular topics. Try to put yourself in the examiner's position. It may be easier to set questions on some topics than others. Some topics may be so central to understanding a subject that it is highly likely that they will be included, directly or indirectly, in the exam.

Make sure that you know the likely format of the paper. How many questions are there usually? How many of these do you need to answer? Are they equally weighted in terms of marks allowed? How many topics does this mean you can afford not to revise? With a little research you should be able to identify areas of the course which it would be dangerous not to know and some which, if pushed, you could more safely afford to revise less thoroughly. But *always* allow a margin. It is extremely dangerous to think that you can completely predict an exam's content, and to revise only the portion of the course you are 'sure' will come up.

Find out from your tutors what *level* of knowledge they expect. Is it fine detail or broad principles? Do you need to remember formulae or will any necessary ones be provided? Find out, too, for subjects where it is an issue, the balance expected between theory and its application. Tailor your revision accordingly.

Find out what you can bring into the exam room and make sure it is in working order. If you are required to handwrite your paper and need a set of coloured pens, pencil and rubber, invest in new ones: during the exam your mind should be on what you are drawing

> **To prepare for exam success:**
> - identify requirements
> - prepare a revision plan
> - revise actively
> - practise writing answers
> - get in good physical shape
> - ensure that you know the time and place of each exam.

or writing, not on whether your pens work. Make sure you have a fresh battery in your calculator or perhaps even a spare machine. I apologise if this sounds patronisingly obvious. It is. But many people still omit these simple precautions, with tragic results.

If you have an 'open book' exam and are allowed to take notes or books into the room, think very carefully about the preparation you need in order to make good use of these materials. You will gain no marks for time spent searching through books for the relevant pages.

Produce an index of best references for likely topics. If you are allowed to annotate books, use this facility to make points briefly in margins. Text which is copied is unlikely to gain you any marks at all, but if you copy a relevant note of your own, the examiner will not know.

### Prepare a revision plan

Plan carefully, and realistically. A revision plan will help you to balance your efforts and make revision more rewarding, keeping your motivation high. Clarify your objectives and decide on how much revision you need to do. Think about the time you have available and the time you estimate you will need. (Remember to build in a contingency factor in case of the unexpected.)

How are you going to revise? Clearly, you cannot read all the books again. Allow extra time to revise topics you found difficult or material you still do not fully understand. If you have already become used to planning your work actively, this stage should be almost second nature to you by now.

Prepare a chart showing when you will work on each part of the course. You can do this well in advance, but once actual dates are announced you may need to reschedule to take into account the timing of specific exams. Remember to allow time at the end for overall preparation and for practice with past papers or other dummy questions. Avoid scheduling revision the night before the exam. There are better uses for that time. Your chart should have spaces for you to tick off topics as you progress. This helps to sustain your motivation.

### Revise actively

Once you have scheduled your time you need to use it to derive maximum benefit. Mere passive reading of books and notes is unlikely to help. Instead, you need to bear the following questions in mind as you tackle each topic:

- What do I need to *learn by heart* (i.e. be able to reproduce from memory – formulae and diagrams, for example)?
- What do I need to *know* (e.g. concepts, principles and techniques and their significance)?
- What do I need to be able to *do* with the above and in what contexts?

You should already have the answers to these questions, but you need to keep them in mind as you work through your notes and other materials.

Even if your notes were taken with revision in mind, you will still need to take further notes as part of your revision. You may find it helpful to extract on to cards those things which you need to be able to reproduce from memory, and learn them (on the bus, in the bath, or wherever you have suitable time at your disposal).

For everything other than rote learning, you should be aiming to *interact* with the materials in as many ways as possible. Draw diagrams of text. Describe diagrams in words. Try to represent relationships with equations. Try to describe equations in words. List possible uses of various techniques. Summarise key parts of the course from memory, then go back to see whether there is anything significant that you have left out. Draw mind maps of possible answers to past questions. Try to invent questions as if you were setting the exam. Then construct outline answers for these. Practise the analysis of requirements and planning of your answer, as suggested earlier for essays.

Aim to do all this fairly quickly. It will keep your brain alert and give you valuable practice in organising your thoughts quickly – a key exam skill. Then go back to course materials and 'mark' your attempts, seeing what you left out and spotting any errors. If you *work* at your revision in this way, rather than sitting in front of your notes and letting your eyes move over them, or merely copying things from one piece of paper to another, you will find that the process is fairly interesting and, more importantly, results in far more learning.

## Practise

Unless you are provided with a word processor for the exam there is one very basic skill you may need to practise: that of writing, quickly, for long periods of time, with a pen. If all your writing is at a keyboard, the connection between brain and pen may have withered. This makes it very hard to write fluently in an exam. Your muscles may cramp, and your thoughts will limp along. Prevent this with 'writing practice'. Pick up a pen and write a diary, letters, or first drafts of essays in order to re-establish your skills.

The next thing to practise is writing for as long as an exam, in order to maintain concentration. Unless you habitually write essays in long stretches and by hand, set yourself 'mock exams'. Draft answers to past papers or to questions you set yourself, allowing the same length of time as you will have in the exam. Start, if you like, with single questions and the time that would be allowed for them, before working up to the whole paper. This gives you a good feel for time and the amount you can write in it and will make time management in the exam somewhat easier.

Feedback on your performance is important here, as with everything else. You can check timing easily. You can if necessary mark your own work, putting it aside for a while so that you come to it fresh. Better still, exchange answers with someone else and mark each other's.

## Other preparation

Your final task is to be in good shape for the exam. If you are on the verge of caffeine poisoning, have worked through the night or have subsisted on biscuits for a week beforehand, you cannot expect your brain to do you justice in the exam. So it is essential to plan to get enough sleep and exercise during the whole revision period. In particular, use the evening before the exam to do something relaxing and have a reasonably early night. (Walk, hot bath, hot milk, bed is a good sequence.) You can waste all your earlier efforts by not taking your body's needs into account.

Do check, too, that you have the time and place of the exam correct. Someone very near to me arrived in the afternoon for a morning exam, an error which prevented him from getting the 'first' he might otherwise have expected.

> **To do well in the exam:**
> - read the paper carefully
> - budget time carefully
> - choose questions you understand
> - read each question very carefully
> - plan your answer
> - monitor progress against question
> - move to next question on schedule
> - relax!

## During the examination

If you have followed the above advice, have checked the time of the exam carefully and arrived in time to relax before entering the room, you should be in good shape during the exam. You merely need to remember the following points.

### Read the paper carefully

Check that the number of questions you have to answer is what you expected. If you have a choice, read all the questions carefully enough to understand what is required before making your choice. It is often better to answer a question you fully understand about something you more or less know than to attack a question on a topic you have revised extensively but where you really are not sure what the question wants you to do. Totally open-ended questions are hazardous: they leave you to guess at an appropriate structure for your answer, with the possibility that you will get it wrong. Questions with a number of parts clearly spelled out make it easier for you to feel confident that you understand what the examiner requires.

### Manage your time

Work out how much time you can afford to allow for each question and monitor your time usage. You must be disciplined about this. More people have failed because they spent too much time on one question and totally failed to answer one or more others than for any other reason. Remember the Pareto principle: here it suggests that you will get 80 per cent of the marks for a question for 20 per cent of the effort that full marks would require. So keeping to time is far more important than aiming for perfection. Move on to the next question when you have used your 'ration' for the current question. You can leave space and come back if you do not use all the time allocated to a subsequent question. Even if you feel forced to choose a question or two on topics where you know your revision to have been inadequate, you should still budget a reasonable time for your attempts. You can gain a surprising number of marks for fairly scant knowledge, if carefully applied to the question. Check your watch and your schedule at frequent intervals to ensure that you allocate your time as intended.

## Read each selected question very carefully

Remember the techniques covered earlier for deconstructing questions. You will need to do this fairly quickly, but it is essential that you identify and understand the instruction words and that you separate out *all* the implicit parts of the question. Any part that you miss will cost you a significant chunk of marks, as it will get zero out of whatever was allowed for that part of the question in the marking scheme.

## Plan your answer

There is a strong temptation, knowing how scarce time is, to leap straight into answering, without any plan. But this is dangerous. It is easy to miss essential dimensions of an answer or to end up with something which lacks much structure, is out of balance and fails to convince the marker of your grasp of the topic. While you cannot afford the leisurely, 'collect everything of potential relevance' approach that may work for essays, you *can* do a quick 'brain dump' of key concepts and points that seem important, each encapsulated in a single word or very short phrase. This captures them so that they do not retreat into the inaccessible parts of your brain once you start writing about something else. You can then spend a few minutes arranging these into a mind map or set of headings and subheadings. Writing your answer will be so much easier once you have done this, and you will more than gain back the time you have spent. (This is provided you did not overindulge in planning – 20 per cent of the available time would seem a reasonable limit for this in most cases.)

A clear structure, with introduction and conclusion and a logical and connected flow between, is essential. It can help to leave space at the start of your answer and add your introduction after you have written the rest. Diagrams may be well worth including. (They need to be clear rather than artistic, so do not spend too much time on making them pretty.)

If you *are* running short of time, do not cross out your notes until your answer is completed. Markers are usually prevented from giving marks for crossed-out work, but will not penalise for notes which are clearly headed as such and *not* crossed out: in case of disaster they may give you some credit for them.

## Remember to monitor progress at intervals

The control loop only works if 'outputs' are sampled often enough that you can take corrective action in time to prevent disaster. This means checking your time management every page or so and also checking that you are still answering the question asked. (Questions have a nasty habit of silently rewriting themselves inside your head into something you would prefer to answer; frequent checking against the original is essential.)

One of your objectives is to demonstrate academic competence, so part of the checking should be that you have noted relevant authors and dates wherever appropriate.

## Above all, DON'T PANIC

Most people pass exams. Almost everyone could have passed by following the guidance above. So if anything feels as if it is going wrong, take a few deep breaths and consciously relax your body while reminding yourself of this. Your brain will probably unscramble itself enough to proceed. If you really cannot answer a question then write *something* that has some tenuous relevance. If you run out of clearly relevant things to say and have not used the time, write something more that has at least some bearing on the subject. If you are running out of time despite everything above, stop and jot down some notes in answer to the remaining questions. And if your problems were because of illness on the day, see a doctor as soon as the exam is over, get a certificate and send it in.

# Viva Voce Examinations

Oral assessment was the earliest examination form of all. In the UK it is uncommon at undergraduate level, though sometimes used for dissertations. It is sometimes used when examiners cannot decide your result from your written papers, perhaps because you were ill and so unable to do yourself justice on the day of an exam. Sometimes a few other people are summoned to a viva to help examiners establish the range of expected standards. You may well need to meet your examiner and discuss your portfolio if you are pursuing an NVQ or other work-based assessment. Such examinations can be tailored to the needs of an individual candidate, but are also very expensive. It is hard to ensure uniformity of standards, so institutions may seek to keep their use to a minimum.

Any viva can be seen as good practice for job and appraisal interviews, so you may like to read what follows with this in mind if you are not expecting a viva.

## Preparing for a viva

Your first requirement is to know *why* you are being examined, and therefore what people are likely to be looking for. You will probably not be told exactly but may be able get some indication at least. Knowing reasons can help you prepare, and may make you less anxious if, for example, the viva is because your work was so good the examiners wish to reassure themselves that you produced it unaided.

> **To do well in a viva:**
> - find out why you are being examined
> - prepare accordingly
> - check that you under-stand each question
> - allow yourself time to think
> - answer clearly and honestly
> - watch responses to your answers
> - check you have been understood.

If the viva is to give you a chance to improve on the marks you gained in a written exam, then you should revise in much the same way as you did for the exam itself, as this is another form of test of the same knowledge. You could also usefully reflect on any exam questions you know you answered badly. It is likely that your examiners will focus on the areas where they think you are weak. Furthermore, if you can demonstrate to them that you are aware of where you went wrong, it will count in your favour. Do not restrict your revision to such areas, however. You may be questioned on any part of the course and, indeed, may not have judged your shortcomings correctly.

If the exam is a routine one in support of a project or thesis, then little preparation should be needed beyond reminding yourself of its contents. If you have sweated blood over writing it, these will probably be indelibly etched in your mind anyway. You might, however, wish to think about your 'reflections' section on lessons learned (assuming there was one – if not, reflect anyway) and about any areas where you know the research was weak so that you can say what you would do about this, given a chance. But much of the exam will probably be directed towards establishing that the work was your own, by looking for the sort of in-depth knowledge you could only have if this were the case.

For a non-routine project viva, or in the case of a borderline written exam, try to find out what the concern was, either from your project supervisor or tutor or from your own reflection. Think of ways in which you can reassure your examiner(s) that such weaknesses either were unavoidable or would be avoided in future because you now fully understand how they arose.

## Answering questions

➤ **Ch 8**

A viva is an example of a spoken exchange where you will be aiming to determine the examiner's concerns and address them concisely. Your goal is to demonstrate your understanding of the material in question. Thus you need the talking and listening skills addressed in Chapter 8. Revisit that chapter before your exam (or interview).

Careful listening is crucial. If you fail to understand a question, you will do yourself as much harm as if you misread a question in a written exam. In a viva you have the chance to check the meaning of a question with the examiner. Take advantage of this. Clarify the meaning and check that your understanding is correct if you are in any doubt.

Thinking is vital too. Do not feel you have to answer a question the instant the examiner stops asking it. It is perfectly reasonable to spend a short time thinking about how to answer it. If this seems odd, ask: 'Can I think about that for a moment?' You will almost always be told that you can. Be honest. If there is a weakness in your project, or you answer something and then realise that your answer was inadequate, say so and then go on to do what you can to make good the shortcomings you have revealed. This is far safer than hoping that the examiner didn't notice. Examiners notice a great deal: that is their job.

Take your cues on formality from the examiner. Some are more informal than others. Aim to match their chosen level. But above all, remember that anything you can do to help the *process* of the interview will help. Look directly at the examiner when talking or listening. You can smile where appropriate. The occasion is one for communication, so treat it as such. Check that you have received the right (question) message. Check that your answer is clear to your examiner. If you are at all unsure, ask whether what you have said is enough, or if there is another angle the examiner would like you to explore, or something which should be covered in more depth. They may not always tell you. But often they will and this will enable you to give a more satisfactory answer.

# Portfolio Assessment

The importance of reflection in learning is now widely recognised and both universities and professional bodies may assess some of your learning and development on the basis of

➤ **Ch 3** personal development files including learning logs, learning journals and other evidence of planning and managing learning. This was discussed in Chapter 3, and if you follow the guidance there, together with that given by your university, and use an appropriate portfolio management system, you should not find compiling this evidence difficult.

If your course includes an element of competence-based assessment, or if you seek such a qualification later in your career, you are likely to be required to produce a more systematic portfolio demonstrating that you have the full range of competences covered in that qualification. Your portfolio will consist of a number of 'exhibits' which demonstrate your skills in some way. Your work on the book thus far should have generated some exhibits. Additionally, you might need to include letters or reports you have written, work schedules you have drawn up, interview plans and/or reports of the interview, training plans, audio or video recordings of interactions of one kind or another, testimonials from people for whom you have worked, examples of things you have made, and so forth. The list is endless, and what is required will depend on the particular qualification which you are seeking.

The *principles* of portfolio assessment are fairly uniform:

- You need to address all, or most of, the aspects of the relevant performance standards.

- Exhibits need to be relevant, fairly recent and to demonstrate your own competence rather than that of other people.

- You need to have organised, indexed, cross-referenced or linked and justified your contents.

In summary, it needs to be easy for the examiner to find the relevant and convincing evidence for each relevant standard.

Having studied the relevant competence framework, the contexts in which assessors want competences to be displayed and the sorts of evidence they want, you can put together suitable materials, together with a 'story' which explains your situation and the contexts in which the competences are used and an index which clearly links exhibits to competences. This is important because a carefully chosen exhibit can often evidence a number of different competences. A project, for example, could show self-management skills, project management skills, written communication skills, information handling skills and possibly others as well. But you cannot merely hand your project in and expect the assessor to work this out. You need to explain which exhibit shows which competence(s) and why, referencing relevant parts of any lengthy exhibit.

If you have been constructing exhibits as instructed in the exercises, you should already be getting a feel for how to do this. You should also be building a collection of evidence which could help you gain qualifications after graduation. It is a good habit to treat everything you do which shows you have mastered a new skill, or can use it in a new context, as a potential exhibit. You will find it helps to consolidate your learning to write your case around the material. Leafing through the portfolio can also be a powerful antidote to depression. When you are depressed it is easy to underestimate yourself. A solid portfolio can counteract this.

# SUMMARY

This chapter has argued the following:

- Doing well in assessment requires clarity of objectives, planning, monitoring and use of feedback wherever possible. It thus closely resembles management in other contexts.

- All assessments can usefully be regarded as communication, so written or spoken communication skills are vital.

- Use of ideas, images or words originated by others, without giving the originators the credit, constitutes plagiarism. Universities exact severe penalties for this, so it is important to clearly indicate and attribute any material which you did not generate yourself.

- Understanding objectives requires that you deconstruct a question and identify its constituent parts, then plan an answer which addresses all parts of a question, in a reasonable sequence.

- Understanding and using tutor feedback can help you improve your marks.

- Both essays and reports need an introduction and a conclusion and clear arguments based on valid evidence between the two.

- Time management is crucial for both written assignments and exams.

- For exams you need a clear revision plan based on identification of the material that it is important to cover. Revision needs to be active and to include frequent tests of recall and of ability to draft outline answers to possible questions.

- During an exam it is important to read questions carefully before selecting, to plan your answers and regularly check both your time usage and the continued relevance of what you write to the actual question asked.

- Should anything go wrong to threaten your success, obtain evidence of the problem where possible and notify the authorities as soon as possible.

# Further information

Race, P. (2007) *How to Get a Good Degree (2nd edition)*, Open University Press.

# HELPFILE
# TERMS COMMONLY USED
# IN ASSESSMENT

## Analyse

To examine part by part. Thus if you are asked to analyse a problem situation you would be looking for the roots of the problem rather than merely describing the symptoms which are presented. You would normally be expected to draw heavily on ideas and frameworks in the course being assessed in order to identify the root causes. The analysis may be the basis for suggesting possible ways forward and deciding among them.

## Assess

To judge the importance of something, or say what it is worth, giving your reasons for your verdict.

## Comment

This terse instruction may appear after a quotation or other statement. You are required to respond in a way that shows that you understand the topic to which the statement refers. Thus you might need to define any terms contained, explain the significance of the statement and possibly evaluate it (see below), or state the extent to which you agree and disagree and give your reasons for this.

## Compare

This means that you should look for both similarities and differences between the (usually) two things mentioned. It is very easy to forget one or the other, thus potentially losing half the available marks. It is safest always to think of 'compare' as shorthand for 'compare and contrast'. Sometimes you will be expected to come down in favour of one of the things compared. One possible approach to comparison is to construct a table with one column for each of the items compared and rows for each relevant aspect. This gives an 'at a glance' impression of aspects where entries are the same and those where there are differences. It will not, however, allow much space for discussion and may need to be complemented by a paragraph or two highlighting the significance of key similarities and differences which appear in the table.

# Consider

This has a similar meaning to comment, though the emphasis on evaluation is likely to be higher.

# Contrast

A subset of 'compare' (see above), requiring you to focus only on differences between the things mentioned.

# Criticise/critically evaluate

To judge the merit of a statement or theory, making clear the basis for your judgement. This might be in terms of the evidence on which the statement or theory is based, the likely validity of any assumptions made, the internal consistency of the statement, or its theoretical, logical or factual underpinning.

# Define

To state, precisely, the meaning of a concept. Normally this will be a definition that you have been given in your course. Sometimes there may be competing definitions, in which case you may need to give both (or all, if more than two), and discuss the differences between them. You will often be asked to include examples of the thing to be defined. Even if not asked for, an example may help to convey to the marker that you understand the meaning of the term in question.

# Demonstrate

This means you need to show something, usually by giving relevant examples, in order to convince the marker of your understanding of something or of its relevance or importance.

# Describe

To give a detailed account of the thing referred to, again with a view to establishing that you know what is being referred to and understand its significance. Diagrams can often help you to describe something and should be included if they add something to your words.

# Differentiate

This is similar to 'contrast', again requiring you to describe the differences between the things mentioned.

# Discuss

To extract the different themes in a subject and to describe and evaluate them. What are the key factors/aspects? What are the arguments in favour of, and against, each aspect? What evidence is there supporting each side of the argument? What is the significance of each aspect?

# Evaluate

This means much the same as 'assess'. If you were asked to evaluate a theory, for example, you would look both at the evidence supporting the theory and at the theory's usefulness.

# Examine

This means much the same as 'analyse', though it might require a slightly higher proportion of description in relation to evaluation.

# Explain

This can mean to make something clear or to give reasons for something, depending on the context. Frequently, you would need to do both in order to answer a question. Remember that your explanation, as with all assessments, is intended to demonstrate to your assessor your understanding of a concept or argument.

# Illustrate

This is similar to 'demonstrate'. It requires you to make clear your understanding of an idea or term by giving concrete examples, or by using a diagram or other figure to add to the word(s) and convey the message that you know what you are talking about.

# Interpret

This normally means to make sense of something, to make it clear, usually giving your judgement of the significance of the thing to be interpreted. You might be asked to interpret a set of figures or a graph, in which case you would need to describe in words the significant features, or messages, contained therein.

# Justify

This means you must give good reason for something, in terms of logic or evidence. It helps to think of the main objections to whatever it is and then show why they are not valid, as well as thinking of the plus points.

# List

This needs to be treated with caution. Strictly it means to give single words or phrases. But sometimes the assessor wants you to give a brief description rather than merely a single word. If in doubt, ask, if it is a written assignment. In an exam, make a reasoned guess from the proportion of the marks allocated to this part of the question and any subsequent instructions. For example, 'List ... Select two items from your list and describe them in detail' clearly does mean a list pure and simple.

# Outline

To give a brief description of the most important features of whatever it is.

# Refute

The converse of 'justify', requiring you to make the case *against* something.

# Review

To go over a subject carefully, giving as much as you can remember or unearth of what is relevant, though as concisely as is appropriate.

# Summarise

Write briefly the main points of something – very similar to 'outline'.

# Trace

This requires you to track a sequence of events which led to a specified state. (Multiple cause diagrams may be helpful here if there is more than a single 'track'.)

# . . . ?

By this I mean questions which seem to invite the answer yes or no, such as 'Do you agree?' after a statement. It is extremely rare for the assessor to expect such a simple answer. Far more often the expectation is that you will discuss the statement and evaluate it.

# CHAPTER 6

# A Brilliant future

To believe in your brilliance is to remove any limitations from your future

To ensure a Brilliant future you really need to understand what employability means to potential employers, your degree discipline and more importantly to you. Despite the fact that both employers and universities make provision for the development of employability skills through the curriculum through the availability of work experience, respectively, ultimately the key driver of your development of employability skills is you. You will determine your level of engagement and to what degree you get involved. As a result it is important to fully understand the 'I' in the I Brand Employability Model as, despite all the opportunities available, students' experiences will vary in relation to their levels of effort and involvement. This further emphasises the importance of your 'individual brand' as everyone will be different: students will differ in the priority they give to developing employability skills and their interpretation of what employability means to them.

## Why is employability important?

The changes in the higher education sector will continually increase the importance of employability not only for students, but will also place the onus on universities to ensure they are producing graduates who can 'hit the ground running'. The increase in fees will raise students' expectations from their institution to ensure 'success' upon graduation. Success will be defined in terms of their ability to secure employment, especially with the expectation that they will become liable to repay tuition fees once their salaries surpass £21,000. Currently universities are required to produce a public statement outlining how they promote employability to students and, by 2012, students will be able to see the employment statistics for each course and so make informed decisions about not only where to study, but also which course.

Employers also place heavy emphasis on employability skills, as, although they recognise their role in the development of graduates, they also see the importance of graduates harnessing and developing their own skills. This shows drive and ingenuity, which will always be valued in any sector. Students who are able to practically demonstrate and draw on examples that show their understanding of generic employability skills will advance far quicker in the graduate market. Do remember that employability does not guarantee employment, but definitely enhances the prospects of graduates to secure employment. The statistics highlighted in 'The graduate market' (High Fliers Research, 2011) emphasised the fact that a third of all graduate vacancies in 2011 will go to graduates who have previously worked at the organisation and students with no work experience will struggle to secure a graduate role.

Employability will continue to increase in importance and universities, employers and students will place more emphasis on developing ways to attain these skills while at university. As stated above, a number of universities have employability awards that both recognise and encourage students to engage with extra-curricular activities. Employers have also developed schemes to circumvent the introduction of fees to maintain access levels for a wider selection of students from all backgrounds who may (due to the increase in fees) have discounted the idea of attending university.

## What is employability?

Mantze Yorke (2006a) defines employability as:

*'a set of achievements – skills, understanding and personal attributes – that makes graduates more likely to gain employment and be successful in their chosen occupations, which benefits themselves, the workforce, the community and the economy.'*

Graduate employers recognise a range of generic employability skills that underpin the ability of a graduate to perform in the workplace. The I Brand Employability Model (reproduced on overleaf for reference) recognises the skills embedded within your course, but also the need to develop practical examples of generic employability skills drawn from your extra-curricular activities, work experience or voluntary work.

The 'I' in the model recognises your individual effort and contribution. The model acknowledges that students' background and personality will influence how they engage with employability both within their course and extra-curricular activities. As mentioned, networking is a key factor in gaining employment and identifying opportunities. The extended network of students is dependent upon their background and their ability to widen their network via their parents' associations and business contacts. This can create a significant disparity in opportunities available to students, as it is dependent not on ability but the social and economic standing of your parents. Your ability to recognise opportunities and take calculated risks is part of your personal make-up and so I Enterprise recognises a students' ability to add value through innovative and creative approaches to tasks. Enterprising skills are highly valued among employers. I Marketing draws heavily on the analogy of marketing a product and encourages students to review all aspects of their marketing strategy. How will they promote their product in the marketplace? How will they stand out?

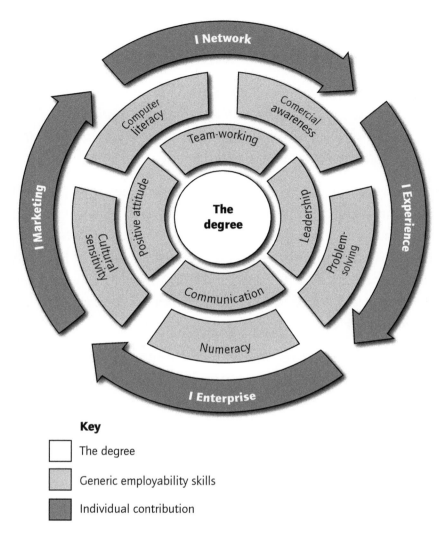

**Key**

☐ The degree

▨ Generic employability skills

▨ Individual contribution

**The I Brand Employability Model**

This is an important aspect of the model as students need to understand their strengths and weaknesses – essentially, their unique selling point – in order to communicate this factor to potential employers. Every student should be able to answer the question 'Why would an employer choose me over another graduate?'

The I Experience highlights and emphasises the different backgrounds, cultural differences and motivational drivers for each student. Student experience is unique and personal to each student, so it is important to recognise this factor when developing employability skills. Students bring their 'personal baggage' to the table and ultimately it will impact their engagement and development of employability skills.

## Whose responsibility is it?

Ultimately the responsibility rests with the student. Universities clearly have a role to play in ensuring students are provided with opportunities to develop employability skills within the curriculum and through the provision of extra-curricular activities. Employers have a responsibility to ensure the provision of varied work experience opportunities. In the end it all comes back to the students' willingness to partake in these opportunities. Each student's level of engagement will vary.

# What opportunities exist to develop employability skills?

Employability is embedded into the curriculum. Through various methods of assessment, students are given the opportunity to develop a range of skills. The key issue is the fact that these opportunities are seldom labelled as such and so few students actually connect the dots and recognise the transferable nature of the skills they develop on their courses and their relevance to the world of work. Vital skills are learnt and honed during assessment, which will not only develop essential skills for the workplace but also for the interview process to secure a graduate role. The table overleaf reinforces the connection between assessment methods and the skills required in the workplace.

The other avenue for developing employability skills is through extra-curricular activities. Both on and off campus, students have the opportunity to develop skills through involvement with the student's union or undertaking internships or voluntary work. It is through this practical application and demonstration of employability skills that students enhance their ability to stand

| Assessment method | Transferable skills |
| --- | --- |
| Group assignments | Students are often required to work in teams to complete a group task. Students develop project management, team-building, negotiation and influencing skills, all highly relevant to the world of work |
| Presentations | The ability to develop a well-structured presentation that communicates the key points effectively and efficiently is a valuable skill, useful in a variety of situations beyond a degree |
| Case-study analysis | The case-study analysis presents a business scenario and requires students to utilise critical thinking, analytical and problem-solving skills not only to identify the key challenges but also make recommendations drawing on both the internal and external environment faced by the organisation. Case-studies are often used within the selection process to differentiate candidates |
| Report-writing | Accuracy and clarity in report-writing is a must! Literacy skills are central to your academic studies and for application forms and writing reports or emails in the workplace |
| Problem-based learning | The ability to resolve problems and provide well-founded solutions is directly transferable to the workplace, where students will be continually presented with challenges |
| Research | Research skills are applicable to all industries. The ability to collate, synthesise, analyse and clearly present information found can add value to all organisations, whether private, public or third-sector. All industries are reliant upon information to provide insights into current industry dynamics, future trends and possible opportunities and threats in the marketplace |
| Personal development planning (PDP) | PDP encourages reflection on your strengths and weaknesses and develops self-awareness, which supports your continual development and learning |
| Examinations | Examinations present the opportunity to apply your understanding to scenarios or questions within a time constraint. Many professions utilise professional examinations to test candidates' knowledge and application of the subject matter. An ability to pass examinations is a required skill within the work environment. Examinations are also used as part of the interview process and so have relevance in many work-related situations |

out. These activities not only enrich the student experience but also provide a wealth of examples that students can draw on in an interview or selection process. Once again it relies on the students' ability to both recognise and connect the skills they are developing to the generic employability skills valued by graduate recruiters. Below is a recap of some of the skills that can be developed through extra-curricular activity and how they relate to the world of work.

- Leadership skills
  - You don't have to be the president of a society to develop leadership skills. Taking ownership of a task or role and demonstrating the ability to influence, negotiate for resources and motivate others to achieve a common goal are all examples of leadership qualities. These skills will resonate with an employer, as one of an organisation's goals is to identify people who have the ability to lead/manage a team.
- Project management
  - Whether you are at university or in the workplace, you will always need to have a clear plan of action of how you will achieve your goals. The ability to plan, adhere to deadlines and identify key milestones to succeed are all part of the organisational skills required within the work environment.

- Event management
  - The co-ordination and planning involved in organising a successful event demonstrate your ability to multitask and strong organisational skills. Event management requires a high level of organisational skills, from liaising with speakers and developing and distributing the marketing communication to negotiating additional resources. The ability to co-ordinate a successful event is an impressive addition to your CV. The busy workplace will always

require the ability to multitask while maintaining standards. Organisational skills and the ability to meet deadlines are musts for successful graduates.

- Budgeting
  - The ability to budget and forecast demonstrates an understanding of how decisions will affect the bottom line. For instance, understanding how to budget for the costs associated with an event and balance these costs in relation to ticket sales to break even and or make a profit are valuable skills. All organisations will value these skills and will especially value your ability to highlight the relationship between decision-making and the impact on costs, as the economy requires all industries to operate efficiently. These skills are directly transferable to all industry sectors.

- Communication
  - Both written and spoken communication can be developed by participating in a university society and their value is transferable to the workplace. The ability to write a persuasive email or report requesting support for the society or the development of effective marketing materials providing members with updates and information are useful skills. Employers will expect a high standard of literacy and communication skills. You will be required to produce reports, communicate with clients and provide information to other departments in the organisation.

- Networking
  - Networking will help the enterprising student secure additional resources for his or her society and generally meet individuals from different backgrounds and interests. Networking is the backbone of all business. The ability to maintain a wide network is useful not only for university but also identifying possible opportunities.

Employability is a continual process. This is reinforced by the circular nature of the model. While at university and beyond you will continue to develop your employability skills and also redefine which skills are important to you and prospective employers.

## Are there jobs out there and can I have one?

Good question. When all is said and done and students have done all they can to develop employability skills, will they be rewarded with a graduate role? The graduate opportunities in 2011 are on the rise and the outlook is more promising, but students cannot afford to be complacent. Companies have raised the stakes and many require an upper second as the minimum for entry to their graduate schemes. More than a third of all graduate vacancies will go to students who have previously undertaken work experience with the companies concerned. As a result, students need to understand the importance of not only developing employability skills but also establishing links with companies during their studies.

Work experience has become a vital ingredient in a graduate's ability to secure employment. As a result, 63 per cent of the top graduate recruiters offer work experience opportunities for graduates in the form of both internships and placements. The competition for these positions is fierce and students will have to undergo a series of selection processes in order to be successful.

## When I grow up I want to be a ...?

Choosing the right career is often one of the most difficult decisions for students. How do you know you will like your chosen career path? Knowing you will be the best starting point! Having a good understanding of what motivates you and what is a priority for you in the workplace will help you not only identify suitable roles but also suitable companies. This can be supported by undertaking research into possible career options, both discipline-related and unrelated. There are many successful professionals who have not taken the automatic career path for their degree discipline. Learning from the experiences of alumni is also another option. Alumni can provide insight into career options and their own experience of the working world. Regardless of your discipline, there will be various roles available to you and it is always useful to speak with professionals in these roles to find out whether the role is suitable for you. Internships and placements also give you a different perspective about a role; there is no substitute for work experience to provide a behind-the-scenes look at possible career options.

This can be easier said than done. Finding work experience and ultimately a graduate position is not an easy feat. An internship provides you with the opportunity to see if a career is for you, but also provides an employer with the opportunity to test-drive your product. If you are not fortunate enough to find an internship there are other ways to gain work experience. Temporary roles or job shadowing are also methods of gaining a practical insight into a potential career choice.

## Communicating your Brilliance

As highlighted above, the ability to translate your employability skills into those valued by employers is an art in itself. Identifying your strengths and weaknesses and areas for development are all essential when trying to find both work experience and graduate roles. The ability to communicate your Brilliance will rely heavily on your verbal and literacy skills and your ability to present yourself both physically and on paper in a manner acceptable to employers. Preparation is central to all of the elements of the selection process, from writing your CV to attending your first interview. Your success will be underpinned by planning, researching the company and the role, reflecting upon your experiences and identifying how they match the selection criteria.

Using the STAR framework – Situation, Task, Action, Result – to review your work experience, tasks undertaken on your course and your extra-curricular activities will help you to match your skill set to the requirements of your employers. You will be surprised at how many examples you will be able to draw upon.

Being meticulous in your preparation in all stages of the selection process is paramount. An error on your CV or arriving late for an interview speaks volumes about your character and creates a bad impression. If you cannot manage yourself, how will you manage any of the clients' business relationships or processes? Researching the company and having knowledge of their main competitors, the challenges they face in the marketplace and a general understanding of the business environment will support you in your interview and add value to your responses. Employers will be impressed if you take the time to find out not only about their company but also any challenges faced by the organisation. Prepare, prepare, prepare, as it can make the difference between a successful application and being overlooked in favour of another candidate.

## A continuous Career Life Cycle

Employability is not an end in itself. Once you begin your career, then you need to continually reflect upon your employability skills to ensure your skills are still aligned with the needs of your employer and your industry sector. For instance, IT is continually changing and influencing sector development. Social media has had an impact on all sectors in some way, with companies utilising social networks both informally and formally. You can't afford to stand still now that you have secured a graduate position, as life is constantly moving!

As you develop, mature and move through your Career Life Cycle, your needs and wants will also change. What you defined as career goals and ambitions may change as you get older or your circumstances change.

The circular nature of the I Brand Employability Model emphasises the continuous process of employability. You will continue to grow and develop and this in turn will inform your employability. Your degree is a three- or four-year course and throughout that time you will be exposed to many different experiences that will influence the direction of your future career. University is a time to explore, research and investigate various career options and the skills required. There are also many opportunities to build and develop your network, both within and external to your university, so don't miss out!

The need to be determined in your search of a career is paramount. Building your employability skills while at university is not an option but a necessity. You cannot afford to ignore your employability until after graduation. Start building and developing your employability skills from day one to get ahead of the game!

## brilliant recap

- Make sure you understand what employability means for your discipline and potential graduate recruiters.

- You determine to what degree you engage with developing employability skills.

- The success of a university is strongly linked to the ability of its graduates to secure graduate employment.

- Ultimately the responsibility of developing employability skills rests with the students, as they have to make an active decision to engage.

- Students need to recognise the opportunities embedded within

▶

their courses to develop transferable skills relevant to the workplace.

- Extra-curricular activities provide students with the opportunity to give practical demonstrations of their employability skills in action.

- Leadership skills, project mangement skills, event management, budgeting and communication are all skills that can be developed through extra-curricular activities.

- Employability is a continual process and each stage of your career will require you to redefine the skills you need to develop in order to progress.

- Take every possible opportunity to network and develop links with companies while studying.

- Take time to explore both discipline-related and non-discipline-related career options.

- Try to gain work experience in your chosen field: this is a good test to see if this career is for you.

- Be meticulous in your preparation at all stages in the application process.

- Employability is not an optional extra – place it at the heart of your university experience.

# Part 2:
# Employability and Careers

**CHAPTER 7**

# The graduate labour market

Increasingly, employers will look for some more interesting skills; things like cultural sensitivity and what makes a global graduate. Sometimes you have to go sideways to get to where you want to be.

Carl Gilleard, Chief Executive, Association of Graduate Recruiters

This chapter will help you to make sense of the graduate labour market. You are going to need to understand how the labour market works if you are to find your way around it – which you need to do as you work towards securing your brilliant career. You need to know that the labour market is both complex and dynamic. This is the chapter you are most likely to turn to when riffling through this book, and it is probably the most difficult chapter to write. Difficult to write, firstly, because we want to present some fairly complex concepts in a very accessible way. Difficult, secondly, because any labour market is not only complex, but also dynamic: it doesn't stand still but constantly shifts and changes in response to a range of factors which shape the supply of and demand for workers. That dynamism means that you may want to consult some online sources of up-to-the-minute data if you want a real-time assessment of what's going on in the graduate labour market when you actually read this.

So this chapter is going to take you through some key concepts in employment, then it will look at why employers want graduates and what graduates have to offer in terms of knowledge, skills and abilities. We will also look at small to medium-sized enterprises (SMEs) as these play a significant role in graduate recruitment, but can be overlooked by graduate jobseekers. We then have a brief overview of what kind of employment sectors graduates have gone into in recent years and the kind of wages they start out with.

 **tip**

The labour market is constantly changing but you can easily get the most up-to-date information online.

# Fundamentals of the labour market: supply and demand

## There are two sides to any market, and that includes the labour market

You'll hear talk of 'the labour market' when issues of employment, unemployment, job vacancies and employability are discussed. 'Labour' here means simply to do with work. The term 'labour market' is used to describe the interactions between employers who need labour (or workers, to put it another way) and employees (those who can supply that labour or undertake that work). The study of the labour market is of interest to economists, and can be seen as a discipline in itself. Understanding how the labour market works and keeping up to date with what's happening with job vacancies and demands is important for careers advisers too.

## Picture a market in your mind's eye

The idea of a 'market' helps us to envisage what is going on. So just take a moment to think of a market (or supermarket or shop) from your own experience. It might be a bustling, chaotic place with people shouting out what they are hoping to sell – or it might be extremely organised into tidy aisles stacked full of goods with special offer stickers pointing out the best buys.

## You are the 'supply' in the graduate labour market

Whatever the setting, there are always two sides in play. On the one hand, there are people offering goods for sale (goods such as a pair of trainers or a bunch of grapes); on the other, people who are looking to buy what's on offer. And that's the first key point: for the market to work, you have to have supply (stuff being offered) and demand (stuff being wanted). Don't be insulted if we now compare you to a pair of trainers or a bunch of grapes, but you are the supply in the labour market. You are available, on show, ready to be snapped up by someone with money to secure you – and a discerning eye to know a quality product (be it trainers, grapes or graduates) when it's up for grabs.

 **brilliant** definitions

The term **supply** refers to all the people who are actively seeking work – which of course includes you.

The term **demand** refers to all the jobs that are looking to be filled – which is, of course, what you want.

## The relationship between supply and demand is critical in your jobsearch

It is clear that 'supply' and 'demand' are the two fundamental forces driving the labour market. So the relationship between supply and demand is critical. As you are part of the supply side, it is important that you think about the market from the other perspective and get a sense of how employers work and what kind of supply they are looking for (demanding). This allows you to tailor your offer (of yourself for hire) to their demand. That could be a relatively simple task: presenting your skills, knowledge and understanding in a way that makes it easy for an employer to understand exactly what you have to offer and how that fits with what they need in their workforce. On making sure that your application gets past the first post. It could, however, require a complex, more lengthy task which might be that you seek to expand your skills, knowledge and understanding (that is, working on expanding your professional repertoire) by undertaking voluntary work or work shadowing, or accepting a job that you don't really want to do now in order to get the job you want in the future: your brilliant career.

> ### ☼ brilliant tip
>
> When you are looking for a job, so that you present what you have to offer in a way that the employer will easily recognise, try to think from the employer's perspective. Look at what they want and why they want it. Then make sure that you've got what they want and you showcase that in your application.

## What's distinctive about the graduate labour market?

### Graduate labour as a distinct sector within the labour market

You may be wondering why graduates are treated as a distinct subgroup within the labour market. Defining sectors is just a way of examining the labour market in more detail, and is helpful in getting a hold on labour market information which could otherwise be unwieldy and overwhelming. Market analysts often drill into data so that they can get the low-down on a particular sector. A sector can be defined by occupation (e.g. Engineering or Business or Creative Arts) or by geography (the South East or Greater Merseyside) or by shared characteristics of the workforce (graduates). We'll look at occupational sectors in more detail 'Labour market information: analysis of what graduates do', but for now we'll look at the graduate labour market: which simply means that the demand is for graduate-level jobs, for which the jobseeker (the supply) must have an undergraduate degree (at least).

## What work do graduates actually do?

Every year the Higher Education Statistics Agency (HESA) asks graduates to report what they have gone on to do after they finished their degree. A questionnaire goes out to all those finishing an undergraduate degree, which includes Foundation degrees. It only goes to people who are resident in the United Kingdom or the European Union, so does not include postgraduates or overseas students who are not UK residents. It only asks about their 'first' destination: that is, what they were doing six months after completing their degree. Destinations include: work (paid employment); further study (perhaps at postgraduate level); looking for work; and not available for work (e.g. travelling). 'Labour market information: analysis of what graduates do' goes into some detail about what graduates from different degrees go on to do. This makes it easy for you to check where people who did the same degree as you ended up. The results are presented by broad subject area (e.g. Social Sciences) then broken down into its particular disciplines (for Social Sciences this would include Economics and Sociology).

### Graduate earnings

One noticeable characteristic of the graduate labour market is that wages are higher. Of course, it is perfectly possible to earn higher than average earnings without a degree, where your skills and talents are in demand. This is particularly true where the supply of skill is very limited, so employers are competing with each other to secure the services of a limited pool of talent. These highly sought-after skills come at a premium, which means the employers have to pay more. A classic example here would be a footballer: the employer's primary concern is ability as a footballer, not the level of formal education achieved.

However, if you look at graduates in the labour market as a whole and compare their lifetime earnings, graduates on average earn more than non-graduates. This is often referred to as the 'graduate premium'. In 2001, the average lifetime earnings of a graduate, when compared to the average earnings of someone with two A levels, amounted to £400,000 or 41%. In the decade from 2001 to 2011, the number of graduates increased hugely, by 41%. This meant that the supply of graduates increased and subsequent research, published in 2007, revised the graduate premium down to £160,000 which still amounts to 20–25% more than someone with two A levels. These are only averages, and the actual earnings of any individual graduate can vary considerably from this average figure. The degree subject you take, the job you go into, the kind of employer you work for and the location of your employment will all have a bearing on your earnings over your lifetime.

## Is the graduate premium guaranteed?

What happens to the graduate premium in the future is largely a question of supply and demand. Even when the supply has increased, although the premium has diminished, it still represents an additional 25% in lifetime earnings. The Office for National Statistics (ONS, 2012) reported average graduate pay at £15.18 per hour, in contrast to £8.92 per hour paid on average to non-graduates in the same age range. There are, of course, big variations in the hourly pay of graduates with medicine and dentistry paying at the top of the range and arts subjects towards the bottom.

Although the recession has certainly affected graduate recruitment, economic forecasts expect the demand for graduates will rise in the coming years, and the graduate premium may have diminished, but it is still there. So there are clear economic benefits to having a degree. This may not ring true if you are battling through difficult economic times when graduate jobs are hard fought and hard won. It may be difficult to think about this now, or to believe that it's important, but when you get towards retirement age you will look back and see what a difference having a degree has made in the long run.

### ⬤ **brilliant** definition

The **graduate premium,** in labour market terms, is the difference in earnings potential for graduates as a sector of the market compared with other groups of workers. The graduate premium requires employers to pay higher wages to secure a graduate to fill their vacancy. The graduate premium means that graduate earnings over a lifetime are likely to be higher than for non-graduates.

*How graduates differ from other occupational sectors*

There are a couple of other significant differences when you compare graduates in the labour market with other groups of workers.

They are more mobile in the labour market, which means that they are more likely to move to another part of the country to take up work and may even work outside their country of origin. Employers are also more likely to move their graduate workers about, though will often offer incentives and rewards for doing so.

Another curious characteristic is that graduates are more likely to be given further training. This can often be in-house or on-the-job training, but can also mean sending graduate workers on specialist and/or postgraduate courses at universities.

 Most graduates now are expected to do regular evaluations of where they are at and where they are going . . . developing the individual to the point where they can take control of their life, their learning and their career.

Carl Gilleard, Chief Executive, Association of Graduate Recruiters

It may seem odd that employers want their skilled people to get even more skilled – but they know that graduates can learn (see below) and a more highly skilled worker is more highly prized because they can do more. The flip side of being offered this kind of opportunity is that employers expect their graduate workers to progress in their careers and invest in their own professional development. Of course, expanding your professional repertoire in this way benefits you because it gives you more leverage in the labour market.

*Not all graduates are the same*

---

### 🔆 brilliant example

'My last job was a stop-gap really: it wasn't the job I wanted and it wasn't the money I wanted. But I wanted to learn, I was interested and, gradually, it built. The longer I was there, the more things were handed over. So then when it came to the pay review I could say: "I'm doing this now, and I want to be paid for it." I'd proved myself. After five years, I was earning nearly three times the salary I started on.'

Sophie, employee in small to medium-sized enterprise

---

---

### 🔆 brilliant example

'I was a (very) mature student, already in my chosen career as a mental health recovery and rehabilitation worker. I decided to study Psychology for several reasons: I enjoyed it at A level, I never had the chance to go to university when I left school and wondered if I could do it, and the subject is closely linked to my work . . . I have much more confidence in decision making and suggestions I make at work now. I feel the knowledge I now have of theories and empirical evidence . . . enhances the experience I already had.'

Linda, BSc (Hons) Psychology

---

We have been talking of a graduate labour market as if all graduates are the same, but that's clearly nonsense. Graduates are different, one from the other, because people are different. Two students may be studying on the same programme, even in the same tutor group, and yet hold very different values and so will be looking for jobs in distinctly different ways. One may be highly motivated by money; the other by job satisfaction and a work–life balance. One may be happy to relocate from one place of work to another within an organisation, or even to move from one country to another if their employer demands it or if a good job offer comes up. For other graduates, family responsibilities, emotional ties or just a strong sense of belonging may keep them in one place, and so they may restrict their jobsearch to a particular geographical area. Some graduates are changing career direction completely and have retrained in order to step out in a completely new career direction. Others will be starting out and their first graduate job may well be their first job. Some graduates will hold out for the job that matches their specification of a dream job. For others, any job will do: they just need to earn money to live. So, even though this chapter treats graduates as a set of workers sharing graduate-level qualifications, there are huge differences for individuals, who will make their own decisions and carve their own path to what is a brilliant career, for them.

 **brilliant** recap

- As a group, graduates earn more over the course of their working life than non-graduates.

- Graduate workers tend to move location and/or employer more than non-graduates.

- Graduates undertake more training and personal development than other workers.

- Employers will pay a premium for highly skilled workers, especially if supply is limited.

- All graduates are individuals who will carve out their own brilliant career.

# What's distinctive about graduates as a labour supply?

## Why would employers pay more for a graduate?

So why are employers prepared to pay more for workers who have a degree? Graduate employees tend to bring innovation and creativity to their work, which solves business problems and can increase productivity. That's not to say that other groups of workers don't do that but graduates, as a workforce and on the whole, have a proven track record for doing so. Broadly speaking, graduates are paid to think, so they add value to their work, which in turn adds value to the organisation they work for, which in turn repays the 'graduate premium'.

## How do employers know what graduates are capable of?

You might think that employers are just taking it on trust that graduates can think, and will be able to apply intellectual and cognitive abilities. Well, yes and no. Employers can take it on trust, because there are clear standards of achievement that are expected before a student can be awarded a degree. Although individual universities award their own degrees, all degrees in England, Wales and Northern Ireland work to the framework for higher education qualifications published by the Quality Assurance Agency for Higher Education. The framework sets the benchmark for what graduates should achieve in their degree, whether Foundation, Honours or Masters.

**brilliant** tip

As a graduate, you are trained to think: to think critically, to think creatively, to think things through. You need to show an employer how your training in thinking can benefit their organisation or add value to their enterprise.

## What graduates should be able to do

For example, on successful completion of their programme, an Honours graduate should be able to:

- understand key aspects of their field of study (including coherent and detailed knowledge);
- conduct analysis and enquiry; devise and sustain arguments, and/or solve problems;
- appreciate uncertainty and ambiguity; and
- manage their own learning.

### What graduates are able to do from the employer's perspective

All of these competencies would relate primarily to the subject or discipline you are studying, whether that is Fine Art, Computer Science or Medicine. From an employer's point of view, that ability to think transfers into the workplace as:

- the exercise of initiative and personal responsibility;

- decision making in complex and unpredictable contexts;

- effective communication of information, ideas, problems and solutions to specialist and non-specialist audiences; and

- the learning ability needed to undertake appropriate further training of a professional or equivalent nature.

So, when an employer specifically advertises a graduate job, and demands that their employee has a first degree, they expect graduate employees to work at this level of sophistication in their workplace.

## How employers view subject discipline

Between 60 and 70 per cent of graduate jobs advertised don't specify the degree discipline – which means you can apply no matter what subject you studied. This statistic has remained fairly constant for a long time, so we can assume that it will hold good for some time to come. What it tells us is that it is your thinking power that employers want, not necessarily the specialist knowledge of your discipline. You might have to help the employer recognise that, despite you studying a very different subject from them, you have got what they are looking for. (Of course, where an employer wants a specialist, such as a doctor, lawyer, dentist or graphic designer, then they will advertise specifically for those roles and qualifications. This accounts for about half the graduate jobs advertised.) The important thing here is to remember to look at things from the employer's perspective. You might well have a degree in a subject about which the employer knows nothing at all. This could be anything, from Classical Civilisation to Sports and Exercise Studies. The employer may even have preconceptions about your degree, thinking, for example, that Arts and Design graduates don't have any commercial under-standing, or not realising that Psychology requires a good understanding of statistics. So you may well have to scrutinise your skills and experience and present what you know in a way that the employer can't fail to grasp. What you can know for sure is that, if you have achieved an undergraduate degree, you have proven thinking power – and that is in demand.

 **tip**

More than half of the graduate vacancies on offer do not specify a particular degree discipline. So you can broaden your jobsearch beyond your field of study.

## Not all employers are big organisations

**brilliant example**

'I've worked in SMEs for several years now. It's actually far more challenging working for a smaller company than it is working for a larger company. You have more opportunity to shine, in fact, and to move up quickly.'

Sophie, Evotel Holdings employee

### Why are small to medium-sized enterprises important?

SMEs play a huge part in the economy: in the EU, 99 per cent of all enterprises are SMEs. In the UK, annual data published by the Department of Business and Skills (BIS, 2015) shows that SMEs accounted for 99.9 per cent of all private sector businesses and 59 per cent of private-sector employment. That means a lot of people are actually working in SMEs (14.1 million at the last count) and that includes graduates. Now do you see why they are so important?

---

⬤ **brilliant** example

Evotel Holdings supplies televisions to electrical retailers in the United Kingdom. They import televisions and they import components which are assembled in the UK and in the European Union. They are in a network of repair agents, working for manufacturers, insurers and retailers. Their market is characterised by high volume and low margin, which means very little tolerance if they are to make a profit. They must deliver on quality, on quantity and on time. A successful small to medium-sized enterprise, Evotel has to stay smart to keep ahead of its competitors.

---

## What is an SME?

SMEs are vital to the economy, both in the United Kingdom and throughout Europe. But what exactly is an SME? The letters simply stand for small to medium-sized enterprise, but we need to define these terms too in order to understand what an SME is.

## What is an enterprise?

There is no one definition, but in economic terms, an enterprise is an organisation created for business venture. So an organisation intends to do business and preferably to do business that makes a profit.

## Small, medium-sized – or micro?

The size of an enterprise can be determined either by the number of people or the amount of money involved. The technical terms here are headcount or turnover/balance sheet total. From an employment perspective it is probably easier to think in terms of how many people are involved in the business: the headcount. In a headcount, no distinction is made between full-time and part-time workers: so if an SME has five full-time and five part-time, that makes ten workers. In the EU, the headcount includes employees and self-employed people working in the enterprise. Whereas in the UK, the headcount applies only to employees (BIS, 2015). But both the EU and the UK agree the headcount categories for SMEs, which are as follows:

**micro** = headcount up to 9

**small** = headcount of at least 10 and up to 49

**medium-sized** = headcount of at least 50, up to 249.

Although we often think of SMEs as small, they can actually be very small indeed, or quite sizeable. They can often be overlooked because the individual enterprises aren't household names. However, the opportunities in SMEs are statistically significant, and certainly worth investigating.

**brilliant tip**

Include SMEs in your jobsearch. You may not have heard their name, but they are a powerful force in the labour market. They are less likely to spend much money on advertising, so do your research and consider making a speculative application to a targeted SME. They really don't have any time to waste, so make sure you focus your application.

## What to do next

There is every chance that you know someone who works for an SME – why not ask them about their work and their workplace? It would be interesting to see if they felt they had had any particular opportunities because of the small scale of their employment – or if they perceived any disadvantage.

## Graduates need employability skills

### What employers want: skillset and mindset

Having said that graduates are in demand in the labour market because of their proven ability to think, and having shown that employers pay a 'graduate premium', graduates are expected to offer more than their intellect: all graduates need good employability skills. This message comes through loud and clear from employers surveyed by the Confederation of British Industry (CBI, 2011) and Universities UK. Now, there is no one agreed definitive list of employability skills – there isn't even one agreed term. Sometimes these skills are called 'soft skills' or 'transferable skills' as well as 'employability skills'.

It is interesting to look at these terms in turn because they give an insight into what is in demand in the labour market, which allows you to pinpoint what you, as the supply, can offer or may need to develop. There is growing evidence that employers also value mindset. This refers to a set of attitudes and behaviours that allow workers to add value to their employing organisation. Some of these attitudes benefit the employee just as much as the employer: taking pride in your work and giving your best makes for greater satisfaction and self-esteem – both key in positive psychology.

 The graduates we employ are over-qualified for work in the warehouse or the call centre. But we employ graduates because they're more attentive, more willing to do a proper day's work. You have to assume they've got the ability to do the job, but if they haven't got it 100 per cent, it's not going to take us long to train them.

Julian Radley, Director, Evotel Holdings

Hard skills refer to such abilities as numeracy and literacy, managing a project or working in a team. It is relatively easy for an employer to check that you have them. In contrast, soft skills are less easy to test for with any scientific reliability, but they can be observed and demonstrated. So 'soft' here doesn't mean that they are easier skills to acquire, but that they are more difficult to pin down for assessment. Transferable skills mean simply that the skills can be developed in one job and taken with you to another job. A good example here would be customer care.

Customer care means dealing with customers: it involves the ability to listen, to question, to understand the issue, to convey that understanding to a customer (without losing your temper!) and to work towards resolving the issue in hand to the satisfaction of both parties. Customer care is important in a wide variety of contexts: looking after patients in a hospital; dealing with complaints from corporate clients; handling irate customers in a queue or on a shop floor. What the customers/clients/patients are concerned about doesn't matter: your skills and abilities can be used effectively no matter what the context. The transferability of these skills also means that you can develop skills in one aspect of your life that may not necessarily be paid work, and can then use them in your employment. An example of this would be the negotiation skills you have to develop as a parent (particularly of toddlers), which stand you in good stead when negotiating in a work environment.

 **brilliant** definition

Employers value a range of behaviours and aptitudes, which can be used in a range of employment contexts. They might be called **transferable**, **soft** or **employability** skills. Their name doesn't matter, but the skills do.

## Employability skillset and mindset

Here is our list of employability skills, drawn from a range of sources including the Confederation of British Industries and the National Union of Students (CBI/NUS, 2011). As they represent employers, this is very much from the demand perspective. They aren't presented in any particular order, because each of these skills is important in its own right, and different employers will place different emphasis on different skills at different times in the lifecycle of their own business. Although we can't give a precise indicator of demand for each of the skills, in an employer survey (CBI, 2011) 36% were not satisfied with foreign language fluency, and 44% of employers were not satisfied with graduate levels of business and customer awareness.

 It doesn't matter what the business is, there are some fundamental principles: cash flow is king; you've got to make sure there's a bottom line for the profit; and you've got to look at risk. Graduates need to ask where they fit into the critical path within the business process.

Julian Radley, Director, Evotel Holdings

## Self-management

Broadly speaking, self-management is the ability to take responsibility for a role or a given task. If you accept responsibility, then a number of attitudes and behaviours will follow from that. You will probably be prepared to be flexible and you may need to be assertive as and when appropriate. You'll need to be a self-starter, getting on with things and not waiting to be asked or to be directed. You'll also have to be aware of the need to manage your time. A key aspect of self-management is that you are prepared to improve your own performance with every task, role or job that you do. This improvement will come from two complementary perspectives. Firstly, your own reflective practice, where you think about what you've done, what went well and what could be done better next time round. Secondly, feedback from others, which is likely to be a mixture of positive and negative feedback. You will learn, and take the lessons you learn with you, no matter where you go next.

---

### brilliant example

'Aside from academic development, personal skills gained through my time at university are arguably as valuable. I've always been fairly confident, and university life allowed me to understand myself better: my strengths, weaknesses and life goals. Within two months of leaving university (in a very tough economic environment) I had secured a great job. I believe my time at university equipped me with the creative problem-solving skills that I need to excel within my industry – online brand reputation management.'

Alex, BA (Hons) Graphic Design

---

## Resilience

Resilience is what sustains you to keep going with a task or responsibility even when the going gets tough and you might be tempted to give up. Resilience requires your commitment to stay involved, some degree of control or influence and a sense of personal challenge to develop. Optimism plays an important part, but it has to be realistic, not hoping for some magic wand you can wave. Knowing what you're feeling and why is also important here, as is the ability to slow down and consider alternatives when you seem to hit a blank wall.

---

### brilliant example

'I was working in France as a runner in a big American-themed sports bar. Although it was an American place, everybody spoke French all the time. I didn't think I was going to take it: it was really busy and I didn't know anyone, not a single person . . . at first it was overwhelming: everyone was older; everyone was French; there was so much to learn, the menu and the ordering, but eventually I made friends and in the end I was sorry to leave.'

Hannah, (undergraduate) Economics and Politics with International Studies

---

## Team-working

This is obviously about working well with others. However, in order to do that you have to be aware that your individual contribution (and success) can be separated out from that of others in your team: you have to be aware of this interdependence and have to be able to manage yourself as a team-worker, not just as an individual. The behaviours that support effective team-working are sharing ideas with others by contributing to discussions and planning, and what follows from that is the need to cooperate with others and to respect them. Negotiating and persuading skills are key here.

---

### brilliant example

'A lot of the course I studied was teamwork-based, which enabled me to increase my confidence in working within a team. We also had to give a lot of presentations, which I found really nerve-racking, but it really did boost my confidence. I actually realised I did have a special talent for talking to groups and this encouraged me to consider teaching as a career.'

Katie, BSc (Hons) Animal Behaviour and Welfare

---

## Business and customer awareness

Although this really is a soft skill, in that you can't necessarily train or test people in it, you can see very clearly when people don't have it. Some employers of graduates say that this is the employability skill most often missing in applicants and new entrants. Although you would expect it to be very much in demand in the retail and business sector, it is actually very important in service and public service sectors too. It means understanding what drives a successful business or service, but that doesn't necessarily mean at the high strategic level. It is very much the bottom-up approach: keeping customers satisfied, understanding why you need to build customer loyalty, understanding how innovation can drive a business forward – and how the lack of innovation can mean a business grinding to a halt. It also includes an appreciation of the need to take calculated risks: not reckless, but bold nonetheless.

Initiative is an important thing in an employee; but they've got to be aware of what that opportunity is, and when the opportunity comes, and then how to deal with it. We needed some marketing expertise – someone remembered marketing was on Seb's CV, so he got the chance to step up to it.

Julian Radley, Director, Evotel Holdings

## Problem solving

Another skill that is pretty obvious, really. It will involve you analysing facts or data, and weighing up the context or situations. You'll need to work creatively, perhaps coming at problems from different angles and looking for a variety of approaches; and in order to solve the problem, you'll need to come up with appropriate solutions. A lot of your undergraduate work gets you to do this kind of thing, even if it isn't immediately obvious: linguists translating unfamiliar phrases need to puzzle things out, not simply reach for the nearest dictionary.

What happens is: we need to do something quickly and the only way to get someone quickly is to use someone that's here. Suddenly we realise someone's got more ability than we realised. Spotting talent is mostly by luck, which I think is wrong; we should be a bit more observant.

Julian Radley, Director, Evotel Holdings

## Project management

This skill is increasingly sought after. As a graduate employee, you may be asked to manage projects – and you need to be clear that you will probably be asked to manage more than one project at time. Effective project management calls on many of the skills listed here: communication and literacy; team-working; problem solving and resilience. You probably will have had direct experience of managing a project on your degree – just think about your final year dissertation or project or end of year show – and you had to do that while managing other 'projects' – your brilliant career included.

## Communication and literacy

This means the ability to read, write and to get your message across, which may seem really obvious. You should be able to write clearly and be able to structure your written work so that it makes sense. You should also be able to modulate the tone of your work to reach your intended readership. You should have good communication skills (sometimes called oral literacy), which means the ability to listen carefully, check your understanding and question appropriately. Poor communication is one of the greatest sources of frustration and irritation to employers; yet you can improve on this every single day, no matter what context you are operating in.

## brilliant example

'I completed a foundation degree in animal management. As well as the huge variety of academic knowledge I gained, I also made a lot of personal developments which have really helped boost my confidence. What was particularly useful was the greater understanding of general writing skills I gained, including grammar and written communication. I feel that my academic writing improved over my time at university and, not only did these skills give me further confidence when completing assignments, but these are skills that I can use in any job environment, whatever the sector.'

Jessica, FdSc Animal Management

## Numeracy

You do need to get your head around what is understood by numeracy. It does not mean advanced mathematical tasks, but fairly general awareness of the importance of maths as a tool in practical day-to-day work. The confidence to tackle mathematical problems in the workplace is in demand by employers. To dismiss this because you think you can't do maths is like saying you can't read and write. If you haven't got a formal qualification in maths (such as Maths GCSE grade A*–C or equivalent), you really should think about doing some basic maths programme so that you aren't cut off from a lot of jobs that need you to have confidence with numbers on a fairly basic level.

## Application of Information Technology

This includes a range of Information Technology skills such as: word processing; using spreadsheets; setting up and managing files; using email and Internet search engines appropriately and using social media for corporate communication. As IT applications develop, it is important to keep up: not just in terms of playing with the latest games or applications, but also in terms of how these new ways of working and communicating and problem solving translate into everyday work.

## Foreign language skills

This is quite a tricky one to get to the bottom of, but an easy one to dismiss if you think that, if you speak English, you don't need to worry about language competence. Languages are in demand in addition to the skill set outlined above: there are few jobs where language ability on its own is the key demand. The level of language skill can vary: in some cases technical mastery and fluency is called for, but everyday conversational ability can be useful, as can a general awareness of cultural differences. Even having a few key phrases in another language can really pave the way for effective relationships, which are at the heart of any business or dealings.

---

### brilliant example

'What's difficult about working abroad? I want to say the language, but it's not that. It's the way of doing things, getting your head around things.'

Hannah, (undergraduate) Economics and Politics with International Studies

---

## Developing employability skills, even when you're not employed

Employers demand that graduates can demonstrate a range of transferable skills which have been shown to enhance their performance in the workplace. This is on top of your degree. The more you develop these employability skills the more attractive you become to an employer, so the greater your chances of success in your jobsearch. It is important to understand that you don't need to be in paid employment to develop all of these skills. For example, if you don't have a job, you can still develop your fluency in a foreign language just by listening to the radio or podcasts in that language, reading an online newspaper or novel, or even watching a film or TV programme. You can develop your customer awareness and business sense just by being aware of what is going on around you: think about how businesses advertise for and treat their customers. What promises do they make about customer service and how do they deliver on that promise?

Observing and analysing behaviours that you come across every day just as a possible customer (not even a consumer) will enhance your understanding. And, of course, if you are struggling to secure a job in a difficult labour market, you are continually practising resilience and self-management; and the real beauty is that, having developed these skills, whether through paid employment, volunteer work or simply on your own, they stick with you and you can use them to move around and progress in the labour market.

## brilliant tip

Seek out opportunities to develop employability skills. You can do this in any job at any level. You can also do it through volunteering and even in unpaid work. Keep a record of your skills development to use when applying for jobs.

# What do graduates earn?

It is perfectly reasonable for jobseekers to ask what graduates earn, but it is a surprisingly difficult question to answer. You will find plenty of answers if you search online, with the figure usually expressed in whole numbers or to the nearest £500. In the same year, three different sources published three different figures for the average graduate salary; ranging from £20,000 to £29,000. The challenge is to look more closely to see what these figures are actually telling us about what graduates earn.

## Average graduate starting salary

Analysis published annually by the Higher Education Statistical Agency (HESA) uses information on what graduates are doing six months after completion of their degree (known as their first destination) to calculate their average salary. In 2014, HESA reported the mean salary as £20,000 and the median graduate salary as £21,000. The difference between these two figures is due to the way in which averages are calculated. The *mean* is the sum total of all the salaries added together then divided by the number of people in the survey. It can be skewed by a relatively small number of extremely high salaries at the top end, or equally by a relatively small number of extremely low salaries at the bottom end. As the *median* salary is the value in the middle of the whole range of salaries, it is less affected by these two extremes. It is reasonable therefore to work with the median salary which happens to be the higher figure of £21,000.

It is important to remember that this is the average of the first destinations of all new graduates, which means that it covers every region of the UK, every single subject discipline and includes every graduate who has found employment, including those who have taken casual or non-graduate jobs which often pay less. The Association of Graduate Recruiters (AGR) also publishes an annual calculation of what their employers are paying graduates as a starting salary. Their most recent figure, published in 2015, also the median, was £28,000. The AGR reported figure is significantly higher than the HESA figure. A number of factors can explain this variation. The AGR report concentrates on graduate recruitment and graduates are, historically, paid more than other employees. Whilst AGR members are located all over the UK, many of them are recruiting in London, where salaries tend to be higher. Finally, AGR members tend to be larger organisations, which again tend to pay more.

## Variations within average ranges

An average salary sits somewhere in the middle of the range; so some actual starting salaries will be higher and some will be lower (a point that is often overlooked by jobseeking graduates when considering advertised jobs). A survey of graduate employers published in 2015 reported median graduate salary at £30,000 and the highest salary (£42,000) offered by supermarket chain Aldi.

It is important to remember all the factors which can, and do, affect starting salaries. We've already seen regional variation, with the example of London generally commanding higher pay than elsewhere in the UK. There are also significant variations by occupational sector: oil and energy, investment banking and law have often appeared at the top end of the scale; while hospitality, retail, the public and voluntary sectors are often to be found towards the bottom end of the scale.

 The work has changed. When I was a kid you wanted to be a bus driver! You learn there are certain job markets and there needs to be a reality check, to learn what job markets pay.

Julian Radley, Director, Evotel Holdings

## Starting, not finishing salaries

It can be disheartening to read news headlines about fabulous starting salaries which seem to be very far from what is actually on offer in your own jobsearch. You can easily find out (from the HESA survey) what the average starting salary was for students from your university, which can be useful in giving you a realistic benchmark of what to expect. Having a better understanding of how these headlines come about leads to a grounded perspective of what is actually happening in the labour market you find yourself in, which in turn helps you to make sense of what is happening to you.

# Points of entry and points of leverage

## Points of entry

It is important here to remember that these are the average starting salaries; that is, the kind of salary you can expect when you are starting out in a designated graduate job. That starting position is your 'point of entry'. In a survey of 16,000 undergraduates in their final year (they were due to graduate in 2010) a third were prepared to accept any (graduate) job they were offered, and a fifth admitted that they had applied to employers they weren't really interested in simply because they felt they didn't have much choice, given how tough the labour market was looking at that time. The key thing for them was to secure a point of entry into the labour market.

---

### brilliant example

'You can't expect to have it immediately – you might do a few jobs and then, suddenly, you know: oh, *this* is what I want to do. For me, it's important to keep your brain going. To keep learning something is always going to be better than doing nothing. And if you can't get the job you want, do any job. Earning some money is better than earning no money.'

Sophie, employee, Evotel Holdings

---

We've looked at transferable skills and how the skills, knowledge and understanding that you develop in one job stay with you. This means that you can evolve as a graduate worker, increasing your know-how and thereby increasing your value to an employer. It is also crucial to recognise that you can start your evolution from day one of an entry-level job. You'll then arrive at a point where you are ready to move on, to look for a greater challenge and a better-paid job. This is what we call leverage in the job market.

## Points of leverage

A longitudinal study tracked graduates not only into their first job on graduation (their point of entry – what is called the first destination in the national data collection), but also as they moved through the graduate labour market for several years further on. The researchers discovered that, three-and-a-half years after graduation, 81 per cent were in graduate occupations (that is, jobs for which a degree is required) and 87 per cent were 'fairly satisfied' or 'very satisfied' with their job. Leverage got them where they wanted to be. So, even if your point of entry is less than brilliant, you will find points of leverage towards your brilliant career.

**brilliant** recap

- Graduates have proven thinking skills.

- They have shown that they are prepared to learn.

- They want to progress in their career and to develop their range of competencies (their professional repertoire).

- They can bring flexibility and innovation to an organisation.

- They bring skills, attitudes and behaviours which can enhance a company's productivity.

- Over half of the graduate jobs advertised don't specify the degree discipline: you can apply no matter what subject you study.

- Include small to medium-sized enterprises in your jobsearch.

- Develop transferable skills in everything you do: paid employment, voluntary work, daily life.

## What to do next

A very simple next step would be to locate your own degree and read through what graduates have done overall, and what kind of occupational sectors they have gone for.

You could make a note of what interests you, and then follow it up by getting more information from your university careers service, or by using some of the other chapters in the first part of this handbook to move you on.

You could also look at the list of transferable skills and see if you can identify examples from your own experience which demonstrate you have that skill. This is as much a help for you yourself as it is for a potential employer. If there is an employability module on offer, have another look at it and see if it could help you – or if it did help you and you didn't realise it at the time.

# 8
# TALKING AND LISTENING

## Networking

Networking in this context refers to the activity of making, maintaining and using personal contacts for professional purposes. Such contacts are invaluable for *all* areas of life. Think about how often you have discovered something important from someone you knew, rather than through official channels. I found my house not through an estate agent but via a friend who told me that a friend of hers was thinking of moving and it sounded like an ideal house. A recent graduate found his (very good) present job by talking to someone in a café. In a pub conversation someone said that they wanted a room to rent and someone else said, 'I don't think Sandy has found a new lodger yet.'

> Networking is strongly associated with management success.

Most jobs are advertised and specified selection procedures are followed. Yet they frequently go to someone who knew of the vacancy in advance and who had contacted relevant people, or exploited existing contacts, before the interview. And despite equal opportunities legislation, not all jobs are advertised. There are many ways of starting to work for an organisation which may grow into jobs if the original project is well handled. For those who are, as is increasingly the case, working for small organisations or for themselves, these informal routes are often the most important ones. One writer on networking (Hart, 1996) claims, though without giving the evidence for this, that networking can be twelve times as effective in getting a new job as answering advertisements.

Networking is valued differently in different cultures. In the UK, some people see it as slightly 'unsporting' actively to develop and exploit personal relationships. In Japan, it is seen as a vital activity in business. Indeed, Japanese managers in the 1980s were sent to major US business schools to study for an MBA not because their superiors felt that the Americans could teach them anything about business, but because of the contacts that they would make with future senior US managers.

Networking is not limited to finding new jobs. It also seems to be of value in progressing within an organisation once you have found the job. The US study by Luthans *et al.* (1988), showed that those managers who were *effective* (i.e. who had satisfied subordinates that performed well) were not necessarily the same as those managers who were *successful* (i.e. who were promoted rapidly).

Indeed, only 10 per cent of managers were in the top one-third on both counts, slightly less than you would expect if the two factors were totally unrelated to each other. If organisational life in the US resembles that elsewhere, and if being successful is something worth aiming for, it is worth looking at the key characteristics associated with success in this study.

The successful managers devoted more time to interacting with outsiders, chatting, joking, passing on rumours, complaining, paying attention to both customers and suppliers, attending external meetings and taking part in activities in the local community. In other words, they spent a lot of time on developing networks of primarily social contacts way beyond their immediate work group but clearly of value to their careers. Note that these exchanges do not need to involve face-to-face contact all the time, though this helps at the start. The telephone can be a useful channel, email is often used in this way to sustain a relationship once established, and even letters can sometimes be used.

So how can you develop networking skills while you are studying? There is a heavy overlap with the skills of talking, listening and the 'valuing yourself' aspect of assertiveness. These lie at the heart of networking, and thus in developing these skills you will inevitably be starting to build a network. By making a point of trying to practise these skills with as many people as possible, you will be starting to maximise the networking potential of your time as a student and to build the foundation of a network that you can develop after graduating. This will be greatly helped if you appreciate just how important networking is. After all, other people will be succeeding because they are networking and may well be including you in their networks. As it is ideally a mutual activity rather than exploitation in the bad sense, you should overcome any inhibitions you may have about becoming good at networking yourself.

## Activity 8.1

Start by establishing the extent of your current potential network. List all the people you know well enough to ask for information on something like accommodation or holiday or job opportunities. (It doesn't matter if they would be likely to know the answer, just whether you would feel comfortable asking them for neutral information of such a kind.) If you are working with a group, compare lists and see whether this prompts any additions. Check that you have included people you know at home, as well as where you are studying, and those you know through all the activities in which you take part. File this list, in order to refer to it at intervals and add to it.

## Activity 8.2

Test the assertion that such networks are more useful than official channels is right. Think of some information that would be useful to you and select from your list of potential network members those who might be able to give that information, or might know people who could. This does not have to be information about a job – it could be anything which you could, in theory, find from an advertisement. See how quickly you can get the same (or better) information just by talking to people.

## Activity 8.3

Draw up an action plan for maintaining your network. Think about opportunities for developing your relationships with people on your list. Could you make a point of having an exchange with them the next time you see them? Remember, Luthans *et al.* (1988) listed joking, social chat, exchanging rumours and complaining among effective networking behaviours. List the people you might have a chance to talk to in the next two weeks. List those you do manage to talk to. (You will be practising your talking and listening skills in the process.) Reflect after each contact on how effective the interaction was in strengthening your relationship and what else you might need to do. Add these comments to your list.

## Activity 8.4

Draw up an action plan for developing your network by making new contacts. Think about activities you can take part in and people you can get to know in order that your net spreads more widely. Members of your network need to be aware of your interests and strengths, so that they will think of you if asked about suitable candidates for an opportunity, or hear something that might interest you. This may help them as well as you. Similarly, you need to know as much as possible about them – the more mutual such relationships are, the stronger and more effective they will be. Again, log thoughts and compare progress with your list and notes already made.

## Activity 8.5

Identify opportunities to use your network. In future, whenever you need to find something out, think about who in your network can help, and approach them. Also, help any people who approach you as best you can. Log your reflections on the process. If your network needs extending, think about who else you need to be able to talk to and deliberately approach them. You will be surprised how often people who do not know you at the start will be willing to tell you things if you make clear why you are asking and that their help would be appreciated. Once they have helped you they will be part of your network.

# CHAPTER 9

# Graduate training schemes

This chapter covers one of the better-known options for graduates, and for many graduates it's the option they aspire to. In case you are not quite clear about what's involved, we will start with a definition, before looking at some examples. Finally, we will show you how to be a strong contender, if a graduate training scheme is your preferred option.

## What is a graduate training scheme?

 **brilliant** definition

A graduate training scheme is a graduate entry position where there is a planned programme of training and development. Usually associated with large organisations of the kind you will meet at careers fairs, they are increasingly also offered by SMEs (small to medium-sized enterprises).

### Sectoral growth and decline

Graduate training schemes can be found in a whole range of job areas, or sectors. Vacancies are currently on the increase in retail, manufacturing and construction, IT and telecommunications and banking.

Note that the term graduate training scheme is sometimes used in professions like law, accountancy, teaching and psychology. In this chapter we are looking at more generalist schemes where the subject of your degree may be less important and the training more broadly based.

## Direct entry

Many smaller organisations or SMEs offer the same kind of opportunity for a graduate entrant, but may not always label it a graduate training scheme. Remember that in Chapter 7 we defined an SME as an organisation with up to 250 employees. These organisations cover almost 60 per cent of the private sector employment in the UK and this includes graduate-level roles, with training.

On the other hand, be aware that many larger organisations also recruit people, who happen to be graduates, to what are called direct-entry jobs, where a degree is not a requirement. This might give you a route in, if your application for a graduate training scheme has been unsuccessful, and you could still work towards a position similar to someone who has come through the graduate training scheme route.

## Three key features

The key defining features of a graduate training scheme are:

- You need a degree.
- You will follow a planned programme which will enable you to sample different work areas and identify your particular strengths and interests.
- You will be employed and therefore paid a salary.

## . . . and three myths

- Graduate training schemes usually lead to a job – but not automatically. You may have to apply for internal vacancies, or wait until a suitable role comes up. In some cases, especially in the public sector, graduate training schemes are offered on a fixed-term contract and offer no guarantee of a job.

- You have to go straight into a graduate training scheme as soon as you leave university. Not so – many graduates apply in the year following graduation – or even later than that. Employers are fine with this, as long as you can show some benefit to yourself, and potentially to the employer, deriving from the time since you graduated. Typically, around half of all graduate trainees recruited across the UK will not be straight from university.

- You have to have a first class or upper second class Honours degree. Not so – although some companies have such a requirement, many do not.

## Some typical graduate training schemes

These examples come from recently advertised graduate training schemes, and help to illustrate the features they have in common, and where the differences might be. You will see that even this small sample covers a range of occupational areas and includes an SME.

 **examples**

### A national pub and restaurant company

- Offers a two-year, fast-track retail management scheme, combining on-the-job experience and formal training, leading to general manager posts with progression to area manager or head office roles.

- The company looks for applicants with strong leadership and team-building skills and the ability to motivate their team, and the self-motivation to develop a business.

- Graduates must have a 2:2 or better and a minimum of 12 months' supervisory experience in a customer-facing environment, and be flexible within two geographical regions (excluding London).

### A global business consultancy

- Offers trainee technology or management consultants a two-year programme with analysts, a balance of workplace, project-based learning and 250 hours of formal training, including online courses, together with the support of buddies and mentors.

- Applicants need 340 UCAS points and at least a 2:1 in any discipline and a strong interest in technology.

- You'll need to be fully mobile to work on client projects that could be anywhere in the country – or even the world – though you would have a UK base.

- An interesting additional requirement is that candidates must prove that they have achieved high performance in other areas of their lives, i.e. outside academic performance. (If you were applying for this training scheme, what evidence could you offer?)

### A regional housing association

- An intensive two-year training programme working in different functions to provide a breadth of experience as a basis for choosing a specialist area after training. All placements will be real business roles. The first year will involve discrete projects lasting 2–4 weeks. In the second year there are two placements lasting six months each in either development, operations or care and support housing.

- Graduates from any discipline may apply. They need to be able to demonstrate energy, enthusiasm and a 'can do' attitude together with good verbal and numerical reasoning, report writing and communication skills.

- You would need to show an understanding of the work of a housing association and be able to explain why you have chosen this area of work.

### A multi-national engineering company

- Offers a structured development programme over the course of 18 months, travelling across various global sites and accessing key training and development modules.

- Training on-site will focus on developing your technical expertise as well as interpersonal skills such as communication, team working and leadership.

- Trainees will be helped to gain appropriate professional accreditations such as IMechE or similar and will be offered a permanent position in an appropriate area of the business.

- Applicants need a minimum 2:2 in mechanical, civil or marine engineering, maths or physics.

# Is a graduate training scheme right for you?

## Meeting the selection criteria

The harsh reality is that, in order to deal with large numbers of applications, recruiters to graduate training schemes set the bar high in terms of degree classification and sometimes, like one of our brilliant examples, even use UCAS points. Sometimes the initial selection is done using computer software. This is highly likely to be the case if you apply online. If you don't meet an essential requirement (for example, you have a 2:2, they want a 2:1) you will be selected out. And all this will happen well before anyone reads your well-crafted personal statement. So you need to consider if, and how, you can achieve what is being asked for. If you can't, then look for other routes.

---

### brilliant example

A large, multinational business consultancy has an alternative graduate training scheme for people who have fallen short of the academic standards normally required but can demonstrate achievement outside their studies.

---

In large organisations you need to be prepared for, and willing to commit to, the full range of selection methods. The entire selection process could last a full day or more and may even require an overnight stay. Have a look at 'Dates and deadlines: your timeline for action' for managing all this alongside your study, and 'Succeeding in selection', for more about what might be involved.

## A chance to find your strengths and interests

You may know that you would like to work in a large organisation of a particular kind – public sector, logistics, retail, finance – but not yet be clear about a specific direction. Many graduate training schemes offer a programme of rotation through various functions and, while you will be expected to make a contribution in each area you work in, you do have the chance to experience different roles first hand.

## Are you flexible?

Large, multi-site organisations will expect you to be prepared to work at different locations. Even if the head office is in your home town, it doesn't mean that you will work there. Make sure you are aware of any requirements to move or work away, and that they fit with your own circumstances.

## Can you commit?

A graduate training scheme is long term – think two years minimum, and that's just for the training programme. So, if you plan to work for six months and then travel, it's not for you at this stage. A recruiting organisation wants a return for the cash investment it's making in selection and training – and you will be giving a lot of yourself to get the most from the experience. So be sure that the time is right for you.

# How to be a strong contender for a graduate training scheme

Much of what we say elsewhere in this book, about researching the labour market, job opportunities, applications and interviews, applies to graduate training schemes as well as to other options you may be considering, so we will assume that you will dip in to the relevant chapters as you need to. What we will do here is look at the particular demands of graduate training schemes on you, the applicant.

## Know the business in context

For every organisation you apply to, you need to know how they generate their revenue, who their competitors are, how they adapt to changes in the market, their strengths, what they are developing, and so on. This knowledge will help you with your application and certainly with your interview. Visit careers fairs, look at websites, talk to anyone who might know anything about the organisations or the sectors they belong to.

## Know about recruitment timescales and where to find vacancies

Some graduate training schemes have an annual or twice-yearly intake, others a rolling programme. For the first group, being ready to apply at the right time is critical. Deadlines can be as early as October of your final year. Sign up for careers fairs, pick up your free copies of graduate directories from your careers service, use your university's online graduate vacancy service and sign up to graduate recruitment websites.

## Know about selection methods

We said earlier that graduate training schemes often use the full range of selection methods, in particular assessment centres, so make sure you know what these are, what to expect and how to prepare for them. Read 'Succeeding in selection', for lots more information about this.

## Be creative

If you don't meet the academic requirements, is there another way you can gain access? You could look for companies like the brilliant example earlier in this chapter, or you could try a direct approach with a good letter or personal contact at a careers fair. Alternatively you could go for direct entry and aim to progress once you are in the organisation.

## Manage your applications

You will almost certainly be applying to more than one graduate training scheme, so keep your applications in order – create a schedule of closing dates and interview dates, make an electronic or paper folder to keep copies of applications, CVs and interview information. Read 'Dates and deadlines' for more about managing your time to hit closing dates and keep your academic work going at the same time.

## Seek and make use of feedback

An unsuccessful application can help you to get the next one better. If you get as far as an interview you should be able to ask the employer for feedback – but do listen to what is said. The employer is telling you how you presented at interview, so try not to defend or justify, because it really doesn't matter – what matters is what the employer saw and heard.

 **brilliant** timesaver

Keep track by making a paper or electronic folder for copies of application forms, CVs and interview information.

**brilliant** dos and don'ts

**Do**

✔ find out about the business and its competitors;

✔ learn about selection methods;

✔ get and use feedback;

✔ look for different routes to where you want to be.

**Don't**

✘ leave it till the last minute to look for vacancies;

✘ lose track of your applications.

## What are the benefits?

We think there are three key benefits of graduate training schemes, and we are not alone. Have a look at the three real-life graduate stories that follow.

In our first example, Paul highlights the benefits of learning to work in a big organisation.

### brilliant example

'My role as a trainee manager on the graduate training scheme of an international car rental company provides me with valuable training on running a business, working as a manager and working your way up a big organisation. The experience has given me such a big insight into the workings of a big company.'

Paul, BSc (Hons) Sport and Exercise Science

In our next example you can see that a good graduate training scheme will support you in further learning, sometimes leading to specialist qualifications.

### brilliant example

'I secured a position with one of the world's biggest banks on their executive management graduate scheme. At university we were introduced to the concept of lifelong learning and with the bank I have the chance to further my studies with qualifications in financial services.'

Phil, BA (Hons) Business Studies

Our final example illustrates the longer-term benefits. Victoria's experience helped her to develop strengths and preferences that enabled her to work out the next stage of her career plan. She is now in her third job after graduating.

### brilliant example

'I joined the graduate programme of a consulting company. In two years I learned masses and I still use the tools and skills I gained with them. I use their methods as a mark of what good looks like in my present company. The IT projects I worked on were for a range of blue chip retail companies. However, after two years I wanted to ▶

try a move away from IT so I moved to another consultancy for more analysis and strategic projects . . . after another two years I realised that I wanted to work in retail, and within the industry rather than through consultancy. Because of my experience I found the job market very responsive, and I got my present job as a business systems analyst with a multinational retail organisation. I get to travel and work with different cultures, teaching and shaping how countries do business.'

Victoria, MA Geography

---

 **brilliant** recap

Graduate training schemes are great for developing your skills and experience. They help you to refine your career plans, and often include the chance for you to gain a specialist qualification.

## What to do next

- Remind yourself of the key features of a graduate training scheme. Could you see yourself as a graduate trainee?

- Think about a job area you might like to work in – marketing, finance, research and development, HR – and see if you can find a suitable graduate training scheme being advertised. Visit websites; useful ones include **www.milkround.com** and **www.prospects.ac.uk**.

- Get hold of a copy of a directory of graduate training schemes from your careers service and look at their online list if they have one. Have a browse and look for similarities and differences among different schemes.

- Sign up for the next graduate careers fair in your area. Find out more from your university website or from **www.prospects.ac.uk**.

**CHAPTER 10**

# Knowing who you are: skills, interests and values

There are two important perspectives when planning your brilliant career. One is what's out there, which we explored in Part 1; the other is who you are, which we cover in this chapter. It's good to try and have both of these perspectives in your mind. Both have enormous value – a sound knowledge of graduate opportunities helps you to be realistic in your plans, while an understanding of your own strengths and preferences will make you a more successful applicant. Even more importantly, this understanding and its application to your career plan will make you a more fulfilled person. When jobs are scarce it's easy to focus on getting whatever is available – and certainly it may be necessary to compromise or to plan for the longer term – but even in a restricted job market there is still scope for choice.

## Skills, interests and values

In this chapter we will help you to analyse your own skills, interests and values.

Here are three fundamental questions: spend a little time thinking about them, making a note of your answers – just words or phrases will be fine. We are giving you some prompts to help.

### What are you good at?

Think about:

● technical skills associated with your degree subject, such as using specialist equipment or software;

- generic or transferable work skills, such as cash handling, working under pressure, meeting targets, supervising others, report writing;
- soft skills, such as working in a team, communication, time management, showing initiative.

## What are you interested in?

This question covers the kind of physical and social setting you want to work in (office-based, a variety of locations, outdoors, production, laboratory, in a team or alone) as well as the subject matter – would you like to use your degree subject in your job? Remember that around half of graduate jobs don't specify a particular subject, so, while it's not necessary for you to use your subject, it might be something you would like to do.

## What do you believe in and how does this fit with your career plan?

At first sight this is less straightforward than the other two questions. To help you, think about which of the following is something you care about:

- protecting the environment;
- improving the life chances of people who are disadvantaged;
- contributing to the economy through provision of goods or services;
- being creative, with words or materials;
- sharing, creating or discovering knowledge;
- achieving a high standard of living.

These are examples of values, or beliefs that guide the way we live our lives. Some people live out their values outside their working life, for example a high-flying business executive whose work role is to contribute to the economy and who gives time and money to a local charity for the homeless; others look for a working life that is consistent with their values, for example an international development worker. Thinking about what matters to you is another way to identify suitable job opportunities.

Make a note of your answers to our three questions.

 **tip**

Think about these three questions:

- What are you good at?

- What are you interested in?

- What do you believe in and how does this fit with your career plan?

## Why does it matter?

Firstly, knowing yourself better helps you to get started if you have no particular preferences about your future career. If you can think and learn about what you are good at, what you are interested in, and what you believe in, you will begin to identify job choices. You will also be able to eliminate jobs from your career plan and this is just as useful, as it helps you to narrow down the possibilities. It also helps you to identify the underlying factors in the jobs you are both choosing and eliminating, which in turn helps you to broaden your range of choices. As you learn more about the detail of job opportunities you will be able to fit this knowledge with what you know about yourself. Remember to refer back to Part 1 of this book to revisit the kinds of opportunities open to you as a graduate.

Secondly, career success and satisfaction are more likely to be achieved if there is a good match with what you are good at, what you are interested in, and what you believe in and believe to be important. Have a look at this brilliant example to see what we mean.

---

### ⏺ brilliant example

'There was so much that my course taught me, including skills that I can use in all aspects of my life. Doing Drama and Theatre Studies encouraged me to be myself and show the world what I had to offer, and this began opening up so many opportunities for me. As well as the content of the course, I developed skills like working to deadlines and self-organisation, which brought with it self-discipline and an increase in my independence. I feel that all these skills have stood me in good stead for the world of work.

Using the wealth of experience I gained at university, along with the academic knowledge, I am now working as an Arts & Cultural Positive Activities Officer for an amazing community interest company delivering activities to children in deprived areas. Workshops range from DJ-ing through drama and graffiti to film production, to raise the aspirations of young people in those communities. The children have the opportunity to work towards an arts award, a nationally recognised certificate which boosts their confidence and gives them something to be proud of. I thoroughly enjoy this role and the satisfaction it gives me in seeing young people, who once may not have had many aspirations, achieve and build in their confidence and outlook on life.'

Joanne, BA (Hons) Drama and Theatre Studies

---

Now read this example again and look for evidence of Joanne's skills, interests and values in her story. All three are critical to her success in, and enjoyment of, her brilliant graduate career.

We noticed her references to:

- working to deadlines;
- self-organisation;
- self-discipline;
- increased independence;
- satisfaction at seeing young people with low aspirations grow in confidence and broaden their outlook;
- her interest in using her degree subject.

## Each of us is unique

Although we referred to Joanne's achieving a good match between her own skills, interests and values and the job she has chosen, this doesn't mean that we are trying to put square pegs in round holes. Two students on the same course, getting the same grades, doing the same kind of part-time work, will each make their own unique and valid sense of their experience – which in turn will impact on their career planning. A skilled careers adviser will help you to 'make meaning' of your own particular experiences and ambitions. So, in addition to considering your skills, interests and values and how these might be fulfilled in particular job roles, you might also think about key turning points in your life so far, how people or events have influenced you, and the extent to which you take a logical, rational approach or an intuitive approach to planning your future. These are all factors that contribute to your uniqueness.

# The skill of reflection

To understand more about your skills, interests and values you need to develop your personal insight and self-awareness. Some people are comfortable describing what they think, feel and believe, others less so – it might not have been encouraged in their upbringing, or they might not find it easy to put such concepts into words. It often takes someone else to tell us what we are good at – perhaps we fear sounding big-headed or overconfident. As far as interests and values are concerned, we might need help in generalising from the specific example to the broader category – 'I really enjoy the voluntary work I'm doing and believe it is making a difference, but I don't know of any paid jobs like this.' Tests, questionnaires and inventories are a great help in learning more about ourselves and we will come to these later. But first let's look at what we can learn just by taking time to reflect on what has happened.

## How reflection works

Watch any post-match discussion of a big football game and you will see the experts taking the game apart, reviewing the successes as well as the weak points of the game and analysing the performance of every player in great detail. If you are a football fan, you might well have evaluated the game in the same way. If not, you might be amazed at the perception of the experts, at the extent to which they notice and interpret what's going on in the game. We can be sure that the manager, coach and players use the same process of review soon after the match, in order to make improvements for next time. What has this got to do with career planning?

- Firstly, the experts and professionals take time to reflect.
- Secondly, they know what they are looking for and can describe what they see.
- Thirdly, they know what this means for future performance.

So let's apply this to something you might do, say working in a group of other students to complete a project. You get an average mark for the work. Which of the following do you do?

1  Say, 'Great, that's a pass', and think no more about it.

2  Take time to read your feedback, talk to your tutor, think about what went well and why, what went badly and why, what your own role was in the group, how you could behave differently next time to get a better result, and then make a note somewhere to remind you.

Option 2 might sound like a lot of trouble – but the gain is that you will have an insight into how you work as a member of a team (a classic area for you to cover in an application and for employers to explore at interview) and a sense of how to become more skilled. You will also find that, if you get into this way of thinking, it will become part of your behaviour and much less of an effort. Your university may have an electronic framework, or e-portfolio, to help you to keep your record. Otherwise, just devise a simple template that you can update as significant events occur.

## Try this yourself

Now try this one for yourself, this time focusing on your communication skills. Take an example – giving a presentation to your seminar group or handling a difficult customer in the workplace – and answer the following questions.

1  What happened? (Describe the setting and the activity/incident.)

2  What went well? Why? How do you know?

3  What went less well? Why? How do you know?

4  What would you do differently next time? What do you need to help you to do this?

Notice that there is a new question here – how do you know? The answers to this question are the evidence you need to show that you have the skill in question. Employers will seek evidence – it's not enough to say, 'I'm really good at communicating with people.'

## Where's the evidence?

Let's go back to the example of giving a presentation. Evidence can come from:

- your own self-reflection ('although I covered the ground, I was running out of time and I felt as if I rushed the last part');

- the response of the audience (they looked interested/stayed awake/asked questions/told me afterwards they understood it); and

- feedback from your tutor (informal comments, written feedback, an actual grade or mark).

Gathering this evidence and being willing to listen to feedback will make a real difference to what you do next time – in other words, it will improve your performance.

So go back to those four steps – what happened, what went well, what went less well, what will you do differently next time and try to apply them. You will learn more about your own skills, and you will get better. Best of all you will develop a skill employers really value, because you will be a person who learns from experience and who actively seeks opportunities for learning.

Most graduates now are expected to do regular evaluations of where they are at and where they are going . . . developing the individual to the point where they can take control of their life, their learning and their career.

Carl Gilleard, Chief Executive, Association of Graduate Recruiters

## More techniques to help you to know who you are

Let's go back to those three questions at the start of the chapter:

- What are you good at?
- What are you interested in?
- What do you believe in and how does this fit with your career plan?

For some people, thinking about their skills, interests and values is enough, especially if they have developed the skill of reflection we discussed earlier in the chapter. However, many people need some help in structuring their thoughts, from talking to someone, e.g. a careers adviser, to completing a questionnaire.

### Talk to people

If your university offers one-to-one careers consultations, you really don't need to know what you want to do before you book your slot! Careers advisers use skilful questioning to guide you through these three areas as a way to help you to develop a career plan. It's surprising how often 'I don't know what I want to do' really means 'I've got a few ideas but I'm not sure . . .'

If you can't get access to one-to-one consultations with a careers adviser, talk to your personal tutor, or a tutor you get on with who knows you well. Just thinking aloud with a good listener can move you forward. Also, try other people you know who might have some time – friends, family, someone you know through a part-time job or work experience. Get them to help you to answer our three questions. If they are in a position to give you feedback, ask them, so that you get a better insight into your skills.

**brilliant** example

'With an idea in mind of the type of career I was interested in, I visited the university careers service to talk to a careers adviser about my options. With the use of interactive software I was able to analyse my skills and get possible career ideas which I was then able to discuss with the careers adviser. She also referred me to a really good website, Graduate Prospects, which contained a wealth of different information for me to research. I found all these processes really useful and realised that my strengths were in communication and teamworking, and that I enjoyed a competitive environment.'

Paul, BSc (Hons) Sport and Exercise Science

## Use psychometric tests

We will be looking at how tests and questionnaires are used by employers during selection. In this chapter we will tell you how to use them to learn more about yourself. Tests used in career planning or selection are often referred to as 'psychometric' tests. This simply means tests that 'measure the mind'. We will look more at the detail of psychometric tests in our companion book, *Brilliant Passing Psychometric Tests* (Mulvey, 2015); for now, here are some quick definitions.

**brilliant** definitions

**Psychometric test** – a set of questions that measure an aspect of mental performance or behaviour. The word psychometric means measuring the mind.

**Aptitude test** – a measure of a particular aptitude or ability consisting of questions with right and wrong answers. Scores are compared with others to assess performance.

**Personality test** – a set of questions designed to explore and describe aspects of personality, or what kind of person we are. There are no right or wrong answers, though when employers use a personality test they may be looking for certain characteristics.

You can use aptitude tests to check out your ability with logic, numbers and words. They may not tell you anything you don't already know – but you might be surprised.

Personality tests, on the other hand, can give you real insight into your characteristics and preferences. They are particularly useful because they contain statements – often multiple choice – that act as prompts. So instead of asking yourself, 'How do I contribute to a team?', a personality test will give you a set of situations to choose from, which, taken together, will indicate how you usually behave. Personality tests and questionnaires are not magic – they only reflect back to you information you have put in, but in a systematic and logical way.

'Career Planner' is a readily accessible and career-specific questionnaire, which can be found on the Graduate Prospects website. Questions are in four sections: first steps; skills; motivation; and desires. Complete 'first steps' and you will see a list of matched occupations; as you complete each further section the list is refined and edited, and there are links to help you to explore the best matches in more detail.

## Employability skills

Skills that have particular currency in the job market are often referred to as employability skills. They are the skills and behaviours that enable you to interact and work with a range of different people, and they can be learned. Here is a reminder of the employability skills we listed and defined in Chapter 7 – look back if you need to remind yourself what some of these terms mean.

- self-management;
- resilience;
- teamwork;
- business and customer awareness;
- problem solving;
- project management;

- communication and literacy;
- numeracy;
- application of IT;
- foreign language skills.

It may not be obvious at first glance, but most degree courses provide opportunities to develop skills that transfer to the workplace. A connection between a degree in Theology and a career in the police might seem unlikely, but read what Andrew says.

---

### brilliant example

'My degree encouraged me to think beyond the expected norms, to challenge ideas and express that thinking. My work certainly demands that I look closely at any given situation and try to look beyond the glaringly obvious . . . whether working with a prisoner or developing new working practices. The close study and intricate dissection of theory, particularly in Theology, was responsible for developing these skills.'

Andrew, BA (Hons) Theology and Psychology, MTh postgraduate student

---

## Find out more

Your university may offer sessions or online materials on how to develop your employability skills. Sometimes these sessions form part of your subject timetable; in other cases they are an optional extra. See what you can find out about what's on offer where you are. Check your university careers service website or Facebook page regularly, or follow them on Twitter. An Internet search for employability skills will also bring up useful questionnaires and checklists.

**brilliant tip**

In addition to the skills needed for a particular job, employers of graduates look for competence in a range of employability skills, so look for opportunities to learn about, develop and show evidence of these skills.

## Making the connections

If you have followed this chapter through, you should now have a clearer idea about those aspects of yourself that help to determine your future choice. You might even have drawn up a summary of your own skills, interests and values. It may be important to add other information about yourself, for example your health and fitness, your family situation and your finances. In the final chapter of this handbook we will explore the impact of these other factors on your career plan. For now, let's think about how to make use of your new insights.

**brilliant dos and don'ts**

**Do**

✔ keep up to date with how your skills, interests and values change over time;

✔ seek out opportunities to develop your skills, through formal and informal learning;

✔ develop your interests with new experiences;

✔ examine job information for skills, interests and values as well as for the activities involved in the job.

**Don't**

✘ stand still – keep on learning, whatever the circumstances.

### Try this exercise

Looking at your own skills, interests and values will help you to look at jobs in a new way. Think about your last part-time or vacation job – you might have taken it 'because it was there', or because you always work there in the vacation, or because your friend works there. For a few moments, think about this job and answer the following questions:

- What skills did you need, or use?

- In doing the job, what did it help to be interested in?

- What values did the organisation hold, either in a mission statement or in everyday working practice?

Now answer these questions for a graduate job you might think about doing:

- What skills will you need?

- What will it help to be interested in?

- What values are likely to be important?

You can find information about skills and interests in the entry requirements or person specification for the job. Information about values is harder to pin down. Though a company website will often quote the organisation's values, you need to think about the detail of a particular job to work out what the associated values might be.

 **recap**

- Knowing more about yourself, especially your skills, interests and values, will help with your career planning and jobsearch.

- Use the skill of reflection to develop your self-awareness and build your evidence.

- Employability skills are important in all jobs – work on yours.

- Get an in-depth insight into job opportunities by using the 'skills, interests and values' headings.

## What to do next

- Use the ideas in this chapter to identify your skills, interests and values.

- Complete the 'Career Planner' on the Graduate Prospects website.

**CHAPTER 11**

# Global business needs global graduates

Study abroad is basic training for the 21st century

Institute of International Education

Today's graduates need to understand the challenges of the global market, but more importantly how to identify opportunities. Both private and public-sector organisations can no longer insulate themselves from the impact of the changing global landscape. Graduates need to understand how these changes will impact their discipline and their future industry.

What threats does the global market present? And what opportunities?

Employers need graduates who can navigate the changing global landscape and provide solutions which can guide organisations to continued success. An organisation's survival will be determined by its ability to be enterprising and harness the challenges of change and reinvent them into positive developments. The global graduate is at the heart of this success.

## Why we need global graduates

In the twenty-first century graduates will work for organisations that operate in a landscape which has no boundaries and is continually changing, evolving and transforming. Friedman (2005) stated that 'the world is flat'.

Technology has transformed the way we communicate, the way we work and the way we do business. No industry has been able to insulate itself from the digital transformation that technology has brought to each and every industry; those that have tried are no longer with us. Many of the jobs which exist today did not exist ten years ago: from app developers, to cloud computing specialists and from sustainability experts to social media managers.

No aspect of the way we do business has remained the same. From the basics of how we select and pay for goods, to how those goods are transported and delivered. Technology has not only transformed industries, but also levelled the playing field (Friedman, 2007), so that competitors are now no longer the usual suspects.

The challenges posed by both BRIC (Brazil, Russia, China, India) countries and MINT (Mexico, Indonesia, Nigeria, Turkey) countries would be impossible without the transformations which have occurred in the marketplace.

So what does this mean for the twenty-first century graduate? With a backdrop of continual change, companies need graduates who can confidently work in diverse teams and often virtual teams located across the globe. As a result, companies need graduates who will not only help to defend their market but assist with both developing and operating in new markets. (Diamond et al., 2008)

Companies are therefore not limiting their graduate recruitment to national boundaries. Graduates face an increased level of competition, where companies seek to source the best talent with a global perspective.

## brilliant tip

Why you should have an international experience

1  Personal development and the opportunity to develop your employability skills.

2  Career opportunities – employers value the skills and attributes gained from students engaging with an international experience.

3  Hone your language skills.

4  Build an international network.

5  It's a life-changing experience.

Despite the importance of an international experience, the data from the Higher Education Statistical Agency (HESA) report on UK Student Mobility do not demonstrate a willingness among UK students to engage with international experiences.

In the academic year of 2014/15 only 1.3% of UK domiciled students undertook an international experience. The rate of adoption by UK students is very low, and not reflective of the level of international students taking advantage of global experiences within the UK Higher Education sector. In 2013 there were 'Nearly 4.3 million students. . .enrolled in University-level education outside their home country'. (OECD, 2013) The UK is one of the second highest destinations of international students globally, but ranks as one of the lowest for sending students abroad, as indicated by the HESA data.

The need for global graduates with a global outlook can be seen in the level of students seeking an international experience. The top five destinations for international students are: United States, United Kingdom, France, Australia and Germany.

**Top 20 Destinations For International Students**

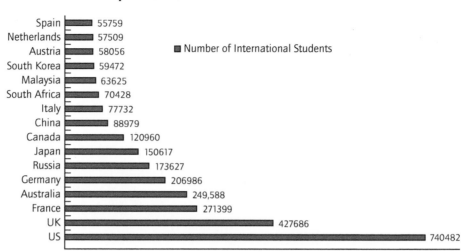

| | |
|---|---|
| Spain | 55759 |
| Netherlands | 57509 |
| Austria | 58056 |
| South Korea | 59472 |
| Malaysia | 63625 |
| South Africa | 70428 |
| Italy | 77732 |
| China | 88979 |
| Canada | 120960 |
| Japan | 150617 |
| Russia | 173627 |
| Germany | 206986 |
| Australia | 249,588 |
| France | 271399 |
| UK | 427686 |
| US | 740482 |

■ Number of International Students

*Source: UNESCO Institute for Statistics (UIS), http://www.uis.unesco.org, extracted July 2016*

## Global competences

Diamond et al. (2008) in a study of 12 graduate recruiters, who represent 3,500 graduate vacancies, identified a list of 'global competencies' which complement the generic employability skills. Regardless of a student's discipline, they would be expected to have generic employability skills as these serve as a baseline for graduates regardless of discipline.

The global competences identified in the study enable students to compete in the global arena. Students who develop these competences will be more able to work in a global capacity participating in global teams.

Employers were asked to rank 14 skills on a scale of 1 to 10, with 1 being the least important and 10 being the most important (and no number was to be used twice). This left four competences scoring zero. The findings of the ranking are listed below.

1    An ability to work collaboratively with teams of people from a range of backgrounds and countries.

2    Excellent communication skills: both speaking and listening.

3    A high degree of drive and resilience.

4   An ability to embrace multiple perspectives and challenge thinking.

5   A capacity to develop new skills and behaviours according to role requirements.

6   A high degree of self-awareness.

7   An ability to negotiate and influence clients across the globe from different cultures.

8   An ability to form professional, global networks.

9   An openness to and respect for a range of perspectives from around the world.

10   Multi-cultural learning agility.

11   Multi-lingualism.

12   Knowledge of foreign economies and own industry area overseas.

13   An understanding of one's position and role within a global context or economy.

14   A willingness to play an active role in society at a local, national and international level.

---

 example

Volunteering in Uganda

I spent the most amazing summer as an International Citizens Service (ICS) volunteer in Uganda. It was a heart-warming, eye-opening and life-changing time where I not only gained perspective on my work (and life) but also gained a new family for life by staying with a Ugandan host family.

The programme allowed me to work with seven entrepreneurs with businesses ranging from a sugar cane farm to selling cosmetics. I worked with them to launch their exciting and innovative businesses to create jobs and improve their lives. As part of my action at home, I currently have the responsibility of selecting the UK volunteers who wish to take part in ICS.

Hermon Amanuel, BA in Business and Enterprise

So how will students develop these skills and do you need to go overseas to develop them? 'Success is all in the global mindset'. (Govindarajan and Gupta 1998)

A global mindset instantly means that you are open to new ideas, willing to step out of your comfort zone, but ultimately curious about the world we live in and the people within it. Alongside the ability to develop a global mindset is the cultural agility and cultural dexterity to adapt your style of working to reflect that of the culture and customs within the country you are operating within.

'I think cultural dexterity is important: an ability not to impose one's own culture on another one, to be sensitive to other cultures and how to do business in different environments. There are certain ways of working with clients in the Middle East that you wouldn't adopt in Japan. (PwC) (Diamond et al., 2008, p. 9)

Central to the global mindset is the need for adaptability in every aspect of the way you work. If you are truly a global graduate, this will be reflected in the way you communicate in an international context.

Naturally you will be mindful of customs and demonstrate a level of understanding when operating in different countries. There is an acceptance that a diverse team is needed to secure an outcome which is globally acceptable and globally competitive. Operating in various countries around the world requires a certain level of flexibility, but an abundance of resilience. There is a definite willingness to go with the flow and accept a different way of doing things. As they say 'When in Rome, do as the Romans do'. In order to appreciate and fully develop solutions, which work on a global basis, it's important to fully immerse yourself into the culture to understand the challenges and the opportunities which exist.

To gauge the level of opportunity in any of the countries in which organisations operate requires a level of knowledge about global affairs. Reimers (2011) stated that commercial and business awareness for the global graduate is 'not just at one country level but at a global level'.

Global decisions are underpinned by a knowledge and awareness of the market which informs the decision-making process at every level. Graduates will be required to understand their industry on a local, national and international basis. Companies operating within this landscape with reduced boundaries need to understand where the next threat will come from or where opportunities are opening. Knowledge is at the heart of global success.

 example

### Have an international experience

The benefits of an international experience – be it studying abroad or combining an international work placement with studying – are well documented. A number of recent studies have re-emphasised the benefits of international experience to students in terms of boosting employability prospects, starting salaries and academic achievement.

The latest Gone International report by the Higher Education International Unit (HEIU, 2016) found that unemployment rates for students six months after graduation were lower among internationally mobile students at 5%, compared with 7% for their non-mobile peers. Black and Asian students seemed to benefit the most from international experience, with their employment prospects showing the biggest improvement: 9.9% of non-mobile, black graduates were unemployed six months after graduation, compared to 5.4% of black, mobile graduates. The corresponding data for Asian students showed that unemployment fell to 4.4% for Asian, mobile students, compared with 9.5% for Asian, non-mobile graduates.

The report also found that employed graduates who had engaged in international experience were more likely (74.8%) than their non-mobile peers (67.1%) to gain employment within one of the top three socio-economic classifications.

Mobile students across almost all socio-economic backgrounds reported higher average salaries than their non-mobile peers. The average salary of a mobile student six months after graduation was £21,349 (compared to £20,519 for a non-mobile student).

The European Commission's Erasmus Impact Study (EIS, 2016) analyses the longer-term impact of mobility on career progression and revealed that former Erasmus students are half as likely to experience long-term unemployment compared to those without international experience.

Students in eastern Europe slashed their risk of long-term unemployment by 83% by taking part in Erasmus (European Commission, 2016). The positive employability impact existed even five to ten years after graduation, where the unemployment rate of mobile students was lower than that of non-mobile students. In particular, work placements were found to have a direct positive impact on employability, with one in three Erasmus students being offered employment by their host company.

Another interesting aspect of the study was the inclusion of personality trait tests for students before and after mobility. The approach looked at six 'memo© factors' that are seen as key employability traits. Ninety-three percent of employers surveyed confirmed that these six traits were key to the recruitment and professional development of employees. Erasmus students from all regions showed higher values for the six personality traits than non-mobile students, even prior to going abroad. Moreover, the mobility experience itself enhanced these traits, boosting the already existing advantage of Erasmus students over non-mobiles by a further 40%.

Here are some ways to overcome barriers to international experience:

- Research funding opportunities: Erasmus mobility grants are available to EU students (https://www.britishcouncil.org/study-work-create/opportunity/study-abroad/erasmus).
- Research scholarships at your university: You may find funding is available for flights or other expenditure linked to mobility.
- Consider a year abroad: This is typically heavily subsidised with students paying just 15 to 20% of annual fees.

- Consider a short international experience: This could be an international summer school. For example, the British Council website has information on short courses (https://www.britishcouncil.org/study-work-create/opportunity/study-abroad).

- Consider combining study abroad with an international work placement: You can seek assistance from companies such as InternshipGuru (www.internshipGuru.co.uk) that facilitate overseas work placements.

    Karen St Jean-Kufuor, Principal Lecturer, Westminster Business School

## Becoming a global graduate

So how do you become a global graduate? CIHE (2008) found that 29% of employers discovered that students were more employable once they had engaged with an opportunity to study overseas. As a result, the UK is challenged in that only 1.3% of the total UK domicile undergraduate students undertake international experiences, and so the opportunity to be fully immersed in an international culture is not sought after by UK students.

On the other hand, as the UK is the second highest destination for international learners, it enables UK students to develop their cultural sensitivity by learning side by side with international students. Despite this opportunity, it still does not outweigh the benefit of the experience of having to adapt to living in a different culture.

 **brilliant** recap

- Global businesses need global graduates.
- Technology has transformed the way we do business.
- No industry has been able to insulate itself from change.
- Competitors are no longer the usual suspects.

- Only 1.3% of UK domiciled students undertake student mobility.

- The top four global competences are collaboration, communication, drive and resilience and an ability to adopt multiple perspectives and challenge thinking.

- Employers value students who have had an international experience.

- Knowledge about international markets underpin global decision-making.

- A global mindset instantly states you are open to new ideas, willing to step out of your comfort zone, and are ultimately curious about the world we live in and the people within it.

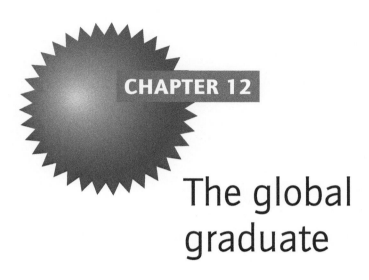

**CHAPTER 12**

# The global graduate

This chapter picks up on the earlier theme of broadening your horizons, first mentioned in Chapter 7, which suggested keeping an open mind and looking at the whole range of jobs and career paths undertaken by other students who have graduated in your discipline. As the title indicates, one way to broaden your horizons is to consider working or studying overseas, and this chapter will help you to think it through, whether you are setting your sights on global leadership of a multinational organisation, or just wanting to take off on your travels.

The chapter will consider what the demand is for the global graduate and how employer and employee both stand to gain. We look at where you can find opportunities, and cover some of the practicalities involved in travelling and living abroad, drawing on brilliant case studies to show how others have fared overseas. Crucially, we show you how to frame your own overseas experience in terms of adding value to your skillset and mindset, even if that was the last thing on your mind when you headed off, passport in hand. So whether you're working as a cleaner in a hostel in South America or as a high flier for a multinational, whether you're about to head off or even if you are reading this now you're back home, this chapter has something for you.

## Demand for global graduates

The concept of supply and demand is an important one for the graduate jobseeker. Chapter 7 explains it in detail but all you need to know here is that you (as a graduate looking for work) are the supply and it is the employers who are the demand. So let's look at the demand for global graduates.

## Employment overseas as graduate choice

The latest published figures confirm that overseas employment is very much a minority destination, accounting for only 3.4% of all graduates across all disciplines. Although that is a very small proportion, it is interesting that this proportion has increased in the last few years, which means more UK domiciled graduates have secured work outside of the UK than before. Roughly four in ten went to Europe, about two in ten went to the Far East and only one in ten went to North America.

Underneath this overall figure are different types of overseas employment, which are likely to include both graduate and non-graduate work. Graduate level entry could be either to a UK multinational company (e.g. Tesco) which then sends the employee to work overseas as part of its international operations, or where a multinational company based outside the UK (e.g. BNP Paribas) takes on a UK graduate and sends them to work as part of its operations which are based outside the UK. Or a graduate might simply seek out graduate work in an overseas location, perhaps to gain job-specific experience, as you will see from our brilliant examples. A graduate may well accept non-graduate work because working overseas is their key driver and the nature of the work is of less importance to them at that time in their career.

Although nobody can predict the future labour market with certainty, it is entirely possible to use economic modelling to get a good sense of how things might turn out over the next few years. Research into future demand across the European Union indicates that between now and the end of the decade, demand for managers, professionals and associate professionals is likely to increase – and these jobs are firmly at graduate level. The same research expects an increase in the employment rates of highly qualified workers within Europe. We need to be cautious here, because this could mean that highly qualified workers (which of course includes graduates) are taking jobs which may not necessarily be at graduate level. Of course that does not mean a graduate stays forever in a non-graduate job; they could easily use the experience of working overseas to develop the skillset and mindset required of a global graduate.

## Specific demand for 'global graduates'

Increasing globalisation and internationalisation of business enterprise and organisations is starting to create a demand for a global graduate. Here's one definition: 'A global graduate is equipped with the skills and competence to succeed in a global marketplace and enable them to perhaps one day become a global leader of a multinational organisation' (CIHE, 2011). Global graduates in this context need to demonstrate that they have all the transferable skills (discussed in full in Chapter 7) but particularly teamwork, communication, resilience and self-management. If we picture a team of employees pulled together from the far reaches of a global organisation for a specific task, then think through what skills they need to work effectively, teamwork and effective communication would of course be top of the list. Resilience and self-management are also going to be in demand for the individuals in that team, because they will be dealing with the new and the unfamiliar, and they are going to have to get on with the job – and with fellow workers.

Multinationals are big organisations and they demand a great deal from their employees, which is why the skillset has to be at high levels; not surprisingly, the multinationals want to attract and retain highly qualified staff so these jobs can be very well paid. Clearly, not everyone is going to fit that specification, and not everyone is aiming for that career goal. Nevertheless, the global skillset is prized by all employers with global connections, not just the big transnationals, which means it is worth considering how you can enhance your total skillset through overseas experience.

### *Employment which demands working abroad*

For some people, their career goal is to take up a role which will, by definition, involve working abroad. Examples include teaching English abroad, working for the European Union, or simply working in the profession for which they have been trained, but in another country. A growing number of people are choosing to work in international development, an interest that may start through volunteering and develop into a paid role. Our next brilliant example, Rachel, spent half of the second year of her degree as an English language assistant in Réunion and Madagascar. She returned to Madagascar as a volunteer soon after graduation, working on building and reforestation projects. After a spell back home to earn some money, she returned to Madagascar, and she continues her story.

---

 **example**

'I led a community health team in a remote region. I did a lot of translating as I was the only French speaker . . . I followed an ecology course as an independent student, being taught by non-government organisation (NGO) professionals . . . on my return to the UK I applied to an international relief and rehabilitation organisation. After a week-long assessment process, I was offered my present post in the Democratic Republic of Congo. I work in French every day, working in medical logistics.'

Rachel, BA (Hons) French and International Development Studies

---

# Demand for language proficiency

For many people, over and above the desire to travel, learning a language is a big draw. Even language students who have studied a specific language to a high level want to deepen their proficiency and immerse themselves in the relevant culture. There is no doubt that learning a language (even at the most rudimentary level) requires you to see things differently and as such increases your cultural agility and sensitivity. But how highly do employers actually value language proficiency?

Employers canvassed by the Confederation of British Industry (CBI, 2011) for their opinion on key issues to do with education and skills reported some concerns about finding people with appropriate skills levels to fill their professional and managerial jobs in the future. This is encouraging for graduates aspiring to such jobs, provided they are prepared to develop their skills base.

As a population, the British are not known for their language ability and the prevalence of English as a common language in business may well have contributed to this. But that does not mean language proficiency is not needed. When asked specifically about the demand for foreign languages as part of the desired skillset, only 27% of the employers in the CBI survey said they had no need for languages; which means 73% do have a need for languages at some level. Only 8% of employers required language fluency. This is a small proportion but a high skill demand because fluency assumes mastery of spoken and written language, which requires constant upkeep and updating.

Even if your language levels are less than perfect, they are still a useful addition to your skillset; employers see their value in making new contacts and building relationships, and of course for international working. There is one final, very important point to grasp about language ability: although it adds value to a skillset, just on its own it offers very little.

---

## brilliant example

'Working at the anti-landmine charity as a translator, interpreter and administrator was a significant learning experience . . . rewarding and challenging in equal measure. (But) I felt I wasn't really helping as much as I had hoped and with my lack of medical, psychological or sociological knowledge it seemed to me I didn't have a place in a charity.'

Claire, BA (Hons) Modern Languages (Arabic and Spanish),
MA International Journalism

---

## brilliant example

'I also thought I was always going to get somewhere with the sheer intellectual kudos of being able to speak foreign languages. It might have been useful if someone had encouraged me to see the merits of business and to appreciate the interesting aspects of jobs that may seem quite boring at first glance. But I was far too concerned with analysing French Occupation literature and learning vocabulary to worry about such piffling things at the time!'

Simon, BA (Hons) French and German, MA Translating

# Looking at travel from the employer's perspective

## Employers value the transferable skills you will develop abroad

Once you're putting your travels behind you and are applying for work or postgraduate study, it is not about where you went and what you saw: it is about how you expanded your professional repertoire and how you can apply what you learned on your travels to your new work situation. It is highly likely that you develop valuable transferable skills through your overseas experience. Chapter 7 takes a detailed look at what transferable skills are, but the most likely skills you will develop as a direct result of your overseas experience are:

- **Self-management:** you will have learnt more about yourself, about how you handle stress and being out of the familiar, or being out of your comfort zone. You may also have had time to think through what is important to you in your life and therefore in your career.

- **Problem solving:** no doubt your overseas experience threw up challenges and problems that you had to solve. Even relatively simple challenges inherent in travel (planning journeys, making connections, getting to the right place at the right time) will make you think through what you are doing and how you are doing it. You may well have found yourself dealing with the unfamiliar and perhaps the unexpected; this in turn demands you find a way through problems.

- **Resilience:** this is the capacity to keep going even when the going gets tough. Living, working, studying and travelling overseas can all be delightful, but can also be challenging. Resilience is how you handle yourself when things seem to be relentlessly challenging. This calls for hope, optimism and being prepared to re-frame things mentally.

- **Foreign languages:** frankly, if you come back from an overseas experience with absolutely zero development in your language ability, that's disappointing. Even if you have mastered nothing but very basic language (greetings, thanks, requests) you will have had the valuable experience of realising how limited you are without language. And for many, the overseas experience allows you to develop fluency and understanding of the language in question and, through that, to develop an appreciation of that country's culture and customs.

## Employers value subject-specific skills

Our next brilliant example is interesting because she already has a job, as a lecturer in animal management at a college of further education. She is travelling in order to enrich her subject knowledge.

---

### brilliant example

'During the summer I plan to travel to Africa to work on an animal conservation project. I am so excited! I look forward to visiting this extraordinary country and working with fellow conservation lovers, caring for wild animals and helping to maintain their environment. I can put my passion into practice and continue to learn in breathtaking surroundings with some of the most magnificent animals.'

Katie, BSc (Hons) Animal Behaviour and Welfare

---

# What opportunities are there abroad?

## Erasmus[+]: short-term study abroad as part of your degree

Erasmus[+] is arguably the best-known university exchange programme: over one million students have participated in the last 20 years. Under the Erasmus[+] scheme, students spend at least one semester studying in a different university in another country. The scheme has operated in at least 28 countries across the European Union (EU) and Switzerland and has expanded beyond the EU to other countries all over the world under the Erasmus Mundus scheme.

### *Erasmus[+] eligibility requirements*

In order to participate, you must be: enrolled as a student (undergraduate, postgraduate or doctoral); eligible to participate (which means broadly speaking that you should have the right to study in the EU); and your home university (here in the UK) must have a bilateral agreement with the host university (overseas). Your course tutor would know if a bilateral agreement with another university is already in place for the course you are on. Your own department might also have some information, but do look both at departmental and university level for the fullest possible information. Even if nothing is in place for your course, your university might already have a bilateral agreement with another university for other courses, and it could be possible for your subject simply to be added to that bilateral agreement.

So if you are interested, the best place to start is the international office or possibly the Erasmus[+] office in your own university. They should be able to advise you on what you can study where, and whether you can apply for a grant. Of course, what you make of those opportunities, and how you transfer your learning to your brilliant jobsearch is very much up to you. Most of what we discuss in this chapter would apply to people taking part in an Erasmus[+] programme: studying abroad gives you a unique opportunity to learn another language, to learn about another culture and to broaden your outlook.

## Work experience as part of your degree

Some courses, especially language degrees, include a chance to spend a year working abroad in a role which will complement the academic content of the course, for example as an English language assistant in a school or college. Others may offer a shorter period of time – the kind of experience Joanne talks about.

---

### brilliant example

'One of the modules I undertook on my course was called experiential learning. I had the opportunity to work in Romania, delivering drama workshops in communities and schools there. This opened my eyes to all sorts of valuable experiences and taught me so much about education in another country.'

Joanne, BA (Hons) Drama and Theatre Studies

---

## Vacation work while you are a student

Most students need to work in the summer vacation, so why not think about working abroad? There are useful reference books on the subject which you will find in your university careers service or library, and some employers come onto campus to recruit.

---

 **brilliant** example

'The university careers team were instrumental in helping me secure a vacation job coaching football in the USA for the summer of my first year, something which undoubtedly benefited me and increased my employability.'

Phil, BA (Hons) Business Studies

---

## How to get what's out there

### Check if you are allowed to work

You can either secure employment and then travel to your new job – or travel to your destination first, then sort out employment. In some cases, you'll have to get the job first because that's what the law requires. You will find there are restrictions to employment depending on the country of employment and the nationality of the employee, so your normal country of residence is important.

There are, however, many opportunities: European Union (EU) nationals are free to live and work anywhere in the EU; some labour markets allow fixed-term work visas for temporary work, or specialised work which can't readily be filled by a local employee; and some international employers can secure work permits for employees who need them.

**brilliant** tip

European Union nationals are free to live and work anywhere in the European Union. In addition, temporary work visas are sometimes available for specified workers, either with key skills or in hard-to-fill sectors.

Before taking on employment you will need to check (a) if there are any restrictions and (b) if these restrictions apply to you. This information is readily available by country – though of course it may not be available in English. The best source of reliable information is the Embassy or High Commission of the country you are interested in. There are also compendium books which pull together a number of destination countries. Your university careers service should have these for reference.

## Check out job opportunities

We take you through the process of finding out what jobs are on offer in great detail, and everything in that chapter applies here. Broadly speaking, you need to look at what's on offer in terms of paid work, and you need to let employers know that you are available for work. You can use printed media (newspapers, bulletins and directories) and online (websites, social networking). Online is particularly useful for overseas work.

**brilliant tip**

Make full use of online resources when looking for work abroad. Use websites, including national newspapers which publish job adverts online. Use social networks to find out about working abroad.

You can also look for work on location. If, for example, you are an EU citizen you can travel anywhere within the EU and then look for a job. You can try the usual labour market channels: local newspapers; employment agencies; speculative applications (i.e. going into an organisation and asking them if they have any vacancies) or word of mouth. It is worth expanding your jobsearch to include some sectors and occupations you wouldn't normally think of; this is particularly useful if the experience of living and working abroad is more important than developing a particular set of job-related competencies.

The problem with looking for a job once you're abroad is that you'll need to stay somewhere, and to fund yourself during your period of jobsearch.

This takes money – almost always more than you expect. And it probably takes a fairly good idea of the local job market, and maybe even a bit of luck once you get there to secure the kind of job you want, as shown in our brilliant example.

## brilliant example

'I started off looking for a job on the Mediterranean coast, because I'd got the chance of accommodation there. So basically I got a load of CVs and went round pretty much every restaurant; that was where I had had most experience, through my Saturday job and work experience at school. It was horrible, really scary, because I didn't really know what I was saying. One place phoned back, invited me for an interview, and gave me a job as a runner.'

Hannah, (Undergraduate) Economics, Politics with International Studies

## Check out whether casual work is worth the risks

Beware that you might be offered casual work that is not legitimate. This can be very tempting: often the pay is cash in hand, and at first sight it does look so much easier to get started working straight away, rather than wade through the hassle of bureaucracy. But working illegally can end up being way more hassle. With no legitimacy and therefore no employment rights or protection, you would be on your own if you had to deal with some of the potential problems of unregulated employment: under-payment; accidents at work; bullying or discrimination.

## brilliant tip

Take the bureaucracy of labour laws (work permits) seriously: protect yourself from the potential problems of unregulated work.

# What you need to know before you go

The Foreign and Commonwealth Office (FCO) spearheads the 'Know Before You Go' campaign, which aims to help British nationals be safe (and in good health) when abroad. It covers a number of key areas – some of which could save your life:

- get adequate travel insurance;
- check the FCO's country travel advice: this is updated very frequently, to take account of emergency situations, e.g. natural disaster or political unrest;
- research your destination – know the local laws and customs;
- visit your GP as soon as you know that you are travelling;
- check your passport is in good condition and valid and you have all necessary visas;
- make copies of important travel documents and/or store them online using a secure data storage site;
- tell someone where you are going and leave emergency contact details with them;
- take enough money and have access to emergency funds.

**brilliant** tip

Use the Foreign and Commonwealth Office (FCO) website (**www.gov.uk/ knowbeforeyougo**) for good information and advice about your destination.

# Once you're away from home

Enjoying the overseas experience

---

### 🔘 brilliant example

'I eventually decided to do TEFL in Germany, especially as I had missed out on the country during my uni year abroad (I had only gone to France) and saw it as a great opportunity to learn the language properly and get some teaching experience. It went really well for me. I really took to teaching and was extremely enthusiastic about living abroad. The Business English context I teach in in Germany has given me a great and interesting insight into so many different companies. I'm very positive about my time in Germany. I've done translating and proofreading work here also, helped set up a website and have worked for a disabled foundation. I had initially thought I could never move back to the UK but lately I've felt more open to it.'

Simon, BA (Hons) French and German, MA Translating

---

You might find the whole experience of working and living away from home is enjoyable from day one: that's brilliant! However, you also might have to put a bit of work into making the experience enjoyable. Having some language is going to help – and acquiring language once you are there will help even more. Being ready to try new things, eat new food, do things in a new way is also going to help you adjust quickly and fit in. You might also need to make more of an effort to make new friends than you would do at home, just carrying on with your normal social circle. People may well make the first approach to include you in what they are doing, but you'll need to show that you are interested in what's going on and are prepared to fit in. So, try to say 'Yes' to any invitations – even if they turn out to be a less than brilliant time, you will at least have clocked up one more experience.

 **brilliant** tip

Be prepared to put a bit of effort into fitting in: try to pick up some language even if you feel self-conscious. Rather than dismissing an invitation or a suggestion, try to give new things a go.

## Surviving the overseas experience

Thanks to social networking sites, you can learn a huge amount, both positive and negative, from other people's experiences. Use them to post questions in advance of your trip, and once you get to your new place. And once there, you can readily tap into the online community, which itself can be a mixture of local people and a more international crew. Your new work mates may also have good advice, which can cover really basic stuff (where to buy food at local supermarkets or markets) to blending in as a local. See what Claire has to say on this:

---

**brilliant** example

'Before I went to Damascus people asked me if I'd have to wear a hijab (headscarf) in order not to offend, or to try and fit in. But I didn't want to wear one, I felt it would be somehow lying, so I decided I wouldn't, and it was absolutely fine that way. The main thing is to dress conservatively, covering elbows, knees and chest, but in a comfortable way. It's important to maintain a level of confidence in how you dress and it's really good to have clothes that suit you and that you like, even if they're not what you'd wear at home. Having said that, even covering yourself from head to toe will not prevent the comments and the staring. It's just something that you have to put up with, walking around as if you're no longer anonymous. Once a young girl of about 10 tapped me on the shoulder and asked incredulously, "Are you from here?" So whether it's men or women doing the staring, it's best to assume it's a harmless sense of wondering.'

Claire, BA (Hons) Modern Languages (Arabic and Spanish),
MA International Journalism

---

## Bureaucracy and accessing key documents wherever you are

Once you are away from home, there are a number of really vital documents which if lost, you would have to replace. Some of these are official: National Insurance documents; passport; visas. Others are personal but equally important: insurance policies; tickets; bank details. You can easily create a document which records all the detailed information you would need if the worst were to happen. It will help enormously if you have someone back home who can access the things you need which you have forgotten to bring: your contact lens prescription; your birth certificate; your European Computer Driving Licence certificate. You could also scan these, and other important documents, and save them on an Internet-accessible website account that you can then access from an Internet connection anywhere in the world. Here's Hannah again.

---

### brilliant example

'The bureaucracy (for working abroad) was tedious, but not impossible. Both my employers did what they could to help. If I needed something I didn't have with me, I phoned home and got it faxed out, or went to an Internet café and accessed stuff that way.'

Hannah, (Undergraduate) Economics, Politics with International Studies

---

## Keeping going when the going gets tough

Even if you have really been looking forward to going abroad, you will have difficult times, when you might feel lonely or homesick. You might feel you have made a big mistake and just want to go home. You might feel you are doing everything you possibly can to get work, make friends and join in with people and it's just not getting you where you want to be as fast as you want to get there. This is perfectly normal, and part of any successful transition from one phase of your life to another. Here is another brilliant example: Claire spent six months in Africa before going to university (three months working in Uganda followed by three months travelling in East Africa), a whole year abroad between her second and final years of undergraduate study (six months at Damascus University and six months working in Colombia for an anti-landmine charity) and now works in Cairo. She shares her experience of feeling low, and what works for her.

## brilliant example

'I learnt to deal with homesickness (in Uganda) – there was just one bout of it, about a month and a half in, and I found the best thing was to go and see friends, or acquaintances, and do something local. To live in the moment and the place, and try and detach. But there's also an element of riding it out. Certainly having had that introduction to living far away from home comforts helped a lot on my (undergraduate) year abroad though. I settled into life in Colombia without too much trouble, and by the time I went to Syria I was a pro at packing and dealing with airports, visas and foreign currency. Settling in, for me, comes with a routine, and I think it's important to feel settled in order to get the most out of a place.'

Claire, BA (Hons) Modern Languages (Arabic and Spanish),
MA International Journalism

*Positive steps to take*

Try to keep a sense of perspective: is the setback you're experiencing going to be such a big deal in five days' or in five months' or even in five years' time? When you feel you've had a really rubbish day, just take five minutes on your own and identify three positive things that have happened. These can be quite small steps, for example:

I got off the bus at the right bus stop/I understood my colleague when he asked me to do something.

Positive things can also be outside of work, for example:

I smelt the gardenia in blossom/I felt so warm in the heat of the day.

It can help to write these moments down in a notebook, so that you build up a store of positive experience, which can help to give a sense of perspective when you're feeling down. Try to keep going: put a bad day behind you and rather than starting the next day convinced things are going to keep going wrong, try to be positive and open to this day going a little bit better.

 **tip**

Try to put negative experiences and feelings to one side and focus on the positive. Take five minutes, each and every day, to identify three positive experiences, no matter how small they may seem.

# Returning

## Securing something to come back to: study or work

*Update your CV in the light of your experience abroad*

Try to capture, on your CV and in your job applications, the ways in which you have expanded your skills and competence. If you have been working, your new skills may well be specific to the work you did, for example.

> I learned to speak fluent Spanish; I can cash up a till; I can operate tools and/or machinery and/or programmes.

Have a look at the kind of employability skills all employers want, but also look at anything an employer specifies in a job advert or person specification.

 **tip**

Rethink your CV in the light of your travelling experience. Think it through from an employers' perspective so you are ready to explain how your travels have added value to you as a prospective employee.

*Include soft skills: look at it from the employers' perspective*

You may also have developed the so-called soft skills, which are just as sought after by employers. These include:

- communication;
- problem solving;
- self-management and resilience.

It is highly likely that you will have found yourself in situations abroad where you had to be flexible, and perhaps also where you had to keep going when things weren't plain sailing. Teamwork skills, such as persuading/negotiating and respecting others are undoubtedly skills you had to develop for a good experience abroad. Try to sell your experiences in terms that are of interest to an employer.

*Foreign language ability*

Many employers are not satisfied with foreign language fluency in graduates. But before you claim you can negotiate high-level deals in another language, appraise your language levels. And if your newly polished language is restricted to ordering food and drink, you might think about picking up some more commercial language applications as part of your jobsearch.

*Get your return destination sorted before you go abroad*

Securing a job or place on a postgraduate programme to pick up on your return is exactly the same procedure you followed to get your job abroad – but in reverse. You might be able to get this all sorted before you even go off on your travels, which means you don't have to think about it at all once you're away from home. Or you might decide to apply from abroad before you return. This is certainly worth exploring for postgraduate programmes, as an interview is not always necessary.

*How to be interviewed at a distance*

Even if you are expected to have an interview you could explore the possibility of doing the interview at a distance – by Skype, for example. This would mean you would miss out on the chance to visit the campus and to meet other people applying for your programme, so it does have its drawbacks.

But the distance interview does have the major advantage of sparing you the expense of travelling a long way. If you do manage to organise a cyber-interview, treat it exactly as you would a face-to-face meeting: prepare for it thoroughly, and present yourself well. Dress formally, look professional. You can always head for the beach once the Internet interview is over.

 **tip**

If you need to be interviewed while you are abroad, ask if an online interview is possible, e.g. using Skype. Remember this is still a formal interview, so dress professionally and present yourself well.

## Aftermath

 **tip**

Don't be too shocked if home seems unfamiliar when you first return: you will adjust to the way of life here, just as you did abroad!

### Reverse culture shock

Coming home after a spell abroad might seem like the easiest thing in the world. But you need to be aware of reverse culture shock. Quite simply, what has always seemed familiar becomes unfamiliar when you go back to it, having experienced something quite different. You might even feel a bit homesick for your life abroad. This can come as something of a shock, and although it's not something people talk about very much, it is quite common. You can draw on the same techniques as you did when you were away: look for the positive in your experiences, however small they may at first appear. You will adjust, and in time, things will fall into place again. Just hold on to everything that was good about your experience. Here's a final word from Hannah.

**brilliant** example

'The best thing about working abroad is when you realise that this is your life. You really do have friends here that you care about. You can go out with them and you can really talk to them in French. And it's as real a relationship as if it was in English. It's just very satisfying, and it's what I wanted. Would I recommend working abroad? Yes, definitely, one hundred per cent.'

Hannah, (Undergraduate) Economics, Politics with International Studies

**brilliant** recap

- Working abroad can be both enjoyable and useful.

- Just a few simple steps will help you to be safe and healthy.

- There are opportunities before, during and after your degree course.

- Make sure that you show clearly how your experiences add value to you as a prospective employee, using the language of employability and skills.

## What to do next

Have a look at the Erasmus+ programme (**https://www.erasmusplus.org. uk/about-erasmus**) to get an idea of what it does. You could also find out what your university offers under the Erasmus+ scheme, by talking to your course tutor, or the international or Erasmus+ office in your university. Use social networks or ask friends who have worked abroad what they made of the experience. Ask employers (at job fairs or alumni events) whether they value overseas experience. Simply think about travelling to enhance your employability, and keep it in mind as a possible option.

# The job market

Developing your I Brand is not
an option: it's a prerequisite for
success!

Don't underestimate the challenge of finding a graduate position. The graduate market is highly competitive and the number of graduates in the marketplace far outstrips the number of jobs available. The key fact to remember is there are opportunities and every year companies recruit to their graduate schemes. You just need to be ready to compete.

One aspect of your preparation is understanding your industry sector. What are the recruiters in your sector looking for? What issues are they facing with current applications from graduates? What areas of the sector do they see in contraction or expansion? Use this information to ensure that you are developing the right skills. How, though, do you access this information?

## What is a graduate scheme?

The majority of top employers offer a graduate training scheme. This is an opportunity for companies to recruit the best graduate talent into their organisations. Graduates are recruited from a wide range of degree disciplines into a wide range of roles. The purpose of graduate training schemes is to offer students the opportunity to experience various roles within an organisation before deciding upon a specialism.

Companies invest in the training and development of their graduate talent, their leaders of tomorrow. As a result, the training presents a range of opportunities and exposure to various departments and individuals, but requires dedication and hard work from graduates. In turn, graduates are rewarded with a competitive salary, career opportunities and a targeted training and development programme.

In order to be successful in gaining a place on a graduate scheme, students need to start their search at least a year before graduation to ensure they are aware of company deadlines and recruitment procedures. A typical recruitment process will include:

- the completion of an online application form
- a telephone interview
- psychometric testing
- invitation to an assessment centre, including a face-to-face interview.

 **brilliant** tip

### Getting the basics right

Every year a significant number of graduate vacancies go unfilled, despite employers receiving over 60 applications per vacancy. Employers search for the mix of knowledge, skills and attributes that will make their organisations perform effectively. Getting the right job may seem a daunting task fraught with uncertainty. But get the basics right and it could be more straightforward than you think.

- **Know thyself.** Socrates may not have realised it but he was disseminating careers advice 2,400 years ago. Reflect on what tasks you are good at, enjoy and can do well even when tired. Then look for an area of work that will let you deploy your talents.

- **Be passionate.** If you enjoy reading the *Financial Times* at the weekend you will probably enjoy a business career. If the sight of blood doesn't make you faint maybe you should be a medic. To be successful you need to work hard and you will only work hard at a thing over a long period of time if you are passionate about it.

- **Understand that a group assignment is not teamwork.** Every student completes a group project at some point in their academic career. When did you get something done with and through others when you weren't told to? This is teamwork.

- **Admit mistakes.** The candidate who has not made a mistake is either lying or hasn't pushed him or herself. It's ok to make mistakes as long as you learn from them and don't repeat them.

- **Try on the shoes of your interviewer.** Recruiters want to hire people. Rejecting a candidate is a negative outcome and, in essence, is wasted time. Think about it. What is your prospective employer looking for? What will make them invest time and resources in hiring you? Would you hire yourself?

Be the candidate that gets the offer call – someone will.

Stephen Isherwood, Chief Executive,
Association of Graduate Recruiters

## Overview of the graduate market

Despite the continued growth in the graduate market since the recession in 2007, the graduate market still remains increasingly competitive. Not only are you competing with current graduates but also with graduates who have not found positions in previous years. The Destination of Leavers in Higher Education Report (DLHE, 2015) stated that in 2013/14 there were 424,375 UK and EU leavers (UK 398,105 and EU 2,270). This represents almost a 50% increase in the number of leavers compared to a decade ago. In 2015 the number of graduate vacancies was the highest since the recession in 2007 with a total of 22,300 vacancies. (High Fliers Research, 2016)

Despite this increase, the Association of Graduate Recruiters also noted that there has been a steady decline in the number of applications received per graduate vacancy. In 2012/13 there were 85 applications per vacancy and this number has decreased every year with only 69 application in 2013/14 compared with 65 in 2014/15. (AGR, 2016, p. 32)

This is good news for students graduating, but when the actual number of applications received is considered it is a staggering 4,522 applications per graduate scheme. The importance of being able to communicate your skills and attributes becomes even more important in order to stand out. As stated previously, there are an increasing amount of graduates (72%) graduating with a 2:1 or a first, which increases the importance of engaging in extracurricular activities to ensure your application has a clear unique selling point.

The graduate market is improving, with a forecast increase in 2014 of 8%, which High Fliers Research states is the 'largest annual rise for four years'. The graduates of 2016 could expect a further 7.5% rise in 2015. The competition is still as fierce as ever, but you always have to keep in mind that there are positions available and you only need one company and one job. You will be rejected on several occasions, but you need to keep going until you find a company that can see the brilliance in you.

 example

Graduate employment

When the global recession took hold in 2008, graduate employment was one of the first parts of the UK economy to be hit. In little more than 18 months, organisations featured in *The Times Top 100 Graduate Employers* cut their graduate vacancies by almost a quarter, leaving tens of thousands of university-leavers either unemployed or in jobs that didn't require them to have a degree.

It has been a long slow recovery since, but by the summer of 2015, graduate recruitment at the country's top employers finally returned to pre-recession levels and several of the UK's most sought-after organisations were reporting a record number of entry-level vacancies.

The outlook for 2016 seems even more upbeat with the number of jobs on offer for new graduates expected to increase by a further 8% (see figure below).

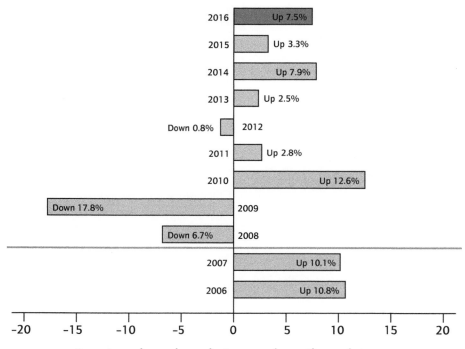

*Percentage change in graduate vacancies on the previous year*

*Source:* The Graduate Marker 2016, © High Fliers Research Limited 2016

Graduate pay is also increasing. After four consecutive years when starting salaries were frozen, the median package for new graduates with one of the UK's leading employers in 2016 is expected to be £30,000, with even more generous salaries on offer from the top City investment banks (an average of £47,000), law firms (£41,000) and banking and finance firms (£36,000). In the table below is a list of graduate salaries in 2016 by industry or business sector.

|                                           | Median graduate starting salaries for 2016 |
|-------------------------------------------|---------------------------------------------|
| Accounting and professional services      | £30,300                                     |
| Armed Forces                              | £30,000                                     |
| Banking and Finance                       | £36,000                                     |
| Consulting                                | £31,500                                     |
| Consumer Goods                            | £29,000                                     |
| Engineering and Industrial                | £26,000                                     |
| Investment banking                        | £47,000                                     |
| IT & Telecommunications                   | £30,000                                     |
| Law                                       | £41,000                                     |
| Media                                     | £27,000                                     |
| Oil and Energy                            | £32,500                                     |
| Public sector                             | £21,000                                     |
| Retailing                                 | £26,000                                     |

*Source:* The Graduate Marker 2016, © High Fliers Research Limited 2016

Despite this upbeat picture, there remains a word of warning. The number of new graduates leaving university from full-time undergraduate degree courses in the summer of 2016 is expected to top 400,000 for the first time – nearly double the number who graduated from UK universities 20 years ago. And yet there are unlikely to be more than 200,000 graduate-level vacancies available across all parts of the UK employment market.

This means inevitably that even in a comparatively buoyant job market, many of those graduating from the 'Class of 2016' – almost all of whom have invested up to £9,000 per year on tuition fees – will still face tough competition to land their first graduate job.

Martin Birchall, Editor, *The Times Top 100 Graduate Employers* and Managing Director, High Fliers Research

## The range of graduate vacancies

The Destination of Higher Education Leavers Report 2015 stated that 68% of the 2013/14 first full-time degree leavers, whose destinations were known, found full-time employment classified as professional.

Although the High Fliers Research report 2016 states that graduate vacancies are at an all time high since the recession, with a further increase due in 2016, the number of vacancies is still not representative of the number of students graduating. Another concern is the fact that in 2015 alone 1,000 graduate vacancies among the top 100 employers were left unfilled. This is an alarming figure as it only represents those companies covered in the survey. You begin to question how many graduate vacancies were left unfilled if we were to consider all of the graduate employers.

In 2016 the accounting and professional services firms, public sector employees, engineering and industrial firms and investments banks will represent 70% of the graduate vacancies. Despite the growth in the number of vacancies, graduates should note that 32% of these vacancies will be filled by those who have already engaged with the company either through work experience, internship or placement. (High Fliers Research, 2016)

It is therefore in students' interest to research carefully companies where they wish to undertake work experience, internships or placements.

The location of 80% of graduate vacancies will be in London, with the second highest region being the south east of England, followed by the south west and north west. Despite companies trying to highlight opportunities in other regions of the country, London still dominates the graduate sector for vacancies.

The other interesting factor about graduate vacancies is the range functions, which are more likely to generate graduate vacancies. IT graduate vacancies top the table at 55%, which is reflective of the digital and technological age that organisations operate within. Finance and human resources are in second and third place with 51% and 39% respectively.

The fact that IT tops the table with the number of graduate vacancies demonstrates that IT skills are wanted at more than just IT companies. It proliferates many sectors and plays an important role within the accounting, public sector, banking and engineering sector.

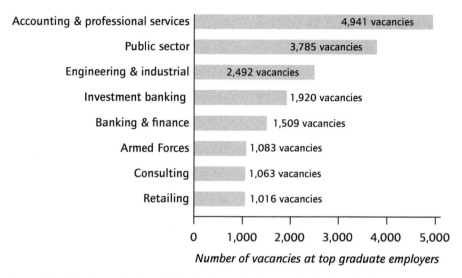

*Source:* The Graduate Marker 2016, © High Fliers Research Limited 2016

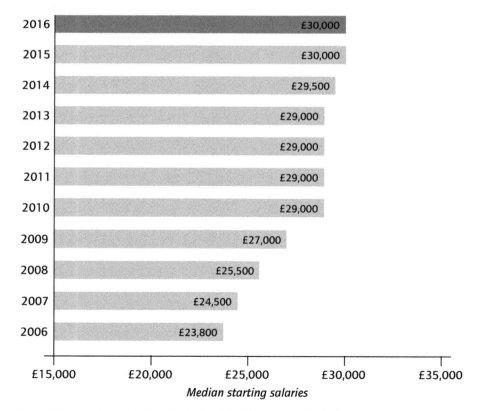

*Source:* The Graduate Marker 2016, © High Fliers Research Limited 2016

## Work experience

The vacancies in relation to placements and internships emphasise the level of importance placed by employers on students gaining work experience. Employers recognise their role in making these opportunities available, in order to develop students' employability skills.

Some 59% of the UK's top 100 graduate employers offered 6- to 12-month industrial placements. Seventy-six per cent of UK's top 100 graduate employers provide paid internships or vacation placements for penultimate year undergraduates.

By engaging with students at this early stage in their studies, employers are able to identify suitable candidates for their graduate schemes. Internships and placements enable organisations to build relationships with promising students. This is further illustrated in the data as a third of all graduate roles are filled by graduates who have already worked for the employer during their degree.

Sixteen per cent of the UK's top employers in 2016 have more than 250 work experience places. This further emphasises the desire of employers to engage with undergraduates, but also illustrates their willingness to provide opportunities for students to gain experience in the marketplace. Graduates with no work experience will find it hard to compete as companies want students to be able to provide practical demonstrations of their employability skills.

The table below lists the number of paid work experience places by industry or business sector.

| Industry/sector | Total work experience places available in 2016 |
|---|---|
| Accounting and professional services | 2,337 |
| Banking and finance | 1,484 |
| Consulting | 210 |
| Consumer goods | 385 |

*(continued)*

| Industry/sector | Total work experience places available in 2016 |
|---|---|
| Engineering and industrial | 1,675 |
| Investment banking | 2,615 |
| IT and telecommunications | 520 |
| Law | 1,030 |
| Oil and energy | 322 |
| Public sector | 2,339 |
| Retailing | 339 |

*Source:* The Graduate Market in 2016, High Fliers Research

It is important to emphasise the need for work experience. Undertaking an internship or placement is a chance for the company to trial your 'product' and, if the company is impressed, you can receive preference for their graduate schemes. It is therefore essential to gain work experience relevant to a sector of interest.

## Diversity and graduate recruitment

Organisations monitor diversity data to ensure that they are receiving applications from a range of candidates and can introduce measures where necessary to increase the diversity of applications and recruits from under-represented groups.

The Association of Graduate Recruiters (AGR) found in its 2015 annual survey that in 2013/14 there was a significant disparity between females hired: 41.6% compared to 58.7% who graduated in the same period. This is not the same when compared to data related to Black, Asian and minority ethnic hires. The disparity between actual hires 15.6% and the number of undergraduates at 18.6% was very minimal.

The other dimension of diversity employers measured was socioeconomic background. Ninety-five per cent gauged socioeconomic background by capturing data on whether graduates were the first in their family to attend university. Other indicators included the attendance at state or private schooling (82.5%) and whether the graduate had claimed free school meals (62.5%).

Nearly 90% of graduate recruiters monitored levels of diversity with almost 80% having an active strategy to monitor and improve the levels of diversity in their graduate hires. It was found that 62.8% of employers focused their efforts on increasing the levels of diversity in relation to gender, compared to 43.9% that actively sought to increase the ethnic diversity of their staff.

## Challenges facing graduate recruiters

To address the continued amount of graduate hires who reneged on graduate vacancies, which on average was 8.2% in 2015, employers made offers to 111 applicants for every 100 positions. The number of graduate hires who reneged once having accepted the position, increased with accounting and professional services to 12.9% and banking and financial services to 12.8%. But it is the engineering and industrial companies that offer the highest with 118.3% of offers for every 100 graduate positions, and 115% for the public sector. This suggests an underlying problem to attract talent or a shortage of candidates.

## Industry or sector

Understanding your industry or sector is paramount. To be successful you need to be aware of the skills needed to compete in your chosen field. There are many ways to develop industry-specific knowledge. Joining a professional body can provide you with regular updates, e-bulletins and networking opportunities with professionals from your chosen industry. The careers service will have specific information on the sector and information on the various roles found within the industry.

Your degree will also provide you with a range of industry-specific links from websites to journals to industry speakers. Using the alumni is another avenue to not only find out about the industry but also possible opportunities for work experience in their organisation.

## Your degree

Employability is embedded in the curriculum and your lectures and assessments will present current trends in your industry. Your assignments will include research into changes in the industry, company-specific case studies and future developments impacting the development of the sector. As a result, your course is one of the first sources of information about the industry.

Reading material will be targeted and provide an insight into industry trends, industry-sector journals and magazines and relevant websites. Lecturers will often invite industry professionals to deliver lectures on challenges facing the industry and changes in the macro-environment impacting the organisation.

## Joining a professional body

All industries have a professional body or network which can provide an insight into the industry. Becoming a member is not as expensive as you may think (student membership can range from £20 to £40). Below is a sample of professional bodies and their membership fees.

### Institution of Civil Engineers (www.ice.org.uk)

Annual student membership: free

Benefits of membership:

- free access to the online version of *Civil Engineering*
- free access to the online version of *New Civil Engineer*
- question and answer support service
- access to the ICE library

- bi-monthly e-newsletter
- free access to ICE virtual library
- eligible for ICE awards and prizes
- eligibility to join the students and graduate network.

## The Writers' Guild (www.writersguild.org.uk)

Annual student membership: £20

Benefits of membership:

- support and advice
- weekly e-bulletin
- *UK Writer* magazine (quarterly)
- events featuring established writers and industry specialists
- discounts.

Do some research to find your professional body as it will keep your industry information and links with industry professionals current.

 **brilliant** example

### British Computer Society membership

I felt so prepared when I started to look for graduate positions. As a member of the British Computer Society I had kept up to date with the industry news and also attended a number of talks by industry professionals. As a result, I had an understanding of the trends and their impact on the current climate. When I went for interviews I could speak quite confidently about the sector and had even formed my own opinions as to forthcoming changes. Interviewers were very impressed with my industry knowledge.

*An information technology graduate*

## Careers service

Don't forget to use the wealth of experience available in your careers service. The advisors will have links with employers and can advise you on the expectations of graduate recruiters. There are also degree-specific graduate industry magazines that can provide you with additional information. The careers service will also organise a number of graduate and placement fairs, presenting opportunities for you to speak directly with employers.

## Alumni network

You are not the first to graduate from your course, so learn from the experiences of others. Use the alumni to field questions about expectations in the graduate market. How hard was it to find a job? What was the interview process? How many jobs did you apply for and when? Alumni are a valuable source of information so either contact your alumni office or speak to lecturers about asking students from previous years to give a talk to the current cohort.

---

 example

The alumni network

I owe my first graduate position to an alumnus of my university. He came to talk to our class about his journey after graduation. We were talking after the event and I asked him if we could go for a coffee one day. He became my sounding board. I would ask him to review my CV or for his view on career pathways. When I graduated, he convinced his manager to give me a three-month temporary contract. At the end of that period I was made permanent. Finding out about the industry from someone who graduated from your course is priceless.

A business graduate

---

## Company annual reports and websites

Annual reports and websites display current information about both the industry and the company. This is displayed in many formats including downloadable reports or video content. It's a valuable online resource and can provide insight into both the company and the sector. Companies need to attract the brightest and the best, so it is in their interest to provide as much information as possible to attract the right candidates.

Review the website of the company you would like to work for. How informative is its website about the company or about the industry? Can you register for any e-bulletins or newsletters?

 recap

- A graduate scheme is an opportunity for companies to recruit the best graduate talent.
- Graduates are recruited from a wide range of degree disciplines into a wide range of roles.
- In 2016 graduate vacancies have risen to pre-recession levels.
- The majority of industries or business sectors are experiencing a growth in their recruitment targets, with public sector, banking and finance employers and engineering and industrial companies experiencing a significant increase.
- The number of graduate positions available in IT and telecommunications has seen an increase in 219% from 2006 to 2016. (High Fliers Research, 2016)
- More than 80% of graduate recruiters offered graduate vacancies in London, followed by 51% in the south east. (High Fliers Research, 2016)

▶

- £30,000 was the average salary with investment banking topping the table at £47,000.
- Companies use internships and placements to trial your 'product' and, if impressed, will aim to offer you a place on their graduate scheme.
- Knowledge is power so make sure you research your industry and leading competitors. Be aware of developing industry challenges and trends.
- Research the professional body associated with your degree and find out what hints and tips they offer to students.
- Use all the resources available to you, such as the university careers service or alumni network.
- Company websites will provide you with an insight into the company and the industry.
- Learn from the experiences of previous graduates on your course. They will be able to give you their experience of the industry and advice on finding a job in it.

# CHAPTER 14

# Tough interview questions

OK, I know that almost any question can seem tough. But compared with 'How long have you been in your current job?', these questions are *really* tough. They're not necessarily intended to make you wriggle (though some are); they may simply be the interviewer's best way of finding out what they need to know.

As far as the interviewer is concerned, this isn't a competition. You're both on the same side, so there should be no element of trying to get the better of you, or knock you down a peg or two; certainly not if your interviewer is professional. Tough questions are generally tough simply because you're not sure how to answer them.

But the point is that, whatever the interviewer's intention, any of these questions might make you feel uncomfortable if you're not prepared for them. Well, that's OK. After this chapter you will be prepared.

---

## brilliant advice

According to professional interviewers, they don't ask deliberately tough questions without a good reason. So what is a good reason? Chiefly:

- To see how you react under pressure.
- To confirm that you are telling the truth (if they doubt it).

▶

Interviewers are particularly likely to see how you respond to questioning under pressure if they have some indication – for example, from psychometric tests – that you don't handle pressure as well as you might.

---

Whether or not the interviewer intends the question to be tough, you should still follow the same ground rules:

- Stay calm.
- Don't get defensive.
- Pause for a moment before you answer if you wish.

The following questions are divided into broad categories to help you find your way around them:

- questions about you
- questions about your career
- questions about this job
- questions inviting you to criticise yourself
- questions inviting you to be negative
- questions about your salary
- unexpected questions.

## Questions about you

Not all the questions in this section will necessarily apply to you. If you're applying for a job that doesn't involve working as part of a team, you're not likely to be asked about your teamwork skills. If you're not applying for a management job, you won't be asked about your management style. But whatever job you are being interviewed for, you'll find that some of the questions here will apply to you and you'll need to prepare answers.

## What will you be asked?

Have a look at the questions in this list, and think about which ones you're likely to be asked for each of the jobs listed. Tick those you think are most likely to be asked for each job.

| | Production manager | Sales assistant | Accounts clerk | Project supervisor |
|---|---|---|---|---|
| 1 Are you a natural leader? | | | | |
| 2 What motivates you? | | | | |
| 3 How do you work in a team? | | | | |
| 4 How do you operate under stress? | | | | |
| 5 What do you dislike most at work? | | | | |
| 6 How well do you take direction? | | | | |
| 7 Do you enjoy routine tasks? | | | | |

Answers: There is no guarantee of what anyone will or won't be asked, but your answers should look something like this.

Production manager: 1, 2, 3, 5
Sales assistant: 2, 3, 4, 5, 6
Accounts clerk: 2, 5, 6, 7
Project supervisor: 1, 2, 3, 4, 5

## What motivates you?

You need to give an answer, as always, that also benefits your potential employer and links into the key responsibilities of the job. So don't say, 'My pay packet'. Give an answer such as, 'I'm happiest when I can see a project through from start to finish', or 'I get a real kick out of running a team that is happy and knows it is successful'.

## How well do you take direction?

Keep in mind the fact that your interviewer may well become your boss if this interview goes according to plan, so it's their direction you'll need to take. The answer, obviously, has to be that you take direction well. You can add credibility to your answer by expanding it to add something like, 'I don't see how a team can function effectively unless its members are happy to take direction from the team leader'.

## How do you handle criticism?

Again, your interviewer may be anticipating being your boss, and inevitably having to criticise you from time to time. They want to know whether the task will be easy for them, or whether you'll make it unpleasant.

So give an answer along the lines of: 'I'm happy to be given constructive criticism. In fact, I think being prepared to take constructive criticism on board is the only way I can hope to learn from mistakes and improve my performance.'

## Do you enjoy routine tasks?

You're not likely to be asked this question unless you're applying for a job which will entail routine tasks. So clearly your answer should be, 'Yes'. However, one-word answers aren't advisable, because your reply will carry more weight if you elaborate briefly to show that you understood the question and have thought out your response.

> one-word answers aren't advisable

So you could add, 'Yes, I have an orderly approach to work and I get satisfaction from carrying out routine work successfully'.

## What is your management style?

There's no point in lying to questions like this, so give an honest answer. But again, make sure it's relevant. You don't need to give a 20-minute rant on the subject; just a couple of clear sentences will do: 'I prefer a carrot rather than a stick approach, and I have an open-door policy', or 'I believe a manager has to be firm with the team, and the team appreciate it so long as you are also scrupulously fair'. It helps to follow this with an anecdote – some example of a problem in your team which you resolved firmly but fairly, for example.

### brilliant tip

Never mention anything at interview that isn't on your CV. You may have managed to miss off those four months you spent stacking supermarket shelves without the gap showing on your CV. But if you make reference to it at the interview, it will call into question the credibility of your whole CV. So either put it on the CV, or make sure you don't refer to it at the interview.

## Are you a good manager?

This is a similar question to the one about your management style, but it is blunter. The answer clearly has to be 'Yes'; if you haven't already been asked about your style you can describe it briefly as we saw in the answer above. Again, it is also a good idea to relate a brief anecdote illustrating your approach to managing people.

## Are you a natural leader?

Since you're only going to be asked this if the job calls for a leader, the answer has to be affirmative. Follow your answer with one or two brief examples, bearing in mind that they don't have to come exclusively from work. You might point out that you were Head Boy or Girl at school, or that you direct your local amateur theatrical society, as well as giving an example from your work background.

Natural leaders, after all, often start young. So if you've been leading groups of people since you were at school, it sug-

> natural leaders often start young

gests your leadership skills really are natural, and people follow you through choice.

## How do you work in a team?

This is another question you need to answer honestly, but pick a relevant way to express your teamwork style. Give a brief answer, such as, 'I enjoy being part of a team, and I like the flexibility it demands. I get a real kick out of collective success.' Follow your remarks with an anecdote or example demonstrating what you mean. If teamwork is an important part of the job, you should certainly expect this question (or a variant of it) and have an anecdote ready.

## How do you approach a typical project?

If you are applying for a project-based job, you should expect to be asked this question. You don't need to give a rambling answer, but show that you take into account the main components of effective project planning:

- Plan the schedule backwards from the completion/delivery date.
- Work out what you need to get the job done effectively and on time.
- Budget cost, time and resources.
- Allow a contingency.

## Best of three

It's a good idea to think of the three personal characteristics you most want to demonstrate to the interviewer. Any more than three, and your message will become diluted. So pick three characteristics (out of your numerous strong points) which:

● are genuinely strong traits of yours

● are important characteristics for the job you're applying for.

Once you have identified the three characteristics you want to promote, prepare examples and anecdotes which emphasise them, as well as making whatever other point you want to illustrate. And when asked questions such as, 'What would your boss say about you?', bring these characteristics directly into play.

Here is a list to give you an idea of the characteristics you could choose from (you may come up with others that aren't on this list):

● Honesty

● Enthusiasm

● Dedication

● Drive

● Attention to detail

● Integrity

● Energy

● Reliability

● Creativity

● Flexibility

● Initiative

● Authority

● Patience

● Leadership

● Diplomacy

● Confidence

● Focus on objectives

● Determination

● Good communication

● Good interpersonal skills

● Calmness under pressure

## How do you operate under stress?

Again, a question you'll only be asked if it applies to the job. A full answer will sell you better than a brief one. So say that you work well under pressure – say you enjoy it if that's true – and give an example of a time you've handled a situation well under pressure. You might also want to add that you practise good time management to make sure that you minimise the stress you have to operate under (but, as always, don't say this if it isn't true).

## How creative are you?

Again, a question for people who need to be creative. So, presumably, you have examples you can give; be ready with them. If you have to do a lot of creative thinking, outline one or two key creative techniques you use, too, to show that you take your creativity seriously.

## How do you get the best from people?

If you're a manager, this is a question you may well be asked. The kind of skills that interviewers want to hear about include:

- good communication
- teamwork skills
- recognising each person as an individual
- setting a sound example
- praising good performances.

## How do you resolve conflict in your team?

You need to answer this question honestly, as always. And find an example of conflict in your team that you can use to demonstrate your skills at resolving it. The kind of techniques you need to demonstrate include:

- fairness
- addressing problems with individuals privately
- making sure you get to the root of the problem
- finding a solution that the people involved are willing to buy into.

Assuming it's true, you would also do well to point out, 'I find if a team is run fairly and the team members are well motivated, conflict very rarely arises.'

### brilliant tip

What do you do if you're faced with an incompetent interviewer? Well, the biggest mistake incompetent interviewers make – by one means or another – is that they don't encourage you to answer questions fully. They ask closed questions (requiring one-word answers), or they never ask you for examples or experiences to back up your claims.

The trick is to do their job for them. Volunteer full answers even if the questions don't demand them. Give examples without being asked. And if you have one of those interviewers who keeps wandering off the point, or stopping the interview to deal with interruptions, impress them by always being able to answer accurately when they ask, 'Where were we?'

## What would your boss say about you?

Your interviewer may well be your prospective boss, so be careful. They want to know that you're an effective worker, but they don't want you stepping on their toes. So describe yourself as any boss would want to see you. For example, 'My boss would describe me as hard working, easy to motivate and loyal. She'd say that I work well on my own initiative, and I'm a supportive member of the team.' Resist the temptation to say 'I *think* my boss would say …'. Be positive and certain in your answer.

If your interviewer is likely to be approaching your present boss at some stage for a reference, make sure that your answer tallies with what your boss is likely to say about you when your interviewer puts this particular answer to the test.

## What do you dislike most at work?

You love work, remember? This interviewer can safely hire you, knowing that you will be well motivated every minute of your working life. So if asked, you can't think of anything you dislike. The only possible exception is if this job is very different from your last, in which case you might say something like, 'I really enjoy my work. But occasionally I get a little frustrated in a small company that I don't get to meet customers as often as I'd like. That's one of the reasons why this job appeals to me so much.'

### brilliant tip

Honesty is the best policy, for several reasons:

- A skilled interviewer may well be able to tell if you're lying.

- Any dishonesty may show up when your interviewer checks references or qualifications, in which case they will certainly be put off you.

- If you succeed in getting the job by being dishonest, your new boss will notice as soon as you fail to live up to the working style or standards you 'promised' at interview. You may have got the job, but once you're in it you'll be off to a pretty poor start.

With intelligent handling of the questions, and following the guidelines here, you should be able to perform excellently at interview without any need to lie.

## Questions about your career

Your interviewer needs to know if you're at the right point on the career ladder for them. But they also need to know where you think you're going. Are you planning to move up the organisation much faster or much more slowly than they expect in this job? So the questions in this section are all designed to tell the interviewer how this job would fit into the broader picture for you in the long term.

This is one of those areas where it is important to be honest. It's not just that interviews can only work on the principle that everyone is honest, quite apart from the ethical aspect of being honest. It's also the fact that, if you mislead the interviewer, you could end up being offered a job which will be detrimental to your career. The interviewer knows far better than you whether this job suits your long-term aims – but only if you tell them straight what those aims are.

> put your answers in the best possible light

At the same time, you want this job, so you will – always – put your answers in the best possible light. But you'll do it without misleading the interviewer.

## Why have you been so long with your present employer?

The answer to avoid is one that implies you were getting stale and should have moved earlier. Any answer which contradicts this unspoken worry on the interviewer's part is fine. For example, 'I've been there for several years, but in a variety of different roles', or 'The job was growing constantly, so it felt as though I was undergoing frequent changes without actually changing employer'.

## Why have you been such a short time with your present employer?

Your interviewer doesn't want to take on someone who is going to leave in six months' time. So show them that you're not really a job-hopper, whatever your CV may appear to show. 'I'd like to settle in one company for several years, but I've found up until now that I've had to move in order to widen my experience and avoid getting stale in the job.'

## You look like a job-hopper to me

This is the previous question but worse. If it is not only your current or most recent employer that you've spent a short time with, but previous employers too, your interviewer will quite understandably be concerned that you'll leave them within a

> nowadays people typically change jobs roughly every two to five years

few months too. Nowadays people typically change jobs roughly every two to five years, but anything more frequent than this looks worrying to a potential employer. And some industries expect their people to stay with them longer than that.

If your CV gives the impression that you barely sit down at your desk before you're off again, you can expect this question. So how do you reassure the interviewer that, this time, you'd be here to stay? The last thing you want to do is launch into a lengthy, defensive justification for each job move in turn. Far better to give a catch-all reason for moving so frequently.

So adopt this kind of approach: 'I'd like to find a company I can settle down in and really make a mark. Until now I've found that I've had to change jobs in order to keep finding challenge in my work. For example …'. Then you can briefly explain just one of your career moves, and why it made so much sense. Finish by saying, 'What I'm looking for is a company dynamic enough for me to find fresh challenges without having to move to another organisation.'

## Why haven't you found a new job yet?

The implication behind this question is that you can't be much good if no one wants to give you a job. So you need to indicate that it has been your choice to spend some time job-hunting. You need to give a reply such as, 'It's important that I only accept a job that seems really right for me, and where I can see that I can make a contribution to the company'.

If you have turned down any offers, say so: 'I have had job offers, but I didn't feel the positions were right for me, and that I was right for the companies concerned.'

## What were your most significant achievements in your current (or most recent) job?

It's unlikely that this job will require exactly the same achievements as the last – although it's great if you can find a clear parallel. So what the interviewer really wants to know about is the qualities you must have exhibited in order to score the achievement. Be ready with something which is:

- recent (or the implication is you've achieved little of note since)
- difficult to achieve
- as relevant as possible to the job you're applying for.

### brilliant tip

You may feel uncomfortable blowing your own trumpet, which is precisely what you need to do at interview. However, you do want to avoid appearing arrogant, so being too cocky is a legitimate worry. There is a tendency to compensate for this by prefixing remarks with phrases such as 'I feel' or 'I think', as in:

- 'I think I'm a good manager.'
- 'I feel my strongest points are ... .'
- 'I think my greatest achievement in my current job has been ... .'

While this may solve the problem of not appearing too arrogant, it creates another problem: it weakens and dilutes whatever you say after it. You're not saying, for example, that you are a good manager – merely that you think you are. You can get round this by substituting a stronger phrase in place of 'I think'. For example:

▶

- 'I believe I'm a good manager.'
- 'I would say my strongest points are ... .'
- 'Colleagues tell me my greatest achievement has been ... .'

## If you could start again, what career decisions would you make differently?

You're on a hiding to nothing if you start trying to think of hypothetical improvements to your past career. Anything you say will suggest that you're not happy with the way things are – and why would anyone want to hire someone who doesn't really want to be where they are?

So the only reasonable answer is that you wouldn't change anything; you're happy with things as they are now. You might add something like, 'I'm not the kind of person to look back with regrets. I like to invest my energy in looking forward.'

## Do you consider your career so far has been successful?

Clearly it's better to be a success than a failure, so unless you've spent long periods out of work and stuck in dead-end jobs, the answer to this question is 'Yes'. To expand on this answer (as you always should on a one-word answer), you can go on to define success in your own terms. This is particularly sensible if your career on paper may look less than outstanding, even if it's respectable.

Perhaps you haven't moved up the career ladder as fast as you might. So you might say, 'What matters to me – more than money or status – is to have a job which is interesting and challenging, and I've been lucky in that respect. So my career so far has been very successful.'

And what if your career has had its low points, and perhaps not brought you as far as it might? There's no point in pretending your CV glitters when it clearly doesn't – so show you are positive and looking ahead: 'I've had one or two career problems in the past, but those are firmly behind me. From now on I intend to build on the good breaks I've had and enjoy a very successful career.'

> there's no point in pretending your CV glitters when it clearly doesn't

## When would you expect promotion?

Don't give a firm timescale here. The answer is, you should expect promotion when you deserve it. 'I would hope to be promoted once I have demonstrated my value to the company, and shown that I'm worth it.'

And show how this job suits your long-term aims: 'That's why I want to join a company that is growing so that the promotion opportunities will be there when I'm ready to move up', or 'That's why I want to join a large organisation so there are plenty of opportunities when I've gained the skills and experience'.

### brilliant tip

Certain questions are technically illegal, or can be if there isn't a sound, relevant reason for asking them. These include questions relating to your race, religion or sex, questions about your medical history, or about your future plans for a family, and that sort of thing. But what do you do if you're asked? You can obviously answer if you wish to, but what if you'd rather not?

While you're perfectly entitled to get defensive and demand that your interviewer retract the question, such behaviour may not help you get this job. Your best bet is to say politely, 'Can I ask why you need to know that?' Unless there's a legitimate reason, this will almost certainly lead to a retraction. If they persist in asking you something totally unreasonable, you will have to choose between refusing firmly or answering anyway (whether truthfully or not).

## Questions about this job

Your interviewer is well aware that there are thousands of jobs being advertised every day. So why have you applied for this particular one? They are looking for evidence that the job really suits you – that it fits in with your general aptitudes, suits your long-term goals, and involves doing things you enjoy.

This is why they will use these questions to delve deeper into how strongly you feel about this job, how enthusiastic you really are about it, and how much you really think you would enjoy it and be able to contribute to the organisation.

### How can you attend this interview while you're employed elsewhere?

The hidden pitfall here is that you must avoid coming across as being dishonest in any way. So if you told your boss you had to stay home for the washing machine maintenance engineer to call, or that you had a doctor's appointment, keep quiet about it. Otherwise your interviewer knows that if they offer you the job, they'll be wondering what's going on every time you ask for time off to go to the doctor.

> you must avoid coming across as being dishonest in any way

Ideally, your boss knows you're looking for work and is aware you're at an interview. However, this isn't often the case. Assuming your boss actually has no idea where you are, the only valid justification for taking time off to come here is that you were owed holiday or time off and you took it in order to be at this interview.

### How does this job fit into your career plan?

It's dangerous to commit yourself too precisely to a career plan. So you might say something like, 'Business changes so rapidly these days, it's hard to plan precisely. But I know I want to get ahead in this industry/in marketing/in management and I think the opportunities to do that in this company are excellent.'

## What appeals to you least about this job?

Careful here. Naming almost anything will give the interviewer the impression that you are less than 100 per cent enthusiastic about this job. So either tell them that it all appeals to you or, if you feel too glib giving this kind of answer, come up with a part of the job which is:

● a small part of it

● of no major importance

● universally unpopular.

One of the best examples of this is filing, or paperwork in a job where the paperwork isn't a significant part of the job (but absolutely not if it's important to the job). But you should still express it in positive terms: 'I can't say I find paperwork terribly inspiring. But it's important to make sure it gets done. And actually, it can be quite therapeutic.'

### brilliant disaster

You're asked what appeals least about the job. You laugh and say 'Probably having to be here by 8.30 in the morning.' You meant it flippantly and the interviewer shares the joke with you, but privately thinks that sort of remark doesn't come from nowhere. If they offer you the job, they wonder, will you get fed up with it because of the early starts? Will you have a time-keeping problem? Will it take you ages to get going once you arrive in the mornings … ? **Whoops!**

### Are you talking to other organisations as well as us?

You want to show your interviewer that you're in demand. It makes you a more attractive prospect, and if you're offered the job it can help to push up the salary you manage to negotiate. At the same time, if you tell them you've had three other offers already, they may be put off you if they still have a long way to go – another round of interviews, for example. So indicate that you are talking to others without suggesting you're on the verge of taking another job. If it's not a downright lie, let them know if you're doing well. For example, 'I've reached the final round of interviews with three other organisations.'

### What other types of job or organisation are you applying to?

There's no need to divulge exactly who you've applied to. Occasionally you may be asked directly where else you've applied, but you can avoid answering by saying that the companies concerned haven't advertised and you don't feel you should divulge the information. That lets you off the hook and shows you can keep a confidence.

But the interviewer can get round it with this question – asking not for names of companies but merely types of job and company. The important thing here is to show that you want this job. If it becomes plain that you're applying for all sorts of different jobs in different industries, it rather casts doubt on your commitment to this post. So indicate that you're applying for similar jobs within the same field.

### How long would it take you to make a useful contribution to this company?

You might be thinking that you can't answer this question without more information. Quite right. So ask for the information you need:

- What would my key objectives be for the first six months?

- Are there any specific projects you would need me to start work on straight away?

You can use the answers to these enquiries to help with your answer. But broadly speaking, you should indicate that (unless there is an urgent project) you would expect to spend the first week or two settling in and learning the ropes. After that you'd expect to be making a useful contribution within the first few weeks, and to show significant successes within four to six months.

## You may be overqualified for this job

The worry the interviewer is revealing here is that if they offer the job you will quickly become bored and leave. You may have reservations on this front yourself, but at this stage you should still be doing your best to get the job. If you're going to turn it down, do it when it's offered – don't write it off half-way through the interview.

So for the moment, you're going to give the best answer you can. Say that strong, dynamic companies can always use whatever talents they have to hand. You want to stay with the company for a while and, if your experience and skills are strong enough, you're sure they will find a way to keep you challenged and making a full contribution.

> so for the moment, you're going to give the best answer you can

## What do you think are the key trends in this industry?

This question isn't difficult so long as you've done your research – which is what the interviewer wants to establish. This question is really the advanced version of, 'What do you know about our company?' So the important thing here is to make sure you do your homework, and identify the key industry trends, ready to impress your interviewer.

Even if you're applying for a job in the industry you already work in, you should still prepare an answer to this question. It won't necessarily come to you, clearly and succinctly, in the heat of the moment.

## brilliant tip

One of the ways in which interviewers can test you is by asking you more than one question at a time. For example: 'How would you approach a typical project, what is the biggest project you have handled in the past, and what were the major difficulties you encountered?'

Unskilled interviewers may do this unintentionally, but skilled interviewers are more likely to do it as a test of your intelligence. The more of the questions you answer (and you have to hold each one in your head while you answer the others), the brighter they will assume you are. If you repeat the question back to them as soon as they ask it, this will help you to fix it in your mind.

## Questions inviting you to criticise yourself

Uh-oh. These are tricky questions, and ones you want to be careful with. You have a bit of a dilemma here: you don't want to admit to any faults or errors but, on the other hand, arrogance is one of the factors most interviewers cite as being particularly irritating. So how can you avoid conceding mistakes without appearing cocky and just too perfect?

> arrogance is one of the factors most interviewers cite as being particularly irritating

One of the classic questions in this category is 'What is your biggest weakness?' – a question so popular we dealt with it in the last chapter. And the recommended type of answer we looked at then applies for all these questions too. Here are the four techniques for criticising yourself without admitting to anything damaging:

1   Use humour – but be careful. This isn't the best approach if you sense that your interviewer has no sense of humour. But if they seem ready for a laugh, and it suits your personality to do it, you can use humour. If you do it every time, however, it starts to look like a cop-out (which it is, of course).

2   Give an example from your personal rather than your work life, where the question allows. For example, 'I used to find getting up in the mornings a real challenge, but since I started walking the dog before breakfast I find I really enjoy getting up.'

3   Pick something from a long time ago, which you can demonstrate that you've learnt from. For example, 'Decisions without a deadline used to be a problem for me – I never got round to making them. Then I discovered the trick of imposing a deadline on myself just so the decision would get made. Now I never delay decisions unnecessarily.'

4   Give an answer which you claim is a fault or a weakness, but your interviewer will see as a strength. For example, 'I can be a bit of a perfectionist. I just can't bring myself to turn out work that I feel isn't as good as it could be.'

---

## brilliant advice

Five phrases that employers hate to hear:

1   'Sorry I'm late.'

2   'I don't really know.' Unless the question is a factual one, employers want to hear you being positive and enthusiastic about answering questions.

▶

**3** 'I don't get on with my boss.' Maybe you don't, but the interviewer wants to hear that you are loyal publicly, regardless of your private feelings. That's a quality they're going to want in whoever they give this job to.

**4** 'What salary are you offering for this post?' This question suggests that you care only about what the organisation can do for you, not about what you can do for it. The same goes for questions about hours of work and all the rest. (Time enough to discuss that after they offer you the job.)

**5** 'You're wrong . . .' or any other form of overt disagreement. If you get flustered or riled into speaking aggressively, it doesn't say much for your people skills. It's quite possible to disagree politely. Remember, the interviewer may be testing you to see how you respond.

---

## Describe a difficult situation which, with hindsight, you could have handled better

Again, the trick here is to be ready with something from a long time ago. And try to prepare an example where it really wasn't your fault you handled it as you did. For example, 'With hindsight, I can see that it would have been quicker to evacuate everyone straight down the main staircase rather than use the fire escape, but because the phones were down I had no way of knowing that the main staircase was safe.'

## What sort of decisions do you find difficult?

You've never found a decision difficult in your life, of course. But the danger with some of these questions is that if you come across as being too implausibly perfect, you risk sounding glib and arrogant. So you have to admit to some minor failings, but make sure they have been overcome or are irrelevant to the job you're applying for – or else make you sound human. So you could say, 'The kind of decisions I dislike most are the ones which other people won't like. They aren't actually difficult, but

I don't like making a decision to sack someone, for example.' If you've never had to sack anyone, find another example of something others don't like.

> you have to admit to some minor failings

## Describe a situation in which your work was criticised

If you pick an instance where the criticism was clearly unfair and you were in the right, you risk looking as if you are simply taking an opportunity to air an old grievance – maybe you're someone who bears grudges (the interviewer will think). So you need to go for the 'distant past' option.

Interviewers may well ask you this question – or a variation on it – if they want to see how you cope with tough questioning. So make sure you have an answer ready in case you need it. You should answer in two stages:

1  Briefly describe the task and the criticism you received for it.

2  Explain how you learnt from it and you haven't repeated such mistakes since.

Not only does this make you sound human, and as though you haven't been criticised for a long time, but it also shows that you can take constructive criticism on board and learn from it.

### brilliant tip

Whatever the temptation, don't argue with your interviewer. If they see you as difficult and argumentative it will put them off employing you. They may even be testing you to see how you respond to their belligerent questioning. So if you tell them you run a team of three people and they say, 'That's hardly managing, is it? This job entails running a team of ten', don't get defensive. Say

▶

> something like, 'I can see that it looks very different on the surface, but I'd say the same principles apply whether you manage one person or a hundred.'

## Questions inviting you to be negative

These questions are intended to find out if you are naturally negative or even bitchy when given the opportunity, or whether your natural instinct is to be positive. So whatever you do, don't take the bait. Refuse to be critical or negative about other people or organisations.

### What is your present boss's greatest weakness?

'Where do I start?' is not the right response to this question. In the last chapter we looked at the popular question, 'What is your present (or most recent) boss like?' This is the tough version of the same question – it really invites you to land yourself in it. So don't fall for it, no matter how long a list of complaints you may privately have about your boss. Remember, this interviewer may one day be your boss. So tell them what they would like to hear about themselves.

> remember, this interviewer may one day be your boss

Say something along the lines of: 'To be honest, I'm lucky to have a very supportive boss who is good at her job and very easy to work with.' Then look as if you're really trying to think of a weakness and add, 'I can't think of anything – if I did it could only be something so picky it wouldn't be worth mentioning.'

### How do you evaluate your present company?

It's a great company which has taught you a lot and given you lots of excellent opportunities. I don't care what you tell your mates, as far as the interviewer is concerned, that's your answer and you're sticking with it.

This reply may understandably be followed with the question, 'Then why do you want to leave your job?' We looked at how to answer this in the last chapter.

## What sort of people do you find it difficult to work with?

As always, you need to resist criticising other people. Don't be drawn into bitching about the PA in your department who's always trying to boss people around, or the programmer who is always moaning about their workload. Start by saying that you generally find most people are easy to work with, but if you had to pick a type you found difficult it would be people who don't pull their weight, and don't seem to care about the standard of their work.

### exercise 3

You're bound to be asked some pretty tough questions during your interview. We all have areas we might prefer not to be asked about, or topics we find tricky. Or maybe we just get nervous when we're put on the spot. So here are a few ideas to help you prepare for the trickiest questions:

- Sit down and think up the five or six questions you'd least like to be asked. Maybe you spent a long time in one job without promotion, and you don't want to come across as a low achiever. Or perhaps you find some people tricky to deal with and you don't want to answer too many questions about how you handle difficult people. Write down your list of 'hate' questions, and then work out answers to all of them.

- Ask a few of your friends or colleagues to fire tough questions at you. Maybe you could ask them to call you out of the blue once or twice in the next few days, and fire tough questions at you.

- Ask a few friends and colleagues to tell you the toughest questions they've ever been asked at interview, and then work out how you'd answer them.

## Questions about your salary

The general rule when it comes to questions about salary is to get them to name a figure rather than allow them to force the ball into your court. If you name a salary, you can bet you'll never get more than the figure you've named. So unless – or

___

don't commit yourself to a specific figure

___

until – you have a very clear idea of exactly what they're expecting to pay you, don't commit yourself to a specific figure.

The following questions are intended to get you to name your price. The recommended answers are intended to sidestep the issue without causing offence or appearing unreasonable. Once you are offered the job, *then* you can negotiate – following the guidelines set.

### brilliant disaster

You're asked what salary you're expecting, so you reply with the figure you had in mind: 'Somewhere around £22,000.' You are subsequently offered the job, at a salary of £22,000 – which you can hardly argue with since you named the figure yourself. Once you start the job you discover that colleagues doing a similar job to you are all earning at least £25,000. **Whoops!**

### What is your present salary?

You don't want to answer this. If you're offered the job, they'll try to get away with paying you as close as they can to your existing salary – at best it will hold the negotiating level down. Say something such as, 'I think salaries can be misleading, as it's really the whole remuneration package that counts. Of course, that's harder to quantify.' Then ask if you can return to the question later, once you get to a point where you need to talk about it in more detail (i.e. when they offer you the job).

## What salary are you expecting?

You don't want to answer this one either, because there's no chance of getting any more than you say now, and a good chance of scaring them off if you ask too much. So answer a question with a question: 'What salary would you expect to pay for this post?' or ask what salary range has been allocated. If they refuse to answer at this stage, you can reasonably do so too.

If they quote a salary and ask for your response, let them know you were thinking of something a little higher, but not out of their reach (assuming you'd agree to that yourself). If they suggest a range, quote them back a range which is higher but overlaps. So if they say £20–25,000 you might say you were thinking of £24–28,000. You're edging them up, but you're not putting them off.

## How much do you think you're worth?

All these salary questions are good news, essentially. Why would they bother to ask unless they were thinking of offering you the job? This particular question is really the previous one again with a nasty twist to it. It's just a matter of justifying what you're asking for – once you've played the previous game of making them go first.

> it's just a matter of justifying what you're asking for

You should already have an idea of the going rate for the job in the industry or the organisation (especially if it's an internal job), so ask for a little more and explain that you've studied salary surveys and so on and, since your experience and skills are above average for the job, you believe you're worth above the average pay. By the way, you can expect the interviewer to respond by saying that the figure you name is too high – that's just part of the negotiating tactic. Don't let it dent your confidence.

> ## brilliant tip
>
> Never drop your guard at an interview. Trained interviewers are very skilled at catching you off guard to see how you react. They may be friendly and relaxed and then suddenly fire a tough question at you, or they may follow a series of easy questions with a trick one, having lulled you into a false sense of security.
>
> So treat every question as a fresh start, and never assume that this is an easy interview. Pause before answering if you need to, so you can't be railroaded into making any unguarded comments.

## Unexpected questions

Some interviewers like to catch you off guard, and many of these questions are intended for just that purpose. They're not just trying to be unpleasant for the sake of it. They either have a good reason for wanting to know the answer, or they want to know how you cope with the pressure of an unexpected question. The key rules here are:

- Pause before you answer if you need to (interviewers rather like this as they can see you're really thinking about your answer).
- If you're unsure what the interviewer means by the question, ask for clarification.
- Stay cool and unflustered, and don't argue with the interviewer.

### Sell me this pen

Some interviewers like asking this kind of question even if you're not applying for a sales post. The aim is to see that you focus not on features ('It's solid silver') but on the benefits to them ('It will impress people'). So give them four or five benefits of the pen (or notepad, or paperclip or whatever they've asked you to sell them), and then finish, half jokingly, with a standard closing technique: 'Shall I put you down for two dozen?' or 'Would you prefer it in black or red?'

## Tell me a story

This is a semi-trick question. You're supposed to demonstrate whether you have a sufficiently logical mental approach to ask for the question to be more specific before you answer it. So ask the interviewer, 'What kind of story?' They will probably ask for a story about you, and are likely to specify whether they want a work-related or a personal story. Then just relate some anecdote which shows you in a good light (so have one ready).

## What do you think about privatisation/global warming/the Balkans (or whatever)?

The interviewer is trying to find out how much of an interest you take in the world in general, and also to get an idea of your values and attitude to life. Whatever the topic, you need to demonstrate in your answer that you can see both sides of an argument, that you don't view things in an over-simplistic way, that you can discuss a subject fluently and that you are capable of making judgements.

So don't rant on about your particular views (if you hold strong views) without acknowledging the other side of the debate. You are most likely to be asked these kinds of questions by companies to whom they are relevant. Pharmaceutical companies may ask your views on supplying cost-price drugs to developing countries; banks might ask your views on interest rates. So take into account their likely view on the subject.

don't rant on about your particular views

Employability Skills for Undergraduate Business Students

## Tough talking

No matter how tough the questions you are asked, if you're well prepared you should be able to take them in your stride. Once you've absorbed the ground rules throughout this chapter (and the last two), you should be able to answer any question – even one you hadn't specifically prepared for. Just remember:

- Stay calm.
- Take your time to answer tricky questions.
- Don't argue.
- Don't admit to any significant weaknesses.
- Don't be drawn into criticising anyone.

# CHAPTER 15

# My decision, my context, my life: why all this matters

This might seem like a very heavy title. Put more simply, the purpose of our final chapter is to help you to recognise and take into account the factors about you and your circumstances that may influence your career choices. Some circumstances might be outside your control, for example a shortage of jobs due to the economic climate but, even if you can't change these circumstances, you can adapt to them so that you gain in the longer term.

---

### brilliant example

'When I started at university I never thought for a second that I would be a teacher. It shows that what you learn along the way is so important to your ultimate career destination, and how much the path changes each day.'

Becky, BA (Hons) French and Tourism, now a primary school teacher

---

## Decisions in context

Firstly, it's important to remember that none of us makes decisions in isolation. You might have a dream holiday destination – but the decision about where you actually go is influenced by cost, your availability, the availability of the holiday, your companions' wishes, and so on.

## Who would you rather be?

Because you are positive and proactive, in planning your holiday you work with each of the factors we have just mentioned, deciding if you can do anything to give you more choice – do some extra hours at work to increase your budget, be more flexible with dates or destinations. Unless things go very wrong, you should still end up somewhere you want to be and be able to look back on an enjoyable experience.

Your friend, however, takes the passive, negative approach. She goes with the flow even if it's not what she wants, because she can't be bothered to get involved, or she opts out because her choice isn't on offer. She ends up spending the whole time resenting the fact that it isn't her choice, or worse, grumbling at home because she isn't going on holiday. Who would you rather be?

 **tip**

Don't opt out, opt in. Be positive and proactive in your approach to career decisions.

## Factors that affect career decisions

If we extend the example of the holiday decision in the last section to career decisions, we can identify aspects of your personal circumstances and preferences that could be relevant to your choice of career. We can call these personal factors.

In Chapter 7 we talked about supply and demand in the graduate labour market; the demand for the kind of job you have in mind is very much influenced by external factors, which are outside your own control, but which have a key impact on your choices.

Here are some examples of these two kinds of factors, and how they might impact on your career plans.

*Personal factors and their impact on career plans*

- **Family circumstances:** is anyone relying on your income? Are you a carer for a child, a younger sibling, a sick or elderly relative? Do you have a partner who is committed to a course or job in a particular area? *Impact:* you may need to look for work in a particular location; your available hours for work may be determined by your responsibilities for others; you may feel under pressure to take any job in order to bring money in; or you may have to delay your entry to the labour market.

- **Finances:** apart from servicing your student debt (which applies to most graduates) do you have any significant debts? Do you have savings, or access to financial support?

  *Impact:* you may feel that you have to take any job to start to pay off debt; alternatively, if you have savings and/or financial support, this could give you freedom to undertake further study or voluntary work.

- **Location:** do you need to stay in or return to a particular area, for example because of family circumstances? Do you have preferences about location and how important are they? Are you willing to move for work? Can you drive?

  *Impact:* opportunities may be more limited if your location is restricted, and conversely more wide ranging if you are willing to move. Housing/living costs in a new location may be relevant.

- **Family influence:** is there an expectation that you will enter an occupation held by your parents, or that you will join a family business? Will your choice of career be a family decision, or one made by you alone?

  *Impact:* it could be helpful to enter an occupation that you know intimately, including understanding the benefits and drawbacks for your way of life. A family business might provide a good start, especially if opportunities are otherwise limited. In either case you can work towards a specialist area based on your interests and preferences.

- **Further study and training:** are you willing and able to commit to further study? If full-time, how will you support yourself financially? *Impact:* some jobs require further study so, if this really isn't an option, you may have to re-plan or defer entry.

- **An existing job:** could you work full-time for the employer you have worked for during university? Are you under pressure from the employer to do so? What's in it for you if you do?
  *Impact:* this route could leave you wondering why you went to university; alternatively, it could give you the prospect of a graduate-level job by another route.

- **A grand plan:** do you have a longer-term aim that is influencing what you do after university?
  *Impact:* sticking rigidly to a set plan can be dangerous if it just leaves you marking time; it can be good if you use the time constructively.

- **Health:** is there anything about your health that might have implications for your choice of job?
  *Impact:* there may be some jobs from which you are excluded (e.g. people with epilepsy cannot usually work with machinery), or some that you need to seek out, for example a job where you are mainly sitting down. Be aware that, if you have a disability, you have certain entitlements by law; if you meet the selection criteria for a job you must be offered an interview; and once you are in employment, your employer is expected to make reasonable adjustments to your workplace and equipment to enable you to carry out your work.

*Reasons, not excuses*

 **brilliant** definitions

A **reason** is an attempt to explain.

An **excuse** is an attempt to avoid.

It might help to assess where you stand in respect of each of these personal factors, both now and in the future, and to consider what is negotiable and what isn't. You might not like working at weekends because it interferes with your social life, but is it a reason? On the other hand, you might coach a junior football team on Sundays and just now there isn't anyone else, it's a tough part of town, and you won't let them down.

Once you have identified honestly what is non-negotiable, be positive, not apologetic, both with employers and with yourself – it's a reason, not an excuse; and review regularly – circumstances change, a new coach comes along, your partner finishes their course so you can relocate – and you can reassess your situation.

## brilliant tip

Review your personal circumstances regularly – a change of situation may enable you to broaden your job search.

### External factors

There is really just one, big external factor affecting graduate jobs and that is the economic climate. More localised events that impact on jobs, such as the opening or closing of finance houses, production plants and distribution centres, are all the result of changes in the economic landscape.

The good news is that the graduate jobs market has improved significantly in the last two years – more graduates have found work than ever before and almost 70% of those going into work are getting jobs for which a degree, though not necessarily in a specific subject, is a requirement. The most recent information (in *What Do Graduates Do?*, October 2015 and published annually) tells us that graduate unemployment is down by 2.5 percentage points compared with two years previously.

A few years ago, at the start of the recession, graduate unemployment had its biggest increase for some years. Even though the picture is much better now, be aware that there are still some negative headlines about, especially stories about graduates doing jobs for which they don't need a degree. However, these graduates are likely to move into a graduate-level job in due course – they are wisely getting some experience of work and some income in the meantime. Later in this chapter you will meet four successful graduates, in graduate jobs, three of whom had an interim job between graduating and their present role.

So do get accurate data, especially about your own subject area and your own university. Have another look for an analysis of what graduates do, and talk to your university careers service for information about recent graduates from your university.

---

### brilliant example

'Within two months of leaving university, in a very tough economic climate, I had secured a great job, providing consultancy to some large firms. I had delivered workshops, presentations and pitches to both sole traders and national companies. I believe my time at university equipped me with the creative problem-solving skills and self-awareness I needed to excel within my industry.'

Alex, BA (Hons) Graphic Design

---

As the economy recovers there are reports of shortages of graduate entrants in some occupational areas. Recent studies by the Bank of England and by the UK Commission for Employment and Skills refer to unfilled jobs in a number of areas including IT and web design, most branches of engineering and, in some parts of the country, marketing and retail management. However, despite the upturn, patterns of recruitment do still mean that there may be a delay between graduating and moving into a graduate job, so be prepared to be flexible:

- it may take longer to get to where you want to be;
- you might go by an unexpected route.

 If you do find yourself in the very unfortunate position of not having a job, not having anything to do and there's nothing in the pipeline, you must do something to get yourself out of that rut. Any job is better than no job. If it's not a job, if it's voluntary work or a training course . . . there's a whole range of things you could be doing.

Carl Gilleard, Chief Executive, Association of Graduate Recruiters

Being a supermarket assistant is not my dream job; however, neither is it beneath me.

Kim, BA (Hons) Christian Youth Work

# If at first you don't succeed

## Mind your language

If you have identified factors in your own context that will influence your career planning, then you need to work with these factors, rather than regarding them as barriers to a graduate job. Even small statements can signal this kind of positive approach. Compare these two:

> I can't drive so I'm limited to jobs in this town.

or

> I'm looking for work that is accessible by public transport and I'm willing to travel for up to 90 minutes each way.

The first contains two negatives – 'can't' and 'limited'; the second, two active positives – 'looking' and 'willing'.

Now these two:

> I can't work in school holidays because of my children, so I probably won't be able to get a job until they are old enough to leave.

or

> I'm exploring all the organisations that might offer term-time-only work – not just schools, but colleges, the local university, and the local authority Children's Services Department. My friend works in Governor Services and has a really interesting job supporting school governing bodies – and it's term-time only.'

Again we can see 'can't' and 'won't', compared with 'exploring'.

There is very clear evidence from psychological research, which shows us that a change in attitude can lead to a change in behaviour. So look again at the second example in each pair. The positive statements are a clear indication of jobsearch behaviour. So, if you can adopt a more positive attitude, this will have an impact on your behaviour.

Can you turn the following statements round to demonstrate a more positive approach?

- 'I want to keep on living here after university because all my housemates are staying, but I don't know if there are any jobs.'

- 'I might as well stay on at the supermarket after I graduate – they've offered me a job and the papers say there aren't any graduate jobs.'

- 'I need to clear my debts so I have to stay on in the bar where I've been working.'

- 'There's no point in doing any voluntary work because I'd only have to give it up if I get a job.'

- 'No one from this university ever gets into a blue chip company so there's no point in applying.'

- 'If only I had a 2:1 instead of a 2:2, it would make all the difference.'

- 'Yes, but what about all the other people who'll apply for that job?'

So, reflect on the language you use – not just in applications and careers interviews, but in informal conversations with your family and friends and, if you hear lots of negatives, try to turn your language around to signal a positive, constructive approach.

 You've got to remain positive. I'll give you one guarantee: if you give up, you'll never get a job. And it's easier to get a job when you're in employment than when you're unemployed. Any job is better than no job. That's the starting point.

Carl Gilleard, Chief Executive, Association of Graduate Recruiters

## Enhance your skills and learning

Increasing the range of opportunities open to you calls for creative approaches. The best counterbalance to an unfulfilling job is to get involved in learning something new. Not only will you maintain the momentum of study you built up during your degree, but you will send a good signal about yourself to prospective employers – and you will ward off boredom. Here are some of the ways you can continue to study:

- Do a short course at your local further education or community college – IT, a language, or a project management course could all be useful in a future job. Get a prospectus online or enquire at your local library.

- Look at postgraduate study. If you can't afford to do a full-time course, you can study part-time or through distance or blended learning. Many universities offer single modules if you don't want to commit to a complete course.

- Maximise your chances of learning from your job. Look at training offered in the workplace – first aid, supervisory skills – or create your own learning – ask if you can assist with a special project or promotion. Look at this brilliant example.

---

### ● brilliant example

'One night the barman seemed to be on holiday, so they put me behind the bar on a busy night. I had done the dispensing bar, which was pretty straightforward, so when it was quiet I asked the bar supervisor to show me the cocktails. But it was like – what the hell am I doing? How can they expect me to do this when I've never done it in my life? I looked like a complete muppet . . . but I'll give anything a go once, and they figured out I could do it and I wasn't that bad, so they put me on the bar a lot more. And it's good because I can show that I've got more all-round experience and I'm happy to learn, and I'm flexible, so I will be able to negotiate a higher rate of pay when I go back next time.'

Hannah (Undergraduate), Economics and Politics with International Studies

---

- Look out for special programmes for graduate jobseekers offered by your university – we gave you an example in Chapter 18.

- Create a portfolio of experience. For example, a psychology graduate interested in working in an advisory role with young people could take a counselling skills course in the evenings, do some voluntary work in an advice centre and support himself with a part-time job in retail or hospitality, both of which are excellent settings for developing skills with people. This three-part package will be far more use in developing his employment prospects than the job on its own.

## Be flexible

It's becoming more common, even for recent graduates, to slot together fulfilling part-time jobs in order to make progress and earn a living. In our next brilliant example, Kim's chosen career of youth work can often be pursued only in part-time or sessional roles. So she paired her youth work post first with a supermarket job, then with a part-time position as a student welfare officer.

---

### brilliant example

'Due to the nature of my career, I often have at least two part-time jobs on the go to "make ends meet". Alongside, I attend job-related training as often as possible and keep up to date with the changes in the sector. I have learned a number of things through this process. To get where I am today, I had to persevere through applying for countless jobs and being rejected for all but one of them. Doing unrelated work allowed me to support myself financially while I searched for more suitable work. Working two high-pressure jobs, being contracted 50 hours a week and often working overtime is not easy. But I love what I do and the long days are worth it. Deciding to pursue a career in an area that I love was the key to my professional success.'

Kim, BA (Hons), Christian Youth Work

---

## Don't be afraid to change your plan

We have talked about the benefit of having a plan, from a longer-term career plan to a short-term weekly jobsearch plan. And we still think this is important. But sometimes the right decision is to change your plan. One reason might be that your initial idea just isn't working out – you've given it a decent and realistic length of time but the signs aren't good and you need to rethink. This might happen if you are in a highly competitive area, such as Forensic Science or Bar Professional Training, where there are far more graduates than jobs. There may be a point when you decide to widen your search or even rethink completely.

Perhaps an even more compelling reason to change your plan is when you realise that your chosen route just isn't right for you. This is hard to face – you have invested time and probably money and it's tempting to feel some pressure to keep going. But have a look at our brilliant example, Steph, who not only changed her plan but believes that she has gained from the round-about route she took.

---

## brilliant example

'For my first degree I studied English Language. I had a couple of wobbles and nearly dropped out twice but kept going and did well. I had been thinking of teaching but because of the wobbles felt I wasn't good enough to teach . . . after doing some research I applied for the Graduate Diploma in Law (GDL) and the PGCE – I got three offers for the GDL and none for the PGCE, so that convinced me I had made the right choice.

I had it in my head that practising law would allow me to talk to people and help them like I'd always wanted to do; but it became more and more apparent that getting a job in law was harder than drawing blood from a stone, unless you were all singing and all dancing. I started to feel like I was trying to be something I wasn't towards the end of the course; I'm very driven, but the course had driven all the drive out of me. I knew in my heart that it was absolutely not for me.

I undertook some work experience at a local secondary school and absolutely knew that teaching was, after all, what I wanted to do, so I reapplied for my PGCE and was accepted. Half-way through the year I had my first job interview at a really good school – and got it! I don't think I'd be who I am or have had the confidence to apply for it again without having done the GDL, and plus it's always another string to the bow!

My advice to anyone in my position would be to do what they think is right. I know education doesn't come cheap, but I truly believe that you need to fall flat on your face before things start working out for you. Try everything and grab every opportunity that comes your way. Life has a funny way of working things out for you: you just have to work your hardest at it and even when it gets tough, you've got to keep going.'

Steph, BA (Hons) English Language

## Be in charge of yourself

We introduced you to the job fairy. It will sometimes seem as if other people get the benefit of this friendly little person, while you miss out; and it's certainly the case that some jobs come out of happy accidents and chance meetings. However, it's also the case that the people this happens to have their ears and eyes open, and respond positively to the opportunity presenting itself. So it's not entirely accidental after all. By all means get help from others – but recognise that you have the control, and no one else. You might have other people to think about, and other people's expertise to draw on, but you are still the person in charge of your future.

> **brilliant** tip
>
> When it comes to your career plan, you are responsible for yourself and nobody else; and nobody else is responsible for you.

*Your first graduate job*

 You move from school and home to experience the freedom and independence of university; then suddenly you are thrust back into an environment where you must abide by much stricter codes of conduct and adhere to an unwritten rulebook of new behavioural expectations that are often difficult to interpret.

Rose, BSc (Hons) Biology

Focusing on your final year and on getting a job can mean that you start work as a graduate without thinking too much about what it will feel like to be a graduate employee, and how your life will change. For example, in many graduate jobs there is no flexibility to your working day – good timekeeping is critical and lunch breaks and time off are fixed. This might seem like a small detail, but it's a big contrast to your student life and one that many new graduates struggle with and find unexpectedly tiring. And you will almost certainly be working at a different level of responsibility from the jobs you have done as a student, as in this brilliant example.

## brilliant example

'Working for an engineering consultancy means you're taking responsibility for expensive, high-profile designs and you're working alongside high-achieving professionals who have spent their careers reaching where they are. It's the complete opposite end of the spectrum from working with other students on a bar at a festival, where your manager is a similar age and on a temporary contract.'

Ed, MEng (Hons) Civil Engineering

There are additional pressures if you have had to relocate for your graduate job, and even making sure that you have suitable, clean work clothes each day adds another new demand. So, imagining yourself in your new job and anticipating some of the challenges might help you to make this crucial transition more smoothly. To help you to do this we have spoken to some recent graduates about their experiences and asked them for their best advice.

The good news is that it really does feel different, and better, to be a graduate employee.

---

## 🔘 brilliant example

'Being a graduate employee (a formulation scientist in a large multinational company), compared with being a student, I felt more grown up and it felt like I had finally joined the real world. I could now start building a career and earning my own money, which I could use or save for whatever I wanted. Compared to the stopgap job I had after graduating – which was useful for earning money and gaining work experience – I felt happier as I was now doing a job relevant to the career I wanted to build.

Sally, MChem

---

For many employers, too, graduate trainees are good news, and ambition is rewarded with support for professional development. In our next brilliant example, Rob talks about the high expectations his employer (a large insurance company) has of graduate trainees.

---

## 🔘 brilliant example

'I am currently a team leader (of nine people in customer service). The expectations, especially with an ambitious graduate scheme like mine, are that you will take responsibility and that you will work and drive your career – which, while it opens up huge opportunities, is also very testing . . . my employer will give me every tool to succeed and I am currently studying for my qualification in insurance, paid for by my employer.'

Rob, MSc International Business and Management

---

When you are applying for jobs and going through the selection process you will hear a lot about the induction programmes employers require new entrants to follow. These can be quite informal, especially in SMEs, or highly structured and lasting several weeks. But what about the unwritten rules? All organisations have these, from coffee routines to protocols for communicating internally and externally, and they can be hard to grasp. Judging how much to use your initiative is a tricky one, especially in the first few weeks, which might feel a bit slow while you are learning the background to your work – yet you are working alongside very busy people, and you may be unsure about speaking up. Our graduates are very clear about the best approach – get to know people and how they work and don't be afraid to ask for help.

 The sooner you build confidence to offer help, be proactive and offer solutions and ideas, the better.

Rose, BSc Biology

 Everyone works in different ways and is motivated by different things . . . you have to key into this and it's important not to rub people up the wrong way.

Rob, MSc International Business and Management

 One thing I have learnt is that you can never ask too many questions, for example don't just do something because you have been asked to do it, ask why and how and try to understand the background . . . always try and do as much as you can; this shows you are willing to learn new things and improve.

Sally, MChem

Don't be afraid to pick up the phone. Our generation is used to instant messaging – but people place a lot of value on speaking to humans and it gets problems solved much faster, especially where there is urgency or scope for confusion.

Ed, MEng Civil Engineering

We mentioned earlier in this chapter that three of our four graduates had intermediate jobs, ranging from restaurant work to unpaid internship, so, if you don't have a job straight after graduating, keep applying and build up your work experience and your skills. Here's our graduates' advice to final-year students:

---

## brilliant tips

- Start early in your job search.

- Look for companies you admire, in the field you are interested in.

- Go for something that will give you training and progression opportunities.

- Make the most of any training and courses you are offered, whether you have a temporary or permanent position in the company.

- Go out of your comfort zone – otherwise you will limit what you learn and the experience you gain.

- Working with people at the top of their game means you have to elevate yours and you can learn a lot, fast, to broaden your skillset for the future.

---

## Moving on

### *Your second graduate job*

This might seem an odd topic to introduce when you are probably still looking for your first one, but by the time this happens to you – two, three or four years down the line – you may feel cut adrift from the sources of help you have been able to use at university, so here are some thoughts for you to keep in the back of your mind till you need them.

✺ brilliant dos and don'ts

**Do**

✔ use the skills of reflection we discussed in Chapter 10 to assess how your first job is going;

✔ record your key achievements along the way – they will be invaluable in updating your CV and in completing future applications;

✔ seek out professional help – some university careers services will help graduates with subsequent job moves for a fixed period of time after graduation. Others offer a fee-charging service to graduates from any university.

**Don't**

✘ move without giving your first job a chance. Discuss with your manager what you need to develop your experience and interest, and how your job will develop in the future, before you decide to move on.

In this example, Victoria, whom you met in Chapter 9, describes moving from her second to her third graduate job, so she is at a point of leverage rather than a point of entry.

◉ brilliant example

'(In my second consultancy) I worked hard to get integrated and continue to pursue retail projects. However, I didn't feel there was much retail opportunity available so, after a year, I decided to leave and then find a new job. It's really hard to find a new job when you are working long days at your existing one!

I put my CV on Internet job boards and used my network of contacts from the two previous companies to find introductions at retail companies and also recruitment agencies.

I began by considering any job opportunity both consulting and "industry" (i.e. for actual retailers) but, as my search progressed, I realised I actually only wanted to work in "industry". I ended up with three offers on the table.'

Victoria, MA Geography

Notice that she was in a much stronger position than when she had first graduated, because she had her own network of contacts. Note too that the actual process of jobsearch helped her to identify her preferred focus.

In our next example, Estee left university seeking a job which made direct use of her psychology degree, but was unsuccessful. However, she made the connections in the job that she did get, so that the next time around she was a much stronger candidate and succeeded in her goal.

---

## brilliant example

'I worked as a university employability assistant for approximately 18 months. In this time I believe I learnt more than when I was a student! I had the opportunity to work on a wide variety of projects, make decisions, and go on courses to improve my skills. I particularly enjoyed giving personalised feedback to students on application forms.

I still had my goal set on a career related to psychology at this point and decided to apply for a trainee psychological wellbeing practitioner role with a local mental health charity. I applied for one of these roles when I first graduated but found that the competition is fierce and candidates straight from university were rarely employed. Therefore alongside my job I volunteered for a mental health charity to be a computerised cognitive behavioural therapy support worker. This voluntary experience coupled with my expertise from my employment allowed me to have the skills needed to carry out the role. I believe my understanding of the role and the ability to reflect on my experience went in my favour at the interview. I really wanted the role so I researched a lot about the project beforehand. In doing this I was also able to ask some questions at the end of the interview that surprised the panel. I started my new role three months ago now and once again I am on a steep learning curve.'

Estee, BSC (Hons) Psychology

---

*Your life and why all this matters*

As a current graduate, you will be affected by two of the biggest changes to working life in recent years.

Firstly, you will be working for longer than your parents did (but you will benefit from flexible working patterns, including homeworking).

Secondly, you will probably have several jobs and many careers during this time. It helps that relationships between health and well-being and job satisfaction are well established, and there is much more recognition of the need for a good balance between working life and life outside work. Some organisations even make provision for staff to have 'career breaks' of a few months' unpaid leave, to go on that trip of a lifetime.

So it's worth investing some time and effort on your career plan, not just now, but at key decision points as they come up. For example, it's never too late to start postgraduate study, and it's often even more rewarding and interesting when you have some experience behind you.

It's impossible to predict now what your working life will look like over the next 40 or so years. It will help if you are open to changes of direction and new opportunities and it's important to recognise that your own interests, skills and values will change over time and that good career progression need not necessarily be upwards.

 Most of those who are graduating now will have two or three careers – not jobs, careers. Be confident enough to step off the career ladder in order to be the best at what you do.

Carl Gilleard, Chief Executive, Association of Graduate Recruiters

We wish you the very best of luck for your future and we hope that our book is there for you along the way – and remember, you are the one in control of your brilliant graduate career.

# Chapter **16**

Handling rejection

It is a sad fact of life that no matter how capable, qualified and experienced you are most interviews will result in rejection for one reason or another. So you had better get used to it! Nearly everybody suffers a few such setbacks when they are hunting for a new job; many job hunters are regularly shot down in flames. Remember: It just wasn't your destiny.

If you were not successful, try to treat the interview as a learning experience. A real, live interview is the very best form of interview practice you can get. We all make mistakes; make sure that you use them to your advantage for your next interview.

If you had your heart set on a particular opportunity and have been through the highs and lows of being invited to a first interview and then to a second or maybe even an assessment centre, then it can be very demoralising to find out the job went to someone else and all your efforts were for nothing.

Or were they...

## Never say never

If you're a philosophical sort of person your initial reaction to receiving a rejection from a prospective employer might be to conclude that it's the end of this particular road and you need to turn your attentions to other possibilities you've got on the go.

However, call me stubborn, but I and many other recruitment professionals still recommend following up on such a rejection with a brief but important letter.

Allow me to explain why.

➤ You have probably worked pretty hard to get to this stage.

➤ They don't want to hire you now but may well be interested in the future.

➤ It should only take you five minutes to fire off this letter.

## Building bridges

Having taken the time to build bridges with this organisation, you'd be wise to maintain those bridges as best you can. You never know when your contacts might come in handy later in your career.

➤ You might end up getting a job where you deal on a regular basis with this organisation.

➤ You may have missed out on the current vacancy but there could be another one in just a few weeks' time.

➤ What if the person who won the job subsequently turns it down?

---

**TOP TIP**

Having invested this much in your relationship, it makes sense to seize the opportunity to spend a few more minutes developing that relationship even further.

---

## Maintaining a positive attitude

The way you approach writing this letter is very important. You might feel a degree of resentment for their having made you jump through lots of hoops only to disappoint you, but you certainly don't want that kind of negative emotion to come through in your letter.

There isn't (or at least there shouldn't be) anything personal about the decision: It's just business. You are not being rejected as an individual; your candidature for this particular vacancy is being rejected. In many cases it could be an extremely arbitrary decision; if an employer is faced with a number of high-quality candidates then it can be very hard to choose between them. Indeed, sometimes there is so little to choose between candidates that, more than anything, success or failure is down to luck.

It is fine to express your disappointment but you should definitely avoid sounding bitter. A negative attitude is unlikely to make a good impression.

You should attempt to extract some constructive feedback from them to help you with future applications you make. Most recruiters won't volunteer this information; you'll have to ask for it. You might just get back the usual canned response that 'it was an extremely difficult decision', etc., etc. You might get no reply whatsoever. But you might just get some really useful advice, which could enable you to address any weaknesses or rectify any mistakes so you have a greater chance of success the next time around.

## Down but not out

You're also demonstrating that you're somebody who doesn't like to lose and who will do their utmost to make sure they're less likely to lose out again in the future.

Remember: There is a job out there with your name on it; if no one has yet recognised your star quality, it's up to you to dazzle them!

Of course, if you're having difficulty getting yourself invited to interview in the first place, then it may very well be that your CV needs some work.

## *The CV Book*

If you would like to learn more about CV writing, then please take a look at my best-selling book on the subject, *The CV Book: How to Avoid the Most Common Mistakes and Write a Winning CV.* You can place your order for a copy via our website: **www.jamesinn.es**

# CHAPTER 17
## Individual differences and diversity

## Emotional intelligence (EI)

Developed originally by *Salovey and Mayer,*[1] EI (or EQ, for Emotional Quotient) is generally attributed to *Goleman* who, in 1955, published his ground-breaking work. Goleman agreed that the classical view of intelligence was too narrow. He felt that the emotional qualities of individuals should be considered. These, he felt, played a vital role in the application of intelligence in everyday life. He identified the key characteristics as:

> *abilities such as being able to motivate oneself and persist in the face of frustrations; to control impulse and delay gratification; to regulate one's moods and keep distress from swamping the ability to think; to empathise and to hope.*[2]

**Emotional intelligence** is the sum of a range of interpersonal skills that form the public persona, including the emotional qualities of individuals. Goleman's model outlines five main EI constructs:

- **Self-awareness**
- **Self-regulation**
- **Social skill**
- **Empathy**
- **Motivation.**

Emotional competencies are not innate talents, but rather learned capabilities that must be worked on and can be developed to achieve outstanding performance.

EI has received considerable attention as a key aspect of managing people effectively. Goleman argues for a more empathetic style of management and suggests that EI predicts top performance and accounts for more than 85 per cent of outstanding performance in top leaders.[3] The Hay Group, working with Goleman, has identified eighteen specific competencies that make up the four components of EI and has produced an inventory designed to measure emotional competence (*see* Figure 17.1). The Emotional Competence Inventory defines EI as 'The capacity for recognising our own feelings and those of others, for motivating ourselves and for managing emotions within ourselves and with others.'[4]

### Significance of emotional intelligence

Research from the Chartered Management Institute identifies EI as one of the key skills managers and leaders will need in the coming decade.[5] According to *Landale*, it should really be no surprise to find EQ so much in demand.

> *After all, we work in structures which are much flatter than ever. We have to be much faster on our feet with both colleagues and clients and, whatever the team structure, there is increasing proximity for us to build the relationships we need – fast. In this context EQ is the glue that holds people and teams together.*[6]

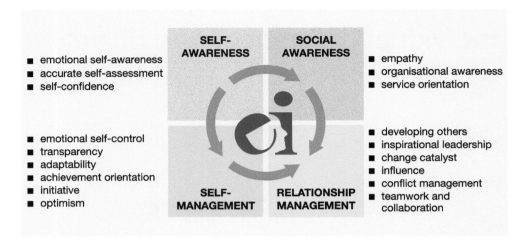

**Figure 17.1** Emotional Intelligence Competence Model

*Venus* makes the point that success in the boardroom is not just down to sound business sense and technical competence; interpersonal relationships also play a key role. The set of competencies known as EI are often overlooked in terms of professional success.[7]

## Developing EI

*Landale* refers to the importance of empathy in EI, which involves how a person self-manages and addresses how to engage with the emotions of others, and suggests a six-step process for developing EI:

**1.** Know what you feel.
**2.** Know why you feel it.
**3.** Acknowledge the emotion and know how to manage it.
**4.** Know how to motivate yourself and make yourself feel better.
**5.** Recognise the emotions of other people and develop empathy.
**6.** Express your feelings appropriately and manage relationships.

> *There seems little doubt that managers and leaders who have trained up in EQ have far more initiative in dealing with organizational life than those who don't. Stress will always exist at work, but EQ gives people the tools and ways of thinking to manage it to their advantage.*[8]

According to *Dann,* becoming highly self-aware allows an individual to recognise inner and outer conflict and develop more proactive self-management. Developing greater social awareness allows the fostering of productive relations and a greater degree of engagement between employees and management. A manager with a high EQ benefits both the organisation and the individual.[9]

However, *Alexander* reports on research concerning the negative uses and dark side of EI, and questions what happens when people start using it to manipulate others in order to further their own careers. Those on the dark side of EI will scrutinise the emotions of others but are adept at controlling their own emotional displays. For example, bosses with negative EI in mind may focus on employees' emotions for cynical purposes. Employees looking to profit by dark EI may constantly scrutinise a superior's emotions for ways to enhance how they are estimated by attuning to the superior's state of mind.[10]

## Critical review and reflection

It is evident that emotional intelligence (EI) is the single most important predictor of the capacity for effective work performance and professional success. Organisations should concentrate their efforts on identifying and developing EI for all managers.

*What is YOUR view? To what extent do YOU have a high level of emotional intelligence?*

**CHAPTER 18**

Work experience:
making it
purposeful

Work experience offers enormous benefits to you in your career planning and job seeking. It sometimes has a poor image – it's associated with school, it's boring, or it's exploitation. We will show you in this chapter that it need be none of these. You can choose and manage your work experience to suit your needs, and make it work for you.

Firstly, we need to be clear what we mean by work experience, and how it differs from work and employment.

**brilliant** definition

Work – a purposeful activity that could be done as a paid job.

Examples from your everyday life include fixing a computer, delivering or collecting something for a friend, decorating a room, braiding someone's hair, giving some sports coaching. Reasons you might do this: to save money, because you enjoy it, are good at it, because friends will return the favour with something they can do, because you want to get more practice. Employment is simply work you get paid to do. So how does work experience fit in?

**brilliant** definition

Work experience – work that you do in order to develop your skills and knowledge. It is usually unpaid but, in some circumstances, such as sandwich placements and some internships, work experience is paid.

In the rest of this chapter, we will look at different kinds of work experience, how to access them and how you can benefit from them, and we'll show you how to get the best out of your work experience.

# Five kinds of work experience

What you choose to do will depend on a number of factors, including how much time you have, what you want to achieve, and whether you really need to get work experience as an entry requirement for a graduate job or course. Later in the chapter we will look at the overall benefits of work experience, but first we need to be clear about the different kinds of opportunities covered in our definition. There are five main categories, each with its own particular benefit, or impact. We will illustrate some of these with real-life stories from graduates.

## Volunteering

Volunteering is, by definition, something you offer to do without being paid. You might think it's about working for a charity, or fundraising for a good cause, but it also includes spending a couple of weeks in a law firm or a primary school in order to learn more about what goes on while making yourself useful. It could be one day a week, a block of time, or just a one-day event like beach cleaning or marshalling for a charity bike ride. A particular benefit is that employers see you as motivated because you are choosing to use your spare time constructively.

---

### brilliant example

'In my second year I had to choose between studying abroad or having a work placement. I went abroad but realised at the start of my third year that I had missed out. I joined the local tourist board as a volunteer for two days a week, and learned many valuable skills which helped me to apply my studies to real-life situations. Towards the end of my third year a full-time job in the tourist board came up – I got it!'

Caroline, BA (Hons) Marketing and Tourism

---

*How to get in*

Some organisations are highly dependent on volunteers and may recruit on your campus with posters and display stands, but other opportunities are less visible. Follow our suggestions to find a really good volunteering opportunity.

## brilliant dos and don'ts

**Do**

✔ find the student volunteering organisers in your university. They help to 'match' volunteers to opportunities – you tell them what you would like to do and how much time you have, and they will make you an offer. You may need a DBS (Disclosure and Barring Service) check, which they will help you with. Be aware that having a criminal record may not rule you out entirely but it may restrict the opportunities open to you;

✔ contact the volunteer bureau in your nearest town or city if you have already graduated – they will do the same job of matching you to what's available;

✔ make a direct approach by letter or email if you have an organisation in mind that isn't on the university's list of opportunities. This works especially when you want to spend a short block of time observing and learning – but make sure that you offer to do some work too. You need not be specific, just show willing! Help them by saying why you want to spend time there and what you hope to gain;

✔ ask people you know. 'Accessing job opportunities'. Friends and relatives are useful as a way in, but remember firstly, that you will be in a work role in the organisation, not as a niece, godson or next-door neighbour; and secondly, that they may have stuck their neck out to get you in – so don't let them down.

**Don't**

✘ let people down. Many organisations rely on volunteers, so if you have made a regular commitment, keep to it. If there's a day when you really can't make it, for a good reason, let them know.

## Work placement as part of your course

Some courses include a work-based or employability module that can either be compulsory or optional. The extent to which you can choose what you do varies according to the university and the subject – but if you have the chance, it's well worth taking. Assessment may be based on the tasks you have carried out for the employer; or it may be about your own learning during the placement. This means what you have learned about yourself – your skills, interests and capabilities – as well as what you have learned about the organisation. The personal insights you get from this process of reflection will help with your career planning, and the particular benefit of a work placement is that it might lead to a job.

### brilliant example

'As part of my Animal Behaviour and Welfare course I did a six-week placement with a charity that trains dogs to assist people with disabilities so that they are able to live more independently. The placement gave me the skills and experience to improve my chances with future job applications, as well as reconfirming that this was the area I wanted to pursue. A year later, the charity contacted me to offer me a temporary post for maternity cover. Four months after that I was offered a permanent post as the charity was expanding.'

Anna, BSc Animal Behaviour and Welfare

### *How to get in*

Some universities have a department or team whose job it is to find placements for all students. This works well because relationships are built up between the university and employers over time and approaches are centrally coordinated. If this is the case at your university, make sure that you provide all the information you are asked for, within the deadlines set. This way you are more likely to get the kind of placement you want.

Other universities expect you to find your own placement. This offers you greater flexibility to tailor the placement more closely to your preferences, but it does also mean that you'll need to be proactive. Here's what to do.

## brilliant dos and don'ts

**Do**

✔ think about the kind of experience you want, based on your career plans, your interests, and the gaps you would like to fill. Do think about talking this over with a tutor or a careers adviser;

✔ identify the organisations that are likely to fit the bill – ask your careers service, your tutors and your contacts. For possible leads, get inspiration from job advertisements and business directories, both in print and online;

✔ write a good letter of application, setting out what you want and why, e.g. 'a four-week work placement to apply the learning from my course in a commercial setting', (don't say 'because I have to do this for my course') and what you can offer while you are there. Check for spelling and punctuation and include your contact details. If you don't hear within say a fortnight, follow up with a polite phone call;

✔ start looking in plenty of time – six months ahead, more for a one-year placement.

**Don't**

✘ settle for an easy option – your old school, your Saturday job, your uncle's firm – unless it really fits in with your career plan and adds value to your CV.

## Work shadowing

This is usually a short spell, from one day up to a week, where you find out more about a job by accompanying someone who does that job in their daily work. The great thing is that you could spend time with anyone in an organisation, from a new graduate trainee to the chief executive. You're not expected to do their job, so you can really concentrate on observing, listening and learning about what they do, to build up your knowledge of a particular kind of work. It's low cost and relatively low effort for organisations, so it can be easier to set up than a longer placement or voluntary opportunity. The gain to you is that it opens up contacts and adds to your networking.

*How to get in*

Some universities offer work shadowing placements so check this out first. Otherwise, just look back at the dos and don'ts for getting your own work placement. The same principles apply, but this time you will be asking for the chance to shadow for a day, or a week, as a way to enhance your experience and knowledge. Also, remember that, for some roles in the public eye, you can observe informally, as Thomas's story illustrates.

---

### brilliant example

'So that I could see what a career as a barrister is like, I contacted various chambers to arrange mini-pupillages, the name given to a few days shadowing barristers in court and in meetings with clients. Not only did this give me an insight into a career at the Bar, but it meant I met barristers at various chambers. In my days off at university or in the holidays, I often went to court and sat in the public gallery observing cases, giving me more opportunity to see barristers in action and sometimes speaking to those I had spent time with on mini-pupillage.'

Thomas, LLB, LLM and Bar Professional Training course

---

The next two categories are a little different as they may involve payment, but are still work experience according to our definition.

## Sandwich and vacation placements during your degree

These placements are either the whole of the penultimate year of your degree, or they fit into a vacation – usually, but not always, summer. They may not be assessed as part of your course. However, a course that is designed to include a sandwich year will require you to carry out the placement in order to pass your degree. Some vocational degrees like Engineering will expect you to undertake relevant vacation placements.

Travel and international trade and commerce have led to a rise in the number of courses with a 'year out', though some of these offer a year of study abroad rather than work experience. Here, we are using the term sandwich course to refer to four-year degree courses, which include a one-year placement in industry, typically in science, business or vocational programmes, such as quantity surveying or dietetics. There are particular benefits – a substantial, one-year placement can make a real difference to your job prospects because you have evidence to demonstrate what you can do. A vacation placement adds to your experience and demonstrates that you are purposeful in choosing how to spend your time off.

## brilliant question and answer

Q What is the difference between a vacation placement and a vacation job?

A The difference is in the intention – the employer is offering you some work that will help you towards your degree, and may signal this with a clear 'vacation placement' label; and you are choosing to do it for the same reason.

*How to get in*

If your placement is a course requirement, there should be some help at the university, even if it's just the contact details of last year's placements. Otherwise, use websites such as Graduate Prospects, get help from your careers service and try personal contacts. Your part-time job in retail just might have something in management or buying if that's your interest.

Be prepared – more is expected of you at the application stage than for the shorter work placements in term-time, which we looked at earlier in the chapter. You may have to go through a full selection process, including application form and interview, 'Making applications: getting past the first post' and 'Succeeding in selection' for pointers. On the plus side, a recent survey of one hundred top employers revealed that they expect one in three graduate jobs to be filled by applicants who have already worked for the organisation, on a placement or during the vacation. So the effort could pay off.

## Internship after graduation

An internship usually refers to a period of planned work experience for graduates. The term is sometimes also used for vacation placements between your penultimate and final year. It was introduced partly to offer something useful to graduates feeling the effects of the recession on their jobsearch; job prospects have now improved, but internships have become established as part of the employment landscape.

Some internships are paid, others are not. Whether you're entitled to payment will depend on what you actually do for the organisation – not what your role is called. If you are performing as a worker, you must be paid at least the national minimum wage. If you are taken on as a volunteer, you're unlikely to receive payment. Even if your internship is unpaid, however, it's worth asking whether the organisation could cover your expenses, such as daily travel costs.

The particular benefit is that some employers use an internship as an extension of the selection process, so you can demonstrate your suitability for the job in the workplace.

*How to get in*

Internships are advertised on websites such as Graduate Prospects and Graduate Talent Pool.

---

### 🔆 brilliant example

'I came to realise that the people who get the graduate jobs are the people who had gained work experience during their time at university . . . I decided to take out a loan to support a political internship . . . Ultimately, it's all well and good having knowledge of a subject, but a practical ability to perform in a working environment is completely different. My eight-month internship involved working for three days a week in every imaginable part of political campaigning. What an eye opener! . . . after the election, I wrote to a dozen or so newly elected MPs explaining what I had been doing. Three days later I had an interview and was offered a job as a parliamentary assistant.'

Kevin, BSc (Hons) Politics

---

# How you can benefit

Whichever kind of work experience you choose there are great gains to be had – and not only because you will be more attractive to an employer, though clearly this is important.

## Personal confidence and transferable skills

Just being engaged in a purposeful activity that has clear outputs and helps other people out, either directly or indirectly, can give you a sense of achievement and a confidence boost. If you pick up some skills for employment, even better. The student in the following example volunteered within her university in a variety of roles, not obviously connected to her graduate job as an innovations researcher. Notice all the gains she made.

---

**brilliant** example

'One of the voluntary roles I took on was as a student ambassador. I introduced new and potential students to the campus and showed them what was available to them on campus and the services open to them. Having been a new student previously myself, I knew how they felt and the need to help them settle in as soon as possible.

I also worked as a volunteer one day a week in a university department. This gave me a chance to experience an office environment and to see the university services from the other side of the counter. I undertook lots of different tasks, including general admin tasks and statistical analysis as well as helping out at different events put on by the department. It was a very team-oriented department, which taught me so much about the need to work as a team.'

Jo, BSc (Hons) Mathematics

---

In this one example, you will have noticed how Jo developed her experience of:

- communication skills;
- administration;
- statistical analysis;
- event management;
- working in a team.

Sometimes you just have to look beyond the surface to find the opportunities for learning. Think about working as a volunteer in a charity shop – a popular choice for people who want to help others. Firstly, there are job-related skills to learn, such as sorting stock, pricing up articles for sale, display, handling money and customer service. Then there are the transferable or 'soft' skills of working in a team, acting responsibly by turning up when you say you will, and interacting with all kinds of people. So what starts out as doing a good deed also becomes a great chance to learn.

## Improving your job prospects

You might have noticed Kevin, in one of our case studies, saying that the people he knew who got graduate jobs were the ones who got work experience at university. It might sound obvious, but why does it work so well?

It works because it enables you to do all of the following.

### Try things out

Firstly, you can try things out so that, by the time you are applying for a graduate job, you are much clearer about what you want and why, and you can say so in your application form and interview. Deciding that you don't want to pursue something is just as valuable as confirming that you do, and you might discover a kind of work, or an interest, that you didn't even know about.

### Get experience

This isn't as obvious as it sounds. For some professional training courses it's essential to have relevant work experience before you can be considered.

Examples are teaching, clinical psychology, physiotherapy; and for jobs and courses where it's not a requirement, it certainly helps to demonstrate your commitment and knowledge.

### Collect and record evidence for your applications

'Making applications: getting past the first post', and work experience is one of your best opportunities. It's hard remembering in your final year the detail of that great work placement you did in your second year, so keep some kind of record of what you did, what you learned and what you achieved for each piece of work experience you have. It will make a real difference to your CV. Kevin, our brilliant example for internships, was able to replace his long list of part-time bar and retail jobs with a section headed 'Political work experience' and a much shorter 'Summary of other work experience'. His CV became targeted and relevant for the kind of job he wanted.

### Enhance your jobsearch

Every work experience opportunity you take will give you some contacts, who may be helpful when you are looking for work. Even if they don't have a job to offer, they might know someone who does, or be willing to look at your CV.

Depending on how long you've been there and what you have done, work experience employers might be great for writing a reference for you. This is useful as most application forms ask for an academic and an employer reference. Remember to ask them first.

### Give yourself structure and focus

This is particularly useful when you have graduated and you are still looking for your graduate job. Even if you are working, using days off or holidays to pursue your career goal with relevant work experience helps to remind you that your goal is still there. Thomas was our brilliant example for work shadowing, and this is how he is using work experience to keep in touch with his career aim of becoming a barrister.

## brilliant example

'Since qualifying I have continued to apply for pupillage. In order to enhance my chances I have continued to complete a number of mini-pupillages at different chambers to broaden my experience and also make myself known to chambers before applying to them.

In order to gain more practical experience, I became a volunteer at an advice bureau. I conduct one-to-one interviews with clients weekly on a variety of different subjects. This has given me experience of dealing with different types of people as well as exploring a client's problem through questioning before advising them on the different options available.'

Thomas, LLB, LLM and Bar Professional Training course

# How to make it work

If you have worked through this chapter you will now know about the different kinds of work experience, how to access them, and why work experience can be a real benefit in your career planning and jobsearch.

In this final section we tell you what to do, and what to avoid, to get the best from your work experience.

## brilliant dos and don'ts

**Do**

✔ take control – be clear what you want and what you can offer and negotiate with the employer so that you both gain;

✔ reflect and review – think carefully about what you are learning and record it somewhere, so that you can refer to your experience in job applications;

✔ be aware that there are limits on hosting work experience in some job sectors, due to factors such as confidentiality and child protection – it may be easier if you use your university volunteering scheme or local volunteer bureau to set up your placement in sectors involving children, vulnerable adults, health services or offenders;

✔ notice and absorb the discipline and protocols of the workplace – what to wear, how people are addressed, how the phone is answered.

**Don't**

✗ give up – if you think that you are not getting any benefit, talk to the person in charge of your programme to see if some adjustments can be made. If it's a placement that forms part of your course, get the advice of your tutor;

✗ assume there's no value in a work experience opportunity without really thinking about it and giving it your best shot.

 **brilliant** recap

- There are five different kinds of work experience, each with a particular benefit.

- There are also benefits that apply whichever kind you do.

- Work experience can help you to develop and learn about yourself as a person, and it can help with getting a brilliant graduate job.

- You can make it work for you – take control, be clear about what you want and what you can offer.

## What to do next

- Think about how work experience could help you with your career plan.

- Consider what you want to (a) learn and (b) achieve?

- Use our 'How to get in' tips to get the work experience you want.

# Part 3: Employability Skills Resources

# Start your Career Journey

Research your Options
Self-Awareness

Develop your Employability
Occupational Research

# STEP 1

UNIVERSITY OF
LINCOLN
CAREERS & EMPLOYABILITY

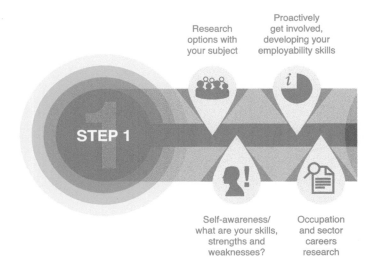

## Stages of Career Development

Self Awareness, Information Gathering, Opportunity Awareness

# Careers &
# Employability
Career Planning Timeline

STEP
UP
STAND
OUT

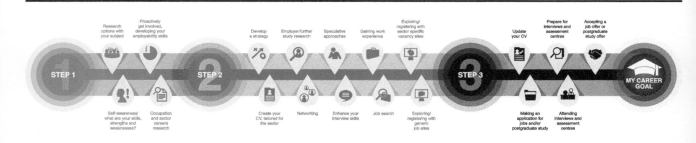

Stages of Career Development

Self Awareness, Information Gathering, Opportunity Awareness     Information Gathering, Opportunity Awareness, Decision Making     Decision Making, Transition Management

# Start your Career Journey

This booklet has been developed by Careers & Employability to help you plan for your future. It will help you to review your skill set, analyse available opportunities and seek support. This booklet is best used alongside the Step One Career Planning Booklet, which you can collect by visiting the Careers & Employability Centre on campus or download from our website: www.uolcareers.co.uk

## In this guide:

- Research Options
- Self Awareness
- Develop Employability
- Occupational Research

Careers & Employability Centre
Ground Floor, Library
Mon-Fri: 09:00-16:30

T: +44 (0) 1522 83 7828
E: careers@lincoln.ac.uk

www.uolcareers.co.uk
www.facebook.com/UOLCareers
www.twitter.com/UOLCareers

# Research your Options

While you may have chosen your degree subject with a specific occupation in mind, all degrees can lead you to a broad spectrum of opportunities. Researching the options available is a great place to start thinking about your own career. You can start a career directly through a standard application process, but it is also worth thinking about your options immediately after graduation that will help you achieve your career aspirations. Such options include:

- Further Study
- Graduate Programmes/Schemes
- Internships
- Work Experience
- Travel Abroad

International Options
- Work internationally
- Return to your home country to work or take up further study

## Finding what suits you

Prospects is a website used by careers services across the UK which offers students and graduates advice and career information for free. As well as offering insights into what kind of jobs are available in various sectors, they also have quizzes that can give you some ideas to start exploring options with your degree. You may disagree or be confused by the results - simply think of them as a place to start your research rather than a guide for life.

Visit www.prospects.ac.uk/planner to start your research - and remember you can visit our Careers & Employability Centre to speak with an adviser if you need help exploring your results and options.

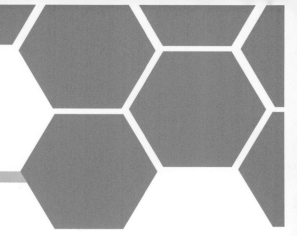

# Self Awareness

## What is Self Awareness?

*Conscious knowledge of one's own character, feelings, motives and desires.*

Although not one of the easiest tasks, the process of identifying your strengths and weaknesses helps you to understand yourself better and identify your career needs. Whilst undertaking volunteering, paid work experience or your course modules, keep a reflective journal on how you felt taking part in different activities within the role. This can take time but will help you discover what you like, what you don't like and identify your strengths and weaknesses

## Things to Think About

**1** — **Likes and Dislikes**
What do you enjoy doing? What would make a job unbearable for you to do day after day? Think about everything from your favourite activities to how you like to interact with people.

**2** — **Strengths and Weaknesses**
What skills do you particularly excel in? Do people often comment on how organised or disorganised you are? If you identify weaknesses, it's worth thinking about what you could do to improve or make up for them - this will help you answer questions about your weaknesses in interviews.

**3** — **Wants and Needs**
Think about what would be simply 'nice to have' for a career and separate these areas from your needs. Addressing these areas will help you narrow or widen your search. Here are some areas you may want to consider:

- Location (Does it need to be close to where you live?)
- Salary (Do you need to earn a certain amount or will benefits make a difference?)
- Working hours (Do you have a maximum amount you can work every week?)
- Industry stability (How stable do you need your work role to be?)
- Company Values (Does the company need to follow an ethos eg. Green energy, importance of family time, etc?)

# Develop your Employability

## Give yourself the best chance

Your University course is enabling you to develop skills and knowledge right now, but it's worth remembering that you may at times be competing with others from your course or similar courses. Being successful in your career path will often mean that you need to gain experience and additional skills to give yourself an edge over your competition.

## Ways to Develop your Employability

### Part-Time or Summer Work
Gain experience to develop your skills whilst earning money. Remember that the skills you learn can be transferable to many areas.

### Work Experience/Work Shadowing
Ask a company who offers the kind of roles you are aiming for if they would be able to give you experience in their workplace.

### Volunteering
Develop your skills while assisting charity, youth or similar organisations. Ensure you have a look at the opportunities advertised through the Student Union: www.lincolnsu.com/work-ready/volunteer-opportunities

### Extra-curricular activities
Get involved in University clubs or society groups outside of your study

### University Course
Take on extra projects, speak to your lecturers about opportunities they may know about to develop your skills

### Home Life
Develop your skills through a hobby, work on a project, assist your friends and family in ways that relate to your degree and career path

### The Lincoln Award
Develop your Employability skills and gain recognition for your achivements whilst learning how to demonstrate your employability skills: www.uolcareers.co.uk/lincoln-award

# Occupational Research

Once you have an idea of the career you would like to achieve, it is time to start researching the different sectors you can go into, and develop a sense of understanding of what would be expected of you.

This additional research could help uncover career paths you may not have considered before! Look out for opportunities to build your network and gain experience to learn directly rather than simply relying on reading.

## Places to start your research:

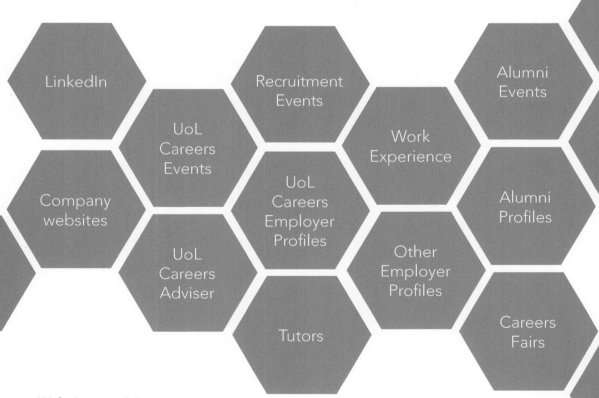

Websites to visit:
www.uolcareers.co.uk/events
www.uolcareers.co.uk/fyf
www.uolcareers.co.uk/employer-profiles

www.uolcareers.co.uk/case-studies
www.targetjobs.co.uk/employer-hubs
www.prospects.ac.uk/employer-profiles

# Work Experience

# STEP 2

## Stages of Career Development

Information Gathering, Opportunity Awareness, Decision Making

# Careers &
# Employability
## Career Planning Timeline

Stages of Career Development

# Work Experience

Use work experience to develop key transferable skills that will help you stand out from other applicants and open up more career opportunities. This experience could also give you the chance to explore whether a particular role or sector is right for you, and improve your awareness of workplace environments.

## In this guide:

- Part-Time Work
- Work Experience
- Volunteering

UNIVERSITY OF
**LINCOLN**
CAREERS & EMPLOYABILITY

Careers & Employability Centre
Ground Floor, Library
Mon-Fri: 09:00-16:30

T: +44 (0) 1522 83 7828
E: careers@lincoln.ac.uk

www.uolcareers.co.uk
www.facebook.com/UOLCareers
www.twitter.com/UOLCareers

# Part-Time Work

Gaining part-time work whilst you are studying can be a good way to not only gain some extra money, but enhance your skills and experience. Any part-time work you do will develop transferable skills such as communication, customer service and teamwork which are useful in most careers. For this reason, It's not vital that you gain work in the field you wish to go into after your studies. However, trying to get work in a role similar to what you hope to work towards (or being able to work closely with someone who is in the role) will allow you to gain some relevant experience and insight.

If you study full-time, it is recommended you work no more than 16 hours a week so as to not interrupt your studies. If you are a non-UK/EEA-domiciled student, there may also be further restrictions to the hours you are allowed to work. For more information, visit UKCISA: www.ukcisa.org.uk or visit Student Support on Campus

## Careers & Employability Part-Time Work Listings

**1** University of Lincoln Careers & Employability Job Search
The Careers & Employability website has vacancies for both Graduate and Undergraduate roles, including part-time work, placements and internships. You will need to register for an account on the system, but once you do you can also receive regular updates about vacancies that may suit you:
www.uolcareers.co.uk/students-graduates/jobs-employment-options/graduate-student-vacancies

**2** Careers & Employability Job Shop
Careers & Employability list part-time roles on-campus and in the local area. Visit: www.uolcareers.co.uk/jobshop

**3** Job Alerts
See the latest opportunities by signing up for Job Alerts. You can do this for both Careers & Employability website's Vacancy system and Job Shop.

**4** Social Media
Find opportunities in your feed by Liking us on our Facebook page www.facebook.com/UOLcareers our Job Shop page www.facebook.com/uoljobshop or follow our Job Alerts on Twitter www.twitter.com/uolcareers_jobs

# Work Experience

## Placements

Many companies (especially large organisations) will offer placements. These roles could lead you to permanent employment with the company. Even if you do not secure a permanent role, you will leave with experience that will attract other potential employers.

Summer placements can be any length or duration and are directed at providing you with the skills and experience to go forward in a role in your particular career path.

Year-long placements are generally taken after completing the second year of your course and usually last a year. It is important when considering a year-long placement that you discuss your options with a tutor or relevant member of staff before you make any applications.

You can also take part in placements in Europe through Erasumus+ with a Traineeship. These placements are funded and will continue to be for at least two years following Brexit. For more information visit www.erasmusplus.org.uk or contact erasmus@lincoln.ac.uk

## Sandwich Placements or Professional Practice Year (PYP)

Some courses will require you to spend a year in industry. This is often referred to as a sandwich placement or PYP, usually taking place between your second and final year at University. These industrial placements are commonly found in engineering, science and construction. You will have a personal/placement tutor to help you arrange your year with an employer.

## Internships

An internship is a fixed period of work experience, offered by an organisation, usually lasting for a fixed, limited period of time. They are typically undertaken by students and graduates looking to gain relevant skills and experience in a particular field.

Internships can last from a few weeks to a year depending on the sector, employer, and the stage you are at of your studies.

The University offers paid Graduate Internships across different departments every year - ask the Careers & Employability team when and how to prepare for these. The Centre also offer support to local businesses, and can help you learn about these:
www.uolcareers.co.uk/students-graduates/jobs-employment-options/internships

Take advantage of work experience fairs to make contact with employers or search for suitable placements online. You can also target employers speculatively* to find and arrange work placements.

*Find our Speculative Application guide at the Careers & Employability Centre

# Volunteering

Volunteering gives you an opportunity to become involved in something different. It shows you have initiative and commitment which may impress many employers. In fact, volunteering can help with your future career in many ways:

- Give your CV a point of difference to stand out
- Gain valuable skills
- Build your confidence and put yourself in new situations
- Gain experience to talk about in an interview
- Learn about new things
- Help the local community
- Expand your network

## Specialised experience

For students wanting a career in areas such as education or with the police, experience in a relevant role is required - volunteering could help you gain this experience. This will be a minimum of a week but in most cases is ten days. As well as meeting the requirement, you find out if the path is for you. Speak to the Careers & Employability Centre about what you will need for your aspirations.

## Volunteering abroad

Volunteering abroad can give you global experience that could truly put you onto your career path. Ensure you do your research into any organisations you are thinking about signing up with to ensure you know everything about them. Research experiences from people who have worked with the organisations you find to see if the organisation is legitimate, right for you and right for your goals.

The Students' Union have a Volunteering team to support you in any volunteering opportunity. They advertise opportunities on campus and in the local area. Visit their website for more information:
www.lincolnsu.com/work-ready/volunteer-opportunities

# Job Search

# STEP 2

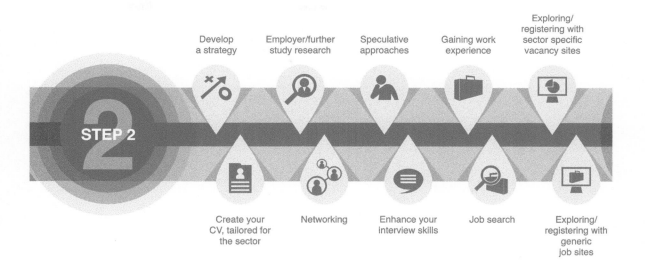

# Stages of Career Development

Information Gathering, Opportunity Awareness, Decision Making

**Careers & Employability**
Career Planning Timeline

UNIVERSITY OF
**LINCOLN**
CAREERS & EMPLOYABILITY

**STEP**
**UP**
**STAND**
**OUT**

Stages of Career Development

# Job Search

Finding a job requires time, effort and a proactive approach. You'll need to tailor your search to your career aspiration and source the best opportunities for you.

## In this guide:

- Begin your search
- Graduate Routes
- Places to Look
- Creative Job Searching
- Additional Tips

**UNIVERSITY OF LINCOLN**
CAREERS & EMPLOYABILITY

Careers & Employability Centre
Ground Floor, Library
Mon-Fri: 09:00-16:30

T: +44 (0) 1522 83 7828
E: careers@lincoln.ac.uk

www.uolcareers.co.uk
www.facebook.com/UOLCareers
www.twitter.com/UOLCareers

# Start Your Search

## Focusing your search

The first step in your job search should be to identify the sort of vacancies you are looking for, and gather as much information as possible about them. Start to think about the following:

- What types of employers recruit for the roles you are interested in?
- Do these employers advertise roles, and if so - where?
- Do these employers use recruitment agencies - which ones?
- Are there trade or professional job sites they appear on?
- What kind of locations are their jobs available in?

Start answering these questions by beginning your research on these websites:

- Prospects Occupational Profiles and Industry Insights
  www.prospects.ac.uk
- Target Jobs
  www.targetjobs.co.uk
- Gov.UK on jobs
  www.gov.uk/browse/working

**Visit the Careers Clinic**
Come see a Careers Skills adviser in the Careers & Employability Centre (Library, Ground Floor) if you are not sure how to start your search

# Graduate Routes

## Graduate Schemes

These schemes are usually run by large companies, tending to follow a structured development plan. These programmes can fast-track you to a senior level role within the organisation and an ongoing career after the programme is finished - as a result, competition for these roles is fierce.

Many schemes are advertised in the Autumn term with closing dates before Christmas. It is beneficial to start your research early:

- www.prospects.ac.uk
- www.targetjobs.co.uk
- www.milkround.com
- www.graduate-jobs.com

The University of Lincoln's Careers & Employability Centre will usually also have free copies of Prospects Guide Books, Times 100 and other guidebooks that you can read in the Centre or take home.

## Graduate Careers Fairs

These are great opportunities to find out more about relevant employers and build your network with different companies.

**1** Find Your Feet
University of Lincoln's Careers & Employability service hold this fair every year, hosting a range of employers: www.uolcareers.co.uk/fyf

**2** External Fairs
You can find opportunities to attend general and industry-specific Careers Fairs around the country, broadening your search. Find out what's on by visiting our events page www.uolcareers.co.uk/events or checking www.prospects.ac.uk/links/careersfairs

When arranging to visit a Fair, ensure you are prepared. Confirm your registration and review any tips you have. Have your CV ready, along with business cards, a pen and a notebook with prepared questions.

# Places to Look

Search engines, generic career search websites and graduate focused websites like Prospects or Target Jobs are great places to start, but use some creative thinking to broaden your search.

**1** University of Lincoln Careers & Employability
We work with employers across Lincolnshire and UK to find vacancies especially for University of Lincoln graduates. Visit our Centre, or explore opportunities on our website: www.uolcareers.co.uk

**2** Recruitment agencies
Seeking out recruitment agencies who work in your sector of interest can give you a useful addition to your search tools. Target your CV to your specific area of interest, and keep in contact with the agency for regular updates.

**3** Social media
Use your online presence to your advantage and seek out what employers are doing online. As well as giving you the opportunity to connect with professionals in your field through various groups, LinkedIn offers a job search function which can tie your hunt to your professional profile. Many employers also advertise roles on platforms such as Facebook or Twitter - many use hashtags like #jobs or #vacancies, but keep an eye on what employers in your sector of interest are using to keep ahead of the curve. Ensure your public-facing online presence is an employable one, and start engaging.

**4** Specialist publications and websites
Consider national & local news publications (whether online or in print) to identify opportunities that may not have made it onto career sites - many have their own careers sections.

Specialist newspapers, magazines or journals can also help find roles within your sector or location. You can even find specialist websites (such as GoingGlobal, found under 'International' on the Blackboard 'My Careers' tab) for international careers and opportunities.

**5** Professional bodies and associations
Many career sectors have professional bodies associated with them. Membership in these associations will often give you access to learning courses, networking events and specialised job vacancy postings among other offerings.

# Information Gathering

Sometimes employers don't widely publicise their vacancies, or aren't fully aware of their employment needs until presented with a suitable candidate. You can take advantage of this through a creative job search (read our guide on speculative applications for more information).

## Identifying contacts

Explore the sector you wish to gain experience or work in, using business directories and current vacancies to find relevant contact details for those in hiring positions. You can also ask family members, friends, lecturers and other people you know if they have any contacts in your area of interest.

## Information Interviewing

This is a process of arranging an informal meeting to ask people about their work - it is a good exercise to gain insight into companies and job roles as well as develop your network. Most people will respond positively to requests to talk about their position as long as you are not going to ask about your own hiring potential. A good approach to arrange an interview is to email a contact - or the company in general - saying that you are interested in working in their field, and are looking to gain more information about the industry. Make it clear that you are after information and insight rather than a position within the company.

Once you have arranged the meeting, think about what you wish to know. Some possible ideas are:

- Details of their job role
- Typical activites
- How they gained their position
- What they would class as good work experience
- Developments within the industry

After your meeting, follow up with a thank you letter. Keep any notes you made for future reference.

# Additional Tips

**1 Take Responsibility**
Make your job search your responsibility. While the people around you can support you, give advice and contacts - it isn't for them to get your job for you.

**2 Maintain Balance**
Your job search is important, but so is the rest of your life. Making time for family and friends, playing sport/exercising and keeping up with your hobbies will save you from feeling too stressed - and additionally help you in being a well-rounded, highly employable candidate. Set time limits for your job hunting to look after your wellbeing.

**3 Develop Resilience**
Everyone has knockbacks. Take this as an opportunity to improve, or simply reflect that it's not your fault - you are up against tough competition, and not everyone can win when there is only one role available. Sometimes being rejected from a role can be a good thing - the role or environment may not have been as appropriate for you as you first thought.

**4 Get Feedback**
Seek as much feedback as you can. Whether it be from your friends, the University's Careers & Employability service or lecturers. If you get knocked back from a role, it's always worth asking for feedback to find out areas you missed - but respect when a company says they cannot provide it.

**5 Stay Focused**
Applying for every single job you come across could hinder your search. You may find yourself confused as to what you've applied for, which could lead to issues when you find that one of your applications has been successful - don't be the person who shows up to a job interview not knowing which role or company you are interviewing for. Taking more time on fewer applications will give you higher quality applications, and an easier time knowing what you have done.

**6 Be Confident**
Push yourself - tell people how good you are. Show employers the value you will bring to their business. A job application is not the place to be humble - developing your confidence and self awareness of your positive qualities is essential to impressing employers with your application.

# Create your CV and Cover Letter

# STEP 2

UNIVERSITY OF
LINCOLN
CAREERS & EMPLOYABILITY

## Stages of Career Development

Information Gathering, Opportunity Awareness, Decision Making

# Careers &
# Employability
Career Planning Timeline

UNIVERSITY OF
LINCOLN
CAREERS & EMPLOYABILITY

STEP
UP
STAND
OUT

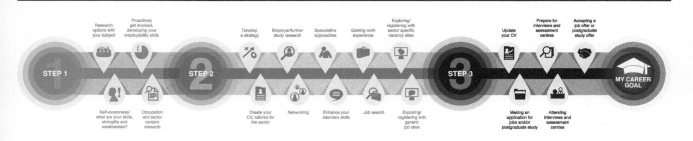

Stages of Career Development

# Create your CV & Cover Letter

A CV is a marketing tool you can use to present your skills, qualifications and experiences to potential employers.

Your CV should be concise, well-structured, up-to-date, and relevant to the organisation or role that you're applying to.

Your cover letter is the first impression an employer has of you – it should be an introduction that briefly covers your interest in the role and sells your suitability.

## In this guide:

- Writing your CV
- Writing your cover letter
- Word bank
- Further reading

Careers & Employability Centre
Ground Floor, Library
Mon-Fri: 09:00-16:30

T: +44 (0) 1522 83 7828
E: careers@lincoln.ac.uk

www.uolcareers.co.uk
www.facebook.com/UOLCareers
www.twitter.com/UOLCareers

# Writing your CV

## You need to tailor your CV

The most effective CVs are tailored to the specific role and organisation that you're applying to. This ensures that the recruiter or employer reading it can easily imagine you in that role. When it comes to CVs, one size does not fit all.

## Before you start

Find out as much as you can about the job role you are applying for and highlight key points to cover; the job description or person specification will usually detail these:

- Required qualifications
- Required or desired skills & knowledge
- Any experience requirements

*If this is not possible (eg. you are making a speculative application) refer to the job profiles on the Prospects website (www.prospects.ac.uk/job-profiles) which give general requirements for various job roles.*

### Remember
All experience counts. Many roles will give you skills that can transfer to many different roles. Use these to your advantage.

## Deciding on a CV style

### Reverse Chronological
A common CV style that goes through each section in reverse chronological order - your most recent qualifications and job roles are listed first to give them more focus and attention. This style of CV is useful to demonstrate a variety of experience and is the one you will most likely use.

### Skills Based
A specialised style of CV which focuses on the specific skills employers are looking for, using skills as headings to demonstrate your relevant experience. You will need to match skill headings to those the employer is looking for. The skills section fills at least your first page and the remainder of your CV can be used to briefly explain your education and employment dates and descriptions. This style of CV is useful when applying for positions not directly linked to previous job roles.

**In most cases, a reverse chronological CV is preferable for a student or graduate.**

# Writing your CV

## Format and layout

Unless instructed otherwise by the employer, your CV should be no more than two sides of A4 sized paper. Your CV should be concise, but not have too much empty space. Be creative with formatting.

Fonts should be clear and professional - think Verdana or Arial instead of Comic Sans. Font size 11 is ideal, anything smaller can be difficult to read.

Avoid using colours on text other than headings, and unless appropriate for the job you are applying for (for example, Graphic Designer), avoid using images or tables. If you are applying for creative roles, however, you may want to use this space to display some of your skills.

Horizontal rules, bullet points, and headings are a useful way of presenting information clearly. If you decide to use any of these, they should be used consistently throughout your CV.

Ensure all text is lined up or in columns and that spelling and grammar is correct.

## References

You should not provide the details of referees until requested. Simply write 'References available on request' at the end of your CV.

You should have two referees arranged, one should ideally be your current or previous employer, and one can be an academic or personal reference such as a lecturer or a senior member of a club you are involved with. Ensure to ask for permission before providing their details.

## Make final checks

Check your CV against the job specifications and description. Have you met every requirement, providing evidence and examples?

If you need some extra help, give your CV a boost by taking a Careers & Employability CV Advice session online. We recommend doing this before you visit us with your CV in the Careers and Employability Centre.

### CV Sessions
Find our CV session on our website:
www.uolcareers.co.uk

### CV Builder
Follow the 'Career Planning' button on Blackboard's 'My Careers' tab to find our CV Builder tool

# Writing your CV

## What to include

This template assumes you are making a Chronological CV, but the methodology used to build each section can be applied to other kinds of CVs as well.

**1** Personal details
Keep this section brief and include:

- Name (this should act as a heading)
- Address (ensure you will be contactable at the address stated)
- Telephone numbers (including mobile)
- Email address (ensure this looks professional, eg. your name, not 'irastronaut@hotmail.com')
- Online portfolio, website and/or LinkedIn profile - if appropriate

You do not need to include a photo, date of birth, nationality, gender, relationship status, religion or the word 'CV'.

**2** Personal profile
Your personal profile is a space to highlight the qualities and skills that are most important to the employer and role you are applying for. Write in the third person and between 3 to 5 lines is recommended. Include your key strengths, as applicable to the role and evidence these with an example.

**3** Education
For a student or graduate CV you will usually place your Education above Work Experience as this is the most recent and relevant experience that you will have. Consider how your degree has prepared you for work.

**4** Work and other relevant experience
Evidence is key: you may have communication skills, but you'll need to prove it by giving an example of how you have used them to assist you in a work situation. Keep sentences short, relevant and in the third person (eg. 'This role involved…' rather than 'I was responsible for…'). Use professional and technical language, including positive sounding verbs and phrases with key words from the employer's role requirements.

# Johnathan Patch

11 Fake St, Lincoln LN6 7TS | **Mobile:** 0711 111 1111 | **Email:** j.patch@email.com
**LinkedIn Profile:** linkedin.com/in/johnpatch

A high achieving, Business and Finance BA (Hons) graduate from the University of Lincoln. A thorough understanding of the accounting and finance sectors, a passion for well-crafted marketing campagins and strong communication skills will help 123 AccountingFinance reach new audiences and maintain relationships with current clients.

## Education

UNIVERSITY OF LINCOLN - Lincoln, UK
**Business and Finance - BA (Hons) - 2015-2018**
- Average of 75% (First Class honours)
- Relevant modules include (among others):
  - Principles of Marketing
  - Financial Management
  - Money, Banking & Financial Markets
  - Strategic Marketing Planning
  - Crisis Management
- Collaborated on major group project to outline strategic marketing plan for a small Lincoln-based business, with the group receiving first-class honours for the project.

LINCOLN COLLEGE - Lincoln, UK
- A-levels: A-grades in Maths, English and Business Studies

## Relevant Experience

DEJUNER ACCOUNTING - Lincoln, UK
**Marketing and Sales Intern - Jun-Aug, 2016**
- Assisted development of key delivery strategy - succeeding in securing a number of contracts, including three worth an annual £15K each - using a range of statistical techniques including regression modelling.
- Maintained client base using interpersonal skills, supported expansion with prompt and accurate responses to client enquiries.
- Analysed relevant industry information to create and distribute a bi-monthly newsletter.

BANKING, INVESTMENT AND TRADING SOCIETY - University of Lincoln, UK
**Marketing Officer- 2015-2016**
- Increased membership by 100% during term by initiating, devleoping and implementing a social media marketing campaign.

## Additional Experience & Achievements

LINCOLN AWARD - University of Lincoln, UK
**Completed 2017**
- Awarded by the University for completing a Careers & Employability program developing teamwork, problem solving, IT skills (social media), communication skills, commercial awareness, leadership & management, organisation, work ethic, confidence and emotional intelligence.

PRIMARK - Lincoln, UK
**Retail Assistant - Feb 2014 - Present**
- Provided tailored customer service to diverse range of customers.
- Handled customer complaints with problem-solving skills including negotiation and escalation where necessary.

*References provided upon request*

Your CV will usually be 1-2 pages long depending on experience

# Writing your Cover Letter

## First impressions matter

This is your chance to show an employer:

**1** Your main selling points

**2** How relevant your skills are to the position

**3** How interested you are in the position

**4** How much you know about the company

The more you target and tailor your letter to a role and employer, the more likely it is to stand out – just like your CV, you will need to make a new one for each role you apply for. Unlike a CV, however, a cover letter has more room to show your personality and tell the story of your career journey.

**Cover Letter Builder**
Follow the 'Career Planning' button on Blackboard's 'My Careers' tab to find our Cover Letter Builder tool

# Writing your Cover Letter

## Addressing your letter

Address your letter to a named individual within the company to ensure that it is read by the correct person. If you have a named contact, you are able to follow-up with a telephone call or email to exactly the right person. Research the company in order to gain a contact, whether it be on the company website, telephoning their switchboard or asking their HR Department.

If you are given someone's full name, e.g. Joe Bloggs, do not address the letter 'Dear Joe' unless you are very familiar with the person. Rather begin 'Dear Mr Bloggs'.

If you find it impossible to get the name of an individual within the company, use 'Dear Sir/Madam'.

If you have a named contact – you should conclude 'Yours sincerely'.
If you use 'Dear Sir/Madam' – you should conclude 'Yours faithfully'.

## Other tips: style, formatting and more

- If you are submitting your letter on paper, ensure the paper you use is good quality. Your letter should come close to filling one A4 page. Keep fonts and text styling consistent with your CV.

- Email will give you less control over fonts and layout, but treat the body of your email carefully nonetheless – use the subject line to give your name and the job role you are applying for, and remain formal. Don't forget to attach your CV, make sure you double check that it has loaded into the email. It is advisable to also make note that your CV is attached, so the employer is alerted that something has gone wrong if it is not present.

- Use positive, active language in the first person ('I did this' as opposed to 'Joe did this'). While you can let your personality through in a cover letter, remain formal and professional. This is not a place for slang or acronyms unless they are relevant to the role or company culture.

- Your cover letter is a summary of highlights which an employer can read more about within your CV. Mentions of your experience and skills should be represented in both your CV and cover letter.

- Ensure that you have included a title - for example the job reference number. The company could have several roles available at any one time and you need to make it clear which role you are applying for.

- Have someone check your spelling and grammar before you submit, or read through it out loud as this will allow you to catch mistakes with greater ease. Keep a copy once you are done so you can refer to it before your interview.

# Writing your Cover Letter

Following a cover letter template could mean your letter will not read naturally to employers. While there are some structures you can follow (including the one you will find on the Cover Letter Builder on Blackboard) you will need to adapt them to suit your unique abilities and how they suit the role. Here are some basic points that you may want to cover. You may choose to order them differently:

**1**   An introduction
A brief and clear paragraph stating who you are, the role you are applying for and perhaps the reason you are applying for it. You can say where you saw the role advertised, establish any links you have with the company (worked for them previously, spoken to a team member at a careers fair) or make it clear that you are making a speculative enquiry about something such as work experience.

**2**   Your interest in the employer
Do your research and show your enthusiasm for working for them. Have they had any recent successes, do they work with particular clients or have any particular values that attract you?

**3**   Your interest in the role
Show your awareness of what the work will involve and establish your suitability for it.

**4**   Your key strengths
Without re-writing your CV, highlight your most relevant skills, qualifications, knowledge and experience that you believe will be of particular importance or interest to the employer or the role.

**5**   Other important information
Make sure you include responses to any specific things asked by the employer to cover in the job advert such as hours of availability or if you have special needs that will need to be catered to in an interview. If you wish to disclose a disability, be sure to read Prospect's advice on doing so:
www.prospects.ac.uk.links/disability

**6**   A positive conclusion
You can thank the employer for their time and express how you look forward to hearing from them. This is also a good time to reiterate your preferred methods of contact and availability for an interview.

Johnathan Patch
11 Fake St
Lincoln
LN6 7TS
j.patch@email.com
0711 111 1111
linkedin.com/in/johnpatch

Winston Briggs
Graduate HR Director
123AccountingFinance
Sparkhouse, University of Lincoln
Brayford Pool
Lincoln
LN6 7TS

23 October 2018

Dear Mr Briggs,

**1** I am writing to apply for the position of trainee accountant with 123AccountingFinance. I am a BA (Hons) Business and Finance graduate from the University of Lincoln. I recently spoke with one of your employees at the University of Lincoln careers fair.

**2** I am extremely enthusiastic about working for 123AccountingFinance. I would love to work within such a fast paced organisation that works on a global level such as your company. I also want to make a difference to people's lives, an ethos at the core of 123AccountingFinance's mission. Being able to work in a financial company which assists its clients to be efficient with their finances and achieve sustainable outcomes are my guiding principles for choosing an employer.

**3** I am looking to gain my first steps in accounting and receive the highest standard of training to complete my accounting qualifications. The varied nature of the role is what interests me, the opportunity to work within the different areas of Tax, Consulting and Transactions so I can fully understand the opportunities available to me upon completion of my accounting training.

**4** The foundation of knowledge I have gained from studying Business and Finance will help me greatly. From my work with the Banking, Investment and Trading society at the University of Lincoln I have developed the analytical ability, methodical approach and problem-solving skills that would be essential for this graduate scheme. My previous experience in a retail environment providing excellent service to customers will be transferrable when working with different types of clients from global companies to individuals. This is also confirmed through my work with Dejuner Accounting where I maintained a client base demonstrating I have the interpersonal skills to work with clients.

**5** As I have now graduated from the University of Lincoln I am available to start with 123AccountingFinance in September on the three year contract that is being offered. Thank you very much for your time and

**6** consideration - I look forward to discussing my application further with you.

Yours sincerely,

Johnathan Patch

*Try refer to a role description if you have one and use similar words that the employer uses.*

# Word Bank

While you should avoid jargon and buzzwords, having a good bank of positive, powerful verbs in your vocabulary will help make your CVs and cover letters sound professional and put your achievements in an active context.

| Leadership | Teamwork & Communicating | Efficiency & Money |
|---|---|---|
| Allocated | Balanced | Accelerated |
| Co-ordinated | Collaborated | Budgeted |
| Delegated | Co-operated | Expidited |
| Directed | Conveyed | Improved |
| Encouraged | Influenced | Marketed |
| Facilitated | Liaised | Reduced |
| Initiated | Moderated | Refined |
| Lead | Motivated | Refocused |
| Managed | Negotiated | Saved |
| Organised | Persuaded | Strengthened |
| Planned | Recommended | Sustained |
| Produced | Volunteered | Yielded |

| Project Involvement | Research and Strategy | General Achievement |
|---|---|---|
| Built | Advised | Attained |
| Delivered | Analysed | Completed |
| Designed | Assessed | Demonstrated |
| Developed | Concluded | Displayed |
| Devised | Conducted | Exceeded |
| Fashioned | Diagnosed | Fulfilled |
| Finalised | Evaluated | Learned |
| Generated | Identified | Performed |
| Incorporated | Interpreted | Presented |
| Implemented | Measured | Solved |
| Launched | Researched | Succeeded |
| Prepared | Solved | Taught |

# Further Reading

## CV Resources

www.uolcareers.co.uk/help-and-advice/writing-a-cv

www.prospects.ac.uk/links/examplecvs

www.targetjobs.co.uk/careers-advice/applications-and-cvs

## Cover Letter Resources

www.uolcareers.co.uk/help-and-advice/your-covering-letter

www.prospects.ac.uk/careers-advice/cvs-and-cover-letters/cover-letters

www.targetjobs.co.uk/careers-advice/applications-and-cvs/271393-covering-letter-essentials-for-graduate-vacancies

You can also use the CV and Cover Letter Builder tools, found in the Careers Tools in the My Careers tab of your Blackboard.

# Get support from your Careers & Employability Service

What we offer

- **Careers Clinic**
  Our Skills Advisers are available to support you with your job search or the recruitment process for any role.

- **Careers Guidance**
  For specific help relating to your degree area, arrange a confidential appointment with one of our Careers & Employability Advisers.

- **Career Events**
  We have daily events running to support your development.

- **Lincoln Award**
  Take part in our employability award to develop and learn how to demonstrate your employability skills.

- **Vacancy Postings**
  Visit uolcareers.co.uk/students-graduates/jobs-employment-options/graduate-student-vacancies for our graduate vacancy system or uolcareers.co.uk/jobshop for local, part-time vacancy listings on the Job Shop.

- **Campus Jobs**
  Come and see the University's Student Employment Agency to learn about all on-campus paid opportunities.

- **Career Information Resources**
  Find information on vacancies and useful advice to build your career in our Centre, on our website and through the My Careers tab on Blackboard.

Careers & Employability Centre
Ground Floor, Library
Mon-Fri: 09:00-16:30

T: +44 (0) 1522 83 7828
E: careers@lincoln.ac.uk

www.uolcareers.co.uk
www.facebook.com/UOLCareers
www.twitter.com/UOLCareers

# WHAT WE OFFER

International

Careers Information

Job Shop

Careers Clinic

Campus Jobs

The Lincoln Award

Graduate Jobs

Group Advice Sessions

Careers Guidance

The Careers & Employability Centre is open
09:00 - 16:30, Mon-Fri
Telephone: 01522 837828
Email: careers@lincoln.ac.uk
Web: www.uolcareers.co.uk

# Chapter **20**

## The ten questions you're most likely to be asked

Here's a list of what I consider to be the top ten questions you are likely to be asked at interview. Make sure you think through your answers to all these questions very carefully before going anywhere near an interview room.

1 Tell me about your work experience – what did you do, what did you enjoy, what were you good at, why did you leave each job?

2 Why have you applied for this vacancy?

3 Why do you wish to leave your current position?

4 Why do you want to work for this organisation?

5 What are your strengths?

6 What are your weaknesses?

7 What has been your greatest achievement in your personal life as well as in your career?

8 What can you, above all the other applicants, bring to this job?

9 Where do you see yourself in five years' time?

10 You've mentioned x under *Interests and activities* on your CV. Can you tell me a bit more about that?

You are absolutely certain to get asked at least some of these questions (or variations of them), if not the whole lot.

I could add an eleventh question to the list: 'And do you have any questions for me/us?' There aren't many interviews that conclude without this question being asked.

For now, let's concentrate on the questions above.

We'll look at them one by one, alongside possible alternatives and other closely related questions. We'll analyse the interviewer's intentions in asking you the question – the meaning behind the question – and we'll discuss how best you can answer it.

## Top question: can you tell me a bit about yourself?

*Alternative and related questions*

➤ Can you talk me through your CV?

## *The meaning behind the question*

This is an extremely popular question, and is just the kind an interviewer might throw at you at the beginning of an interview to get the ball rolling. They are quite simply placing you centre stage and hoping you will open up to them. Alternatively, they are hopelessly overworked, haven't yet had time to read your CV, and asking you this question will buy them some breathing space!

## *Your answer*

This is a very broad question, and you might, therefore, be at a loss as to the approach you should take to answering it.

They are not asking for an autobiography. Focus on discussing major selling points that feature on your CV or application form; selling points that are directly relevant to the job for which you are applying. Don't start telling your whole life history.

Whilst they do want you to open up and paint a picture of yourself, you're not on the psychiatrist's couch here! Keep it professional and avoid getting too personal.

Besides talking about your career, make sure that you have something to say about your education and qualifications and even your hobbies and interests.

---

**EXAMPLE**

---

I'm a highly driven individual with extensive management experience acquired principally in the aviation sector. Following completion of my degree in International Business (which included a couple of years in Germany), I started my career in administration and have worked my way up to become an export sales manager. I believe I combine a high level of commercial awareness with a commitment to customer care, which helps me to achieve profitable growth in a competitive market. I enjoy being part of, as well as managing, motivating, training and developing, a successful and productive team and I thrive in highly pressurised and challenging working environments. I have strong IT skills, I'm fluent in German and I'm also a qualified first aider. In my spare time I undertake a wide range of activities; I'm particularly keen on squash and I am also currently working towards my Private Pilot Licence.

It's vital to practise your answer for this in advance, and try to limit your answer to one minute. If you can't successfully 'pitch' yourself in under a minute you risk losing the interviewer's attention.

How have you described yourself in the professional profile at the top of your CV? A lot of this material can be recycled to help you draft your answer to this question.

# 2  Why have you applied for this vacancy?

## Alternative and related questions

> ➤ Why do you want this vacancy?
> ➤ What attracted you to this vacancy?
> ➤ Why do you think you're suitable for this job?
> ➤ What is it that you are looking for in a new job?

## The meaning behind the question

The interviewer is probing to see

> ➤ If you fully understand what the job entails
> ➤ How well you might match their requirements
> ➤ What appeals to you most about the job

## Your answer

This is another open-ended question where you might be tempted to say too much. By taking the time to think through your answer to this question in advance, you will be able to remain focused on a few key points.

Your emphasis should be on demonstrating to the interviewer precisely how you match their requirements and, in doing so, demonstrate that you fully understand what the role entails.

If you've done your research properly then you will have a good idea of what it is the company is looking for.

You have been asked what your motivations are in applying for the vacancy, but try to turn the question round so that the answer you give indicates why you are the right candidate for the vacancy.

**EXAMPLE**

I've applied for this vacancy because it's an excellent match for my skills and experience and because it represents a challenge I know I'll relish. I already have extensive experience as a senior quantity surveyor, including previous experience of rail and station projects – an area I'm particularly interested in. I enjoy managing multiple projects simultaneously. I also enjoy overseeing and coaching junior and assistant quantity surveyors. I'm used to dealing directly with clients; developing productive working relationships with clients is definitely one of my strengths. This is exactly the type of role I am currently targeting and I am confident I will be able to make a major contribution.

## 3  Why do you wish to leave your current position?

### Alternative and related questions

➤ Why do you wish to leave your current employer?

➤ What do you plan to say to your current employer in your letter of resignation?

### The meaning behind the question

The interviewer is trying to understand your motivation for changing jobs. They clearly want to know why you want to change jobs but they also want to know how serious you are about changing jobs. Are you really committed to moving or are you just wasting their time?

### Your answer

There are a multitude of reasons for wanting to leave your job; however, they won't all be positive selling points for you.

Positive reasons include:

➤ Wanting a greater challenge

➤ Wanting to diversify

> ➤ Seeking greater opportunities
> ➤ Seeking further advancement
> ➤ Taking a step up the career ladder.

Negative reasons include:

> ➤ Problems with your boss
> ➤ Problems with a colleague
> ➤ A financially unstable organisation
> ➤ Personal reasons.

If your reason for wanting to leave your job is a positive one, then your answer will be easy enough to construct. Explain to the interviewer what your motivations are and how the move to your next job will help you to achieve your goals. You are making a positive move for positive reasons and intend to achieve a positive outcome simple as that.

If, however, your reason for leaving your job is in my list of negative reasons, then giving the right answer is going to be somewhat trickier. Because each situation is so different, I will deal with each of them in turn.

Problems with your boss: Having problems with the boss is the top reason people give (in surveys) for changing jobs. However, you should never say anything negative about either a current or a previous employer. It isn't professional, it doesn't portray you as someone who is particularly loyal, and it will reflect badly on you. In almost all cases, I would recommend that you avoid citing this as a reason. Criticising your current employer is considered one of the top mistakes you can make at interview and will most likely cost you the job regardless of whether or not your criticism is justified. Aim to give an answer that focuses on the benefits you will experience in moving to your new job rather than making any reference to your having had problems with your boss.

### BLOOPER!

Having delivered a particularly devastating critique of his current employer, one candidate was rather shocked to discover that his current employer was in fact the interviewer's brother-in-law!

Problems with a colleague: Maybe you want to leave because of a persistently unpleasant colleague? However, explaining this to the interviewer will most likely open you up to expressing bitterness or recrimination – traits that are not attractive to a potential employer. Again, you should aim to give an answer that focuses on the benefits of moving to your new job rather than drawing attention to your problems.

A financially unstable organisation: You may well have decided to leave your job before your employer finally goes bankrupt, but you don't want to be labelled as a rat leaving a sinking ship. It doesn't say much for your loyalty. Avoid giving this as a reason.

Personal reasons: There are many different personal circumstances that might cause you to wish to leave a job. For example, you might simply want a better work–life balance. However, if possible you should avoid giving 'personal reasons' as an answer and instead leave the interviewer to believe you are leaving in order to pursue a more promising opportunity.

As for asking what you would write in a resignation letter, you should remember that when it comes to resignation letters it is well worth being as nice as possible about the matter. Harsh words in a letter of resignation could easily come back to haunt you in the future – not least if you ever need a reference from this employer.

---

### EXAMPLE

After careful consideration, I have made the decision to move on to a new challenge. Naturally, I'd thank them for the opportunities with which they presented me during the course of my employment, reassure them that I will do my best to help ensure the seamless transfer of my duties and responsibilities before leaving and wish them all the very best for the future.

---

## 4  Why do you want to work for this organisation?

*Alternative and related questions*

➤  What is it about our organisation that attracts you?

## The meaning behind the question

The interviewer is analysing your motivations and probing your expectations of the organisation. Why do you want to work for this one in particular? Whilst this question doesn't directly ask what you know about their organisation, in order to be able to answer it effectively you are clearly going to have to demonstrate that you have done your homework.

## Your answer

If you have done your research properly, you will already be fairly well informed as to the organisation you are applying to join. However, the key to answering this question is how to communicate that knowledge to the interviewer whilst tying it in with why you want to work for them.

Focus on what in particular attracts you to the organisation. We'll cover the closely related but more generalised question, 'What do you know about us as an organisation?'

---

**EXAMPLE**

---

I'm particularly attracted by how progressive an organisation you are. I've seen how your sales levels have grown the past few years and I'm aware of your plans to expand into the United States. Yours is an organisation that is rapidly developing and evolving, that's exactly what I'm looking for. I want to work for an organisation which is forward-thinking and isn't afraid to tackle new challenges.

---

# 5 What are your strengths?

## Alternative and related questions

➤ What are you good at?

➤ What do you consider yourself to be good at?

## *The meaning behind the question*

With this question the interviewer wants to achieve the following:

➤ Identify what your key selling points are.

➤ Establish whether or not these strengths are relevant to the role they are interviewing for.

➤ Gain some insight into your character – how self-confident (or arrogant) you are.

## *Your answer*

Everyone has their strengths. The key to answering this question is not to rattle off a long list of what you consider your strengths to be. Instead, you should be looking to highlight a smaller number of specific strengths, discussing each one briefly and, most importantly, identifying how these strengths relate to the requirements of the job you are applying to undertake. You can even elaborate on one of your strengths by mentioning a specific relevant achievement.

Choose your strengths carefully. It can be hard to say anything very interesting, for example, about the fact that you are very meticulous and pay great attention to detail. However, if the recruiter is looking for someone to lead a team, then you can mention team leadership as one of your strengths, citing an appropriate example or achievement.

## *Word of warning*

If you don't give the interviewer at least one specific example to back up your statement, be prepared for them to ask for one!

---

### EXAMPLE

I believe my key strength is that I combine experience of traditional film production with extensive experience in the online arena. I'm very aware of current trends in new media and am able to demonstrate excellent creative judgement. I'm also very good at juggling multiple projects simultaneously; in my current role I frequently have as many as half a dozen different projects on the go at any one time, and I'm committed to completing them all on time and on budget. This clearly requires extremely strong project management skills.

# 6 What are your weaknesses?

## Alternative and related questions

➤ What are you not good at doing?

➤ What do you find difficult to do and why?

➤ In what areas do you feel you need to improve?

## The meaning behind the question

With questions of this kind the interviewer wants to achieve the following:

➤ Identify any weakness which might actually be detrimental to your ability to undertake the role.

➤ See how you react when faced with a somewhat tricky question.

➤ Assess how self-aware you are and how you define weakness.

## Your answer

Yes, this is a tricky one. Whilst it is superficially a somewhat negative question, it is in fact full of opportunities for you to turn it around to your advantage and make your answer a positive point.

Don't be perturbed by the question or let it throw you off balance. Your answer should be right on the tip of your tongue. You should only ever discuss a professional weakness, unless the interviewer specifically requests otherwise (unlikely).

Your first thought might be to say, 'I don't really have any particular weaknesses.' But this is definitely not the answer the interviewer is looking for – and is definitely not the answer you should be giving.

### BLOOPER!

Telling the interviewer your weakness is 'kryptonite' – as one candidate did – is unlikely to amuse an interviewer. But it may possibly be better than the candidate who said he was a 'work**alco**holic'!

The interviewer wants to know that you are able to look at yourself objectively and to criticise yourself where appropriate. If you honestly don't think you have any weaknesses and say so, then you risk coming across as arrogant, and nobody wants a perfect candidate anyway.

Clearly, you don't just want to come up with a straightforward list of what you consider your weaknesses to be, so you have two choices:

➤ Talk about a weakness that's not necessarily a weakness at all.
➤ Talk about a weakness that you turned (or can turn) into a strength.

The problem with the first option is that you risk running into cliché territory. I'm talking about the kind of people who answer:

➤ I would have to say that my main weakness is that I'm a perfectionist.
➤ I have a reputation for working too hard; I often push myself far too hard in my work.

You risk sounding as though you plucked your answer straight out of a 1990s manual on interview technique.

Personally, I prefer the second option: talking about a weakness that you turned (or are turning) into a strength because you are answering the interviewer's question by highlighting a definite weakness, before reflecting positively on it by outlining the active steps you are taking to overcome it. You are demonstrating a willingness to learn, adapt and improve, and you are showing that you have the initiative required to make changes where changes are due.

Choosing a weakness that has its root in lack of experience and has been (or is being) overcome by further training is ideal because it is a weakness that is relatively easily resolved.

## EXAMPLE

When I started my current job my first few months were an uphill battle dealing with a backlog of work I inherited from my predecessor. I recognised that I have a weakness when it comes to time management. I have since been on a time management course, read a couple of books on the subject and I believe I've made a lot of progress. But it's something I'm still very vigilant about. I make a concerted effort to apply the principles I've learned every day and to put in place procedures which enable me to most effectively prioritise and process my workload.

This example is a good and comprehensive answer meeting all the objectives we've outlined above.

## Word of warning

Do be prepared for the interviewer to ask the follow-up question, 'OK. That's one weakness. You must have more than one weakness?'

---

# 7  What has been your greatest achievement/accomplishment?

## Alternative and related questions

> What are your biggest achievements?

> What are you most proud of?

> What was your biggest achievement in your current/last job?

> What has been the high point of your career so far?

## The meaning behind the question

Unless the question is qualified by specifically mentioning, for example, your last job, it is important to remember that the interviewer isn't necessarily looking for a work-related achievement. They are looking for evidence of achievement, full stop. However, a work-related achievement is normally what they will be expecting.

## Your answer

Make sure you have thought this question through carefully before the interview and have selected both a key professional achievement as well as a key personal achievement to cover both bases.

Try not to go too far back; try to pick a recent achievement. If you've included an achievements section in your CV (which I would recommend you do) then this will be a good starting point for you to generate ideas.

Describe clearly to the interviewer

> What it is that you achieved

> What the background and circumstances were

> What impact it had on your career/life

What was the benefit? Try to phrase this in such a way for it to be self-evident that this would also be a benefit to any prospective employer.

> **EXAMPLE**
>
> My greatest achievement so far in my career would probably be winning the manager of the year award last year. I made numerous operational changes at my branch, including a massive reduction in stock levels, which significantly boosted our working capital. I also drove up sales levels, especially by increasing the uptake of after-sales insurance packages. The net effect was that we smashed the previous branch sales record by an impressive 37 per cent and profits rose in line with this. This directly resulted in my promotion to the management of the flagship Edinburgh branch.

## 8  What can you, above all the other applicants, bring to this job?

### Alternative and related questions

➤ What makes you the best candidate for this job?

### The meaning behind the question

The interviewer is directly asking what your 'unique selling point' is. They are looking for at least one significant reason that you should be their No. 1 choice for the job.

### Your answer

Well, what does make you the best candidate for this job?

I'll level with you – this isn't necessarily a top ten question in terms of how likely you are to get asked it. However, it is very much a top ten question in terms of the importance of your having prepared an answer to it. You need to go into every interview with a thorough understanding of what it is that you have to offer. If you don't know what it is that you're offering then how can you hope to sell it effectively?

If you do get asked this specific question, then don't be afraid to answer it quite candidly. It's a bold question and warrants a bold answer. The interviewer is putting you on the spot to sell yourself. But do be very careful to avoid coming across as arrogant because that's the last thing you want to do. It's a fine line you need to tread.

Feel free to cite an example from your past where you demonstrated that you are someone who is capable of going the extra mile. It's all very well to say that you're someone who gives 110 per cent (although it is a bit of a cliché), but if you can actually throw an example at your interviewer then you're going to be a whole lot more credible.

### BLOOPER!

An ex-army candidate for a management role replied, 'I can shoot someone at 300 yards.' What is more amazing is that he actually got the job! This is a rare example of a sense of humour working to the candidate's advantage.

### EXAMPLE

Having now been working in this industry for over a decade, I have developed successful relationships with key decision makers in numerous companies, enabling me to achieve a sales conversion rate much higher than average. This is undoubtedly a very challenging role, requiring considerable drive and determination, but I believe my previous sales record is clear evidence that I am more than capable of achieving what it is that you need.

## 9 Where do you see yourself in five years' time?

*Alternative and related questions*

➤ How long do you plan to stay/would you stay in this job if we offer it to you?

➤ What are your long-term career goals?

➤ How does this job fit into your long-term career plans?

➤ How far do you feel you might progress in our organisation?

## The meaning behind the question

The interviewer is trying to ascertain what your long-term career ambitions are and to get a better understanding of your motivations. They will invariably be looking for someone who is keen to learn, develop and progress. However, they are recruiting for a specific role and will want someone who is prepared to commit to that role for a reasonable period of time.

You may think this question is just a cliché and doesn't really get asked in practice. Trust me it does and far more frequently than you might imagine.

## Your answer

Lots of people think they're displaying a great sense of humour/ ambition/self-confidence to reply, 'Doing your job!' I wouldn't recommend it because it may come across as arrogant and aggressive.

Avoid being too specific. It's very difficult for most people to know exactly what job they will be undertaking in five years and so it can be unrealistic to quote a specific job title you are aiming for. Try to present your answer more in terms of what level you hope to have reached – what level of responsibility, of autonomy. It's also a good idea if you can phrase your answer to communicate that you hope still to be with this same organisation in five years' time.

**EXAMPLE**

Five years from now I expect I will have progressed significantly in my career and be making an even greater contribution. Having proved my value to the organisation I would hope to have been given increased responsibilities and greater challenges. I've clearly given a good deal of thought to working for you and I can see that there are indeed a lot of opportunities both for promotion and for ongoing professional development. My career is very important to me and I want to push myself hard to deliver the very best of which I'm capable.

# 10 You've mentioned x under *Interests and activities* on your CV. Can you tell me a bit more about that?

## *Alternative and related questions*

> ➤ What activities do you enjoy outside work?
> ➤ What are you interested in outside work?

## *The meaning behind the question*

There are a variety of possible reasons interviewers might ask this question.

> ➤ They're trying to get some insight into your personality and character.
> ➤ They're testing to see how truthful you've been on your CV.
> ➤ They've run out of other questions and are killing time!

Besides knowing whether you're capable of doing the job, most employers are keen to know what sort of a person you are to work alongside. Employers are generally keen to have a diversity of characters within their team and are always on the lookout for someone who can add a new dimension.

Whilst nobody has yet conducted a survey specifically to research this, there is plenty of anecdotal evidence of recruiters deciding to call someone in for an interview purely as a result of what they have included in their CV under interests and activities. I, for one, will admit to having done so when hiring.

## *Your answer*

This is a very simple question to answer provided, as always, that you've prepared for it in advance. If you have a hobby that makes for an interesting talking point at the interview then it will reflect positively on you as an individual.

Remember, you need to be able to back up everything you've listed on your CV. If you mention playing chess to give your CV some intellectual clout, but haven't played since you were at school, then you could well come a cropper in your interview if your interviewer turns out to be a chess fan and asks you which openings to the game you favour!

It's always a good idea if you can subtly slip in mention of any positions of responsibility you hold outside work. If your passion is, for example, football, and you're also the captain of the local team, then do say so.

Besides the obvious selling point of football being a team activity (and hence your being a team player), you've immediately communicated your leadership qualities, your ability to take responsibility for others, your ability to commit yourself to a project etc.

## EXAMPLE

I've always been fascinated by planes. I remember my first flight as a child; it was a thrilling experience. Even though I understand the science behind it, I'm still in awe each and every time I see a plane clear the runway. It's quite an expensive hobby to pursue but, as soon as I could afford to do so, I started taking flying lessons. I gained my Private Pilot Licence, went on to qualify as an instructor and I'm now a senior member of my local flying club. Whilst it's not something I've ever wished to pursue as a career, I do enjoy giving the occasional lesson and generally participating in the club community. It's definitely something about which I'm very passionate.

# CHAPTER 21

# What are psychometric tests?

By the end of this chapter you will understand five different types of tests which are commonly used by employers as part of the selection and recruitment process.

## 21.1 What are psychometric tests?

Having to take psychometric tests when applying for a job you want can seem a lot to take on, and it is fair to say that where such tests are routinely used for recruitment, it is likely to be part of a selection process which is both thorough and highly competitive. Getting your head round what the tests involve will help you to approach them with a degree of confidence, which should in turn allow you to perform at your best. That is, after all, the ideal outcome both for you as a job applicant and also for the employer: you get a job you really want and they get a new recruit who is well suited to the job they wanted to fill.

### What does a psychometric actually do?

Fundamentally, a psychometric (or psychometric test) is a measure of the mind. It might measure ability or aptitude; this is the case where the answer can be deemed right – or wrong. Or it can simply measure – just as a thermometer measures temperature. A psychometric should measure objectively, without bias.

### Can I trust a psychometric test?

The simple answer is: yes, you can trust a psychometric test. Just as a thermometer was developed out of scientific work, so psychometrics are developed by psychologists working to exacting scientific principles and constraints. This process will involve close consideration of what questions are included and how they are worded. Everything in the test will be refined, using sophisticated analytical techniques. The design of the test will focus resolutely on the aptitude or ability under scrutiny; a maths test should not be a test of reading ability.

This scientific discipline ensures that the measure is both reliable and valid. That means the measure will produce similar results when used over time and with different groups, and that it will be relevant to its intended purpose and will measure only what it sets out to measure.

Psychometrics are also designed and tested to be objective and it is this quality of treating everyone who completes them in the same way which makes them a valuable part of the selection and recruitment process.

*Do psychometrics tell us everything we need to know?*

Although we can rely on psychometrics as an objective measure, they can't tell us everything we need to know. That goes both for the applicant and the recruiting employer. Let's use the concrete example of measuring height. If height is measured, we can be confident that we know, for sure, someone is 5'6" tall. That's all we know. But if we know that they are applying to be cabin crew in an airline for which the minimum height is 5'2" and the maximum height is 6'3" then we know that their height fits within those parameters, which means they can be considered as a viable applicant, if only on the height criterion. Of course, we don't know how the person measured feels about being that height, or even if they think themselves quite tall or not tall enough. That's not what was being measured. So psychometrics can't tell us everything we need to know, which is why they are often used alongside other selection tools in a recruitment process.

## 21.2 Five types of psychometric tests commonly used in selection

There are hundreds of psychometric tests used across the world every day, but what you really need to know about are the handful of measures which are very commonly used in selection, particularly where the selection is relatively non-technical and non-specialist – a graduate management trainee scheme for example. These include ability/aptitude tests for:

1  Verbal reasoning

2  Numerical (also called non-verbal) reasoning

3  Inductive (also called abstract or diagrammatic) reasoning

4  Situational judgement tests (including in-tray exercises) and

5  Personality tests or indicators

## Testing reasoning ability in three different ways: verbal, numerical and inductive

It makes sense to look at the first three of these tests as a cluster, because they share a common purpose. Each of them tests how you reason: how you solve a problem by working through it systematically, using logic and reason to get to the right answer. In all of these reasoning tests there is only one correct answer. That may come as no surprise when you think about working with numbers (in the numerical tests) and diagrams (in the abstract or inductive tests) but might seem less likely for the verbal tests. It is nevertheless the case: you have to work out what is the only correct answer you can deduce from reading a piece of written text. It isn't about how well you understand the text (although that does come into it) and it certainly isn't about how well you can express yourself in writing, as that would be measured by a different test altogether. Verbal reasoning, just as much as numerical and inductive reasoning, is about working through a thinking process logically so that you identify a statement which is correct as a conclusion derived from the text you are given.

### *Reasoning ability doesn't change across employer*

The reasoning tests are standard across many different organisations and employment sectors; the same tests tend to be used no matter if you are working in the private sector or the public

> ### brilliant definition
>
> **Reasoning tests**
> There are three different types of reasoning test: verbal (which uses words), non-verbal (which uses numbers), and inductive/abstract/diagrammatic (which all use diagrams). All of them are designed to test how you work through a problem systematically, using logic and reason to get to the right answer. There is only one right answer in reasoning tests.

sector, in finance or retail or education or health. This makes sense, because it is your ability to reason which is being tested; no matter what capacity or context you'll eventually work in, this demand stays the same.

## Testing your judgement of complex or competing demands

The situational judgement test (SJT for short) measures your core competencies by examining how you react to a number of scenarios or imaginary episodes. The kind of competencies would typically be: working in a team, leading and managing people, effective communication, problem-solving, and prioritising tasks. These competencies are transferable across jobs and employers and sectors, so SJTs are used widely.

> ### brilliant definition
>
> **Situational judgement tests**
> Situational judgement tests reproduce the kind of real-life problems you are likely to encounter if you were actually doing the job you are applying for. Often the test is looking for the most effective answer for that particular company in its particular context.

*Testing whether your judgement fits with
the organisational values*

An SJT is often developed very specifically from the business and/or experience to be found on a day-to-day basis in a particular job. SJTs test how you approach the kind of problem you are likely to encounter in the workplace of the organisation you are applying to, and how well the way you would most likely tackle this problem matches up to how the company would want the problem to be tackled. Some SJTs are designed to probe both for competence and for personality; either way, the test will have been designed to ensure that it looks at exactly what is needed for the job – nothing more, nothing less.

There will be a preferred answer that the test is looking for, but there will also be a close second answer which might be an effective way of tackling the problem you've been presented with, but won't be the answer the company is ideally looking for. Just as much science lies behind SJT questions and answers as in the battery of reasoning tests; this is to ensure that the tests are reliable. The preferred answer will have been rated in the test design phase by a panel of experts who understand the scenarios presented, often because they have had direct experience in that work role or in that employment sector.

'SJTs are not at all technical. They're a lot about pressures and judgements and team-working and doing the right thing. No prior knowledge is needed and no work experience is needed.'

Sara Reading, Royal Bank of Scotland

You can get a good sense of how the organisation thinks and the skillset and mindset it values by looking at information on its website or in its recruitment brochure. Employers are often explicit about their values and the skills they prize in their employees; this is because they want a good fit between the employee and the job, and they don't want to waste either your time (as an applicant) or their time (as a recruiter) if the fit just isn't there.

## brilliant recap

- SJTs test your judgement of typical work scenarios.
- One answer will reflect most closely how the company likes to operate.
- Some SJTs probe for personality type as well as competence.

## 21.3 In-tray exercise to see how you actually manage competing demands

The in-tray exercise is included here because again it asks you to put yourself in the kind of position you are applying for and tests how you would tackle a typical day's work in that business. The in-tray exercise is very practical. You'll start off as if you were working at that company in the job you are applying for. You'll be presented with a set of tasks and some documents you'll need to work on. Once the test starts you may well receive emails or notifications which make new and competing demands on your time. This is a good way to put you under the kind of pressure you will encounter in the job – and see how you manage.

## brilliant tip

Do notice the organisation's values, the skills and attitudes they prize, and keep them in mind when doing SJTs and in-tray exercises.

## 21.4 Personality tests and indicators

Personal qualities are also very important in a job, so personality tests (sometimes called personality indicators) are used to measure your beliefs, values, motivation, drive and – personality. With personality tests, there isn't really a right or wrong answer; the test is there simply to measure. Being a psychometric, the test does of course give an objective measure against a range of personal qualities, and the strength of those qualities may be important for the job advertised. However, the recruitment process may be looking for the scores in a personality test that fit the job profile of the vacancy they are recruiting to fill. If the job requires a lot of interaction with the general public, a level of extraversion would be sought. If the job requires that care is taken and a certain amount of vigilance then a level of conscientiousness is called for. Taking a personality test can offer fresh insight into what makes you tick, or you may find the test confirms what you have always known about yourself.

 **brilliant** recap

Personality tests look at what makes you tick and give a sense of how you might fit into the job and the company. You don't have to work out the right answer, just be honest about who you are.

## Responding to personality tests

There are two slightly different ways in which personality test questions are presented, but in both cases there will be a set of statements. You might be asked to indicate to what extent you think these statements apply to you, putting your answer on a scale running from 'agree strongly' through a neutral position to 'disagree strongly' at the opposite end of the scale. Alternatively, you might be asked to rank your responses, so you will indicate which statements you most agree or most disagree with, as applied to you. The technical difference is that ranking responses is ipsative and rating responses is normative. Normative tests are more common, so you are more likely to be asked to rate yourself along a scale of agreement with a set of statements. There isn't a right answer, so all you have to do is read the question carefully and give your response. You do need to keep your concentration levels up and that can be hard when there are lots of questions, some of which will be asking pretty much the same thing but in slightly different ways. Going by instinct is a good approach; you don't want to over-think your answer because that might distort the picture.

### *You, just the way you are*

You might hear people say that a strategic approach is to work out what kind of personality the employer is looking for and choose the answers that will make you out to be that type. That's really not a good strategy. Firstly, personality tests are carefully designed and you'd need to be very smart indeed to fool the test. Secondly, what would be the point of making up a version of you that might fit with your idea of what the company wants – that just means you'll end up in a job that doesn't really fit with the kind of person you are. What both you and the employer want is an accurate sense of what makes you tick. The real you, not a manufactured identikit or replica; you, just the way you are.

## brilliant dos and don'ts

### Do

✔ Take tests seriously; they are used to select for the next stage.

✔ Practise reasoning tests so you are confident.

✔ Check on employers' websites for which tests they use.

### Don't

✗ Over-think personality tests; just relax and be yourself.

✗ Ignore the advice about practice – just have a go!

## 21.5  What's it like, doing the different sorts of tests?

### Reasoning tests

It is hard to say what it's like to take these tests; the only way you're going to know for sure is by – well, by taking a test. That's why practice tests are included here for you to try out. The reasoning tests (verbal, non-verbal and inductive) tend to be more stressful in that you know you are trying to work out which is the right answer, and you are doing so against the clock. You'll also be using a calculator for the non-verbals and possibly some scrap paper for notes so that's another thing you have to learn to handle. When these tests are taken online there is a count-down timer running down on the screen which can be distracting and unnerving. Practice tests help you get used to both of these pressures.

 'Reasoning tests are no fun, but they're not meant to be. You can prepare, and I would advise it.'

Hannah, BSc Economics and Politics

### Situational judgement tests

In situational judgement tests you'll be doing a lot of reading. The challenge here is to think yourself into the situation and to pay attention to what kind of answer you're being asked for. The time pressure might not feel so great but you still need to get through everything; again, practice can help you to pace yourself in reading, thinking and choosing.

### Personality tests and indicators

Many people find the personality tests the easiest of all the psychometrics; there's no right answer and there isn't the same kind of time pressure you find in the reasoning tests. Of course, it is possible to feel anxious about personality tests too and to start stressing out about whether the answer you are drawn to is the answer the test is looking for. There is no point going down this path; the tests are designed in such a way as to be rather difficult to second-guess or to manipulate. And even if you were to work out what answer was the one being looked for (and honestly, that is a very difficult thing even for chartered psychologists to do) all you'd achieve by distorting your answers to fit would be to get closer to a job that actually you are temperamentally unsuited for. Far better to work through the questions calmly and answer them honestly. It can feel like there are a lot of questions to get through, and it can feel like some of the questions repeat themselves. If you find yourself tripping up over a question, just take another moment to read it through and go with your instinct; your first answer is probably the best one. Relaxing into the personality test while keeping alert is probably the best approach.

## brilliant recap

- Psychometric tests are used to measure ability and aptitude.

- Reasoning tests are commonly used in graduate and other formal training schemes.

- Reasoning tests can be verbal (words) or non-verbal (numbers) or inductive (diagrams) but all of them need you to think logically.

- In situational judgement tests you decide what action you would take in a workplace scenario.

- In-tray exercises simulate a typical work scenario; you are often presented with new tasks and/or information over time.

- Personality tests are all about you; they can enrich your self-knowledge and insight, and help you work out if the job in question is really what you want.

## 21.6  How do I know what tests an employer uses?

Employers don't make a secret about what tests they use and many of them not only tell you what to expect but make a point of telling you to familiarise yourself with the tests they use by doing some practice tests before you apply for their advertised job. Usually this information can be found in their promotional or recruitment literature (very often you can find this online in the company's website, typically in the Careers or Vacancies or Working For Us section). Once you've identified which tests they use, you can read about each type of test in more detail. There are worked examples of each of the five test types later in this text. You can take a whole test in the practice section of this text (Tests, Brilliant practice) and find all the answers, along with full explanation of how to get to that answer, in the final section (Answers, Brilliant answers). There is also a list of websites for your practice; some of these offer online tests under timed conditions.

### ✖ brilliant  dos and don'ts

**Do**

✔ Check the employer's website for which type of test they use in recruitment.

✔ Read more about each test in this text.

✔ Try the practice tests included in Tests, Brilliant practice.

**Don't**

✗ Avoid practice – work through the example questions.

✗ Forget online practice tests will have a built-in timer.

### Practice helps performance

Throughout this text, you will be encouraged to practise. This is so you become familiar with what the tests want and how you tackle them. This should give you the confidence to perform authentically when you are taking the test for real. That means you are able to perform as you would if nerves didn't get in the way.

 'The key is practice, practice, practice, practice.'

Sara Reading, Royal Bank of Scotland

You don't need to take a practice test immediately after you've read about it, but you do need to take the practice test included in this text at some time. This is so you know for sure what you know, which means that when you come to tackle the tests for real you know what you need to do and you're confident you can do your best.

---

### brilliant practice

Now check what you've learnt about psychometric tests by taking the Chapter 21 true/false quiz in Tests, Brilliant practice. It should only take 5 minutes.

---

# Tests

## Chapter 21  What are psychometric tests?

The brilliant learning from Chapter 21 was that you would *understand five different types of tests which are commonly used by employers.* Check your understanding of what are the most common psychometric tests used by employers by taking this true/false quiz. The answers are given in "Answers".

For each of the following statements, decide whether it is true or false.

21.1  **If an employer uses psychometric tests as part of the recruitment process they will use the whole range of tests available.**

|                    True                    False

21.2  **Verbal reasoning tests only look at your understanding of the passage you have to read.**

|                    True                    False

21.3  **You will come across the same kind of reasoning tests whether the employer is in public or private sector and even across engineering and banking.**

|                    True                    False

21.4  **Either you get reasoning or you don't – practising won't help.**

|                    True                    False

21.5  **Situational judgement tests measure skills like problem-solving and team-working, which can transfer across employer and sector.**

|                    True                    False

**21.6 Personality tests can give you a real insight into the kind of person you are so can be useful if you don't get the job in telling you something about whether that job would have suited you.**

True          False

**21.7 Psychometrics are the best way of selecting for a job.**

True          False

**21.8 You can't really do a situational judgement test unless you've already worked in that role.**

True          False

**21.9 Public and private sector use the same reasoning tests.**

True          False

**21.10 Personality tests help you check whether the job is really right for you.**

True          False

## Verbal reasoning tests

The brilliant learning that you would *understand what the questions in verbal reasoning tests are asking you to do* and that you would *have a clear strategy to minimise your stress and maximise your performance.* Try this set of six tests, on your own, within the time limit set (25 minutes). The answers are in Brilliant answers.

Founded in 1954, the Bilderberg Group holds an annual conference of 120 of the world's most powerful and influential people. Participants, invited by a steering committee comprised of two people from each of 18 different countries, typically include financiers, industrialists, politicians, royalty and newspaper editors. Past delegates have included Tony Blair and Bill Clinton, shortly before becoming heads of state.

▶

Reporters, however, are not invited: the Bilderberg Group's meetings are conducted in privacy, with strict confidentiality rules to foster open discussion. The Group was established to promote understanding and cooperation between the United States and Europe and to create an informal network for the global elite. No votes are taken at the conference and no policies are agreed. However, the secrecy surrounding the conferences has given rise to numerous conspiracy theories. Right-wing critics believe that the Bilderberg Group is a shadowy global government, with some conspiracy theorists holding the Group responsible for organising events including the overthrow of Margaret Thatcher, the Bosnian War and the invasion of Iraq. Left-wing activists, who call for greater transparency, accuse the Group of being an unelected capitalist cabal controlling world finance. While opponents view the Group as undemocratic, supporters argue that modern democracies depend on cooperation between banking and politics, and that organisations such as the Bilderberg Group help ensure their success.

**Q1  The Bilderberg Group has critics on both sides of the ideological spectrum.**

True        False        Cannot say

**Q2  Representatives from the media are not allowed to attend the Bilderberg Group conference.**

True        False        Cannot say

**Q3  The Bilderberg Group was created as a private forum to set Europe and America's political and financial agenda.**

True        False        Cannot say

**Q4  Topics discussed at Bilderberg Group conferences have included the invasion of Iraq.**

True        False        Cannot say

**Q5  Because its delegates are not elected, the Bilderberg Group's activities are widely believed to be undemocratic.**

True        False        Cannot say

▶

Although today used to describe any movement to claim back territory for ethnic, linguistic, geographical or historical reasons, the term irredentism originally came from the Italian nationalist movement Italia irredenta. Meaning 'unredeemed Italy', Italian irredentism was an opinion movement rather than a formal organisation. It sought to unify ethnically Italian territories, such as Trieste, Trentina, and Istria, that were outside of Italian borders at the time of the unification of Italy in 1866. The annexation of these Italian territories from Austria provided Italy with its strongest motive for participating in World War I. The Treaty of Versailles in 1919 satisfied most of Italy's irredentist claims, however new borders delineated by the treaty gave rise to new irredentist claims. Dividing the German Empire into separate nations created German minority populations in the new countries of Poland and Hungary. German irredentist claims to these territories, as well as to Austria, resulted in the Second World War. The Treaty of Versailles created Yugoslavia to be a Slavic homeland, but ethnic and religious differences between Bosnians, Serbs and Croats eventually led to war in the 1990s. The artificial political states created by the Treaty of Versailles in East Africa failed to take tribal boundaries into account, and thus remain subject to irredentist claims. Similarly, borders drawn up in the Near East are still contentious today.

Q6 **Trieste, Trentina and Istria were reunified with Italy following the Treaty of Versailles.**

True        False        Cannot say

Q7 **Borders imposed in 1919 by the Treaty of Versailles resulted in twentieth century conflicts.**

True        False        Cannot say

Q8 **Irredentist movements advocate the annexation of territories only on the grounds of prior historical possession.**

True        False        Cannot say

**Q9** Yugoslavia was created following the Second World War to provide a homeland for Bosnians, Serbs and Croats.

                                              True          False          Cannot say

**Q10** Although originally an Italian movement, irredentist claims are now being made in other countries.

                                              True          False          Cannot say

Many organisations predict that the global water crisis presents this century's biggest threat. Today 84% of people in developing countries have access to clean water, 2 billion more than in 1990. However, millions still lack clean water for drinking and sanitation, posing a major health threat. In the developed world, water consumption is unsustainably high, doubling every twenty years. Agriculture accounts for 70% of the world's fresh water use, and an increasing population to feed means this demand will only increase. Groundwater sources, used to irrigate crops, are running dry because of overuse. While limiting the use of groundwater is a possible solution, it would have a financial impact on farmers and result in lower yields. While climate change has resulted in increased precipitation in some areas, it is contributing to water shortages in other regions. Rising temperatures have caused the Himalayan glaciers, the source for all of Asia's major rivers, to retreat. A reservoir for nearly half of the world's fresh water, these glaciers are predicted to lose four-fifths of their area by 2040. The solution to the global water crisis lies predominantly in new technologies. Desalination plants, which convert seawater into fresh water, have now been built in countries including Israel and Singapore. The process's high costs however limit its widespread adoption. Organising bodies and treaties are also needed to ensure that cross-border water sources are managed properly and do not become a source of conflict.

Q11  The global water crisis has resulted in less of the world's population having access to fresh water.

|  | True | False | Cannot say |

Q12  The irrigation of crops comprises the majority of groundwater usage.

|  | True | False | Cannot say |

Q13  Despite increasing rainfall in some areas, climate change is the main cause of the global water crisis.

|  | True | False | Cannot say |

Q14  The main impediment to desalination is expense.

|  | True | False | Cannot say |

Q15  Both technological innovation and diplomacy are needed to tackle the world's water crisis.

|  | True | False | Cannot say |

# Inductive, abstract and diagrammatic reasoning

The brilliant learning that you *would understand what the questions in inductive, abstract and diagrammatic reasoning tests are asking you to do* and that *you would have a clear plan of attack to minimise your stress and maximise your performance.* Try this test, on your own, within the time limit set (25 minutes). The answers are in Brilliant answers.

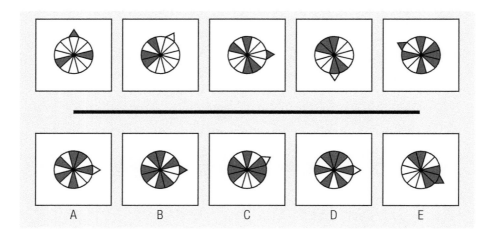

Q1 **What comes next in the sequence?**

(a) A        (b) B        (c) C        (d) D        (e) E

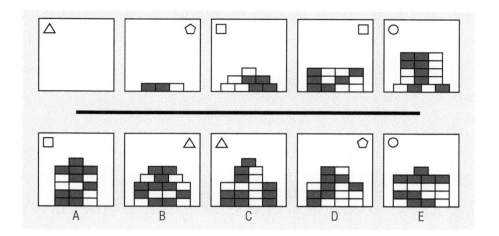

## Q2  What comes next in the sequence?

(a) A          (b) B          (c) C          (d) D          (e) E

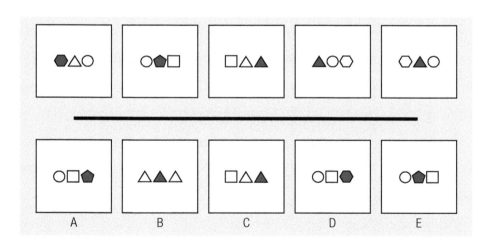

## Q3  What comes next in the sequence?

(a) A          (b) B          (c) C          (d) D          (e) E

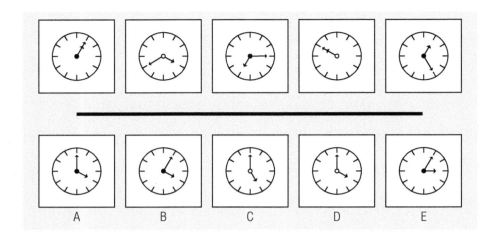

## Q4 What comes next in the sequence?

(a) A          (b) B          (c) C          (d) D          (e) E

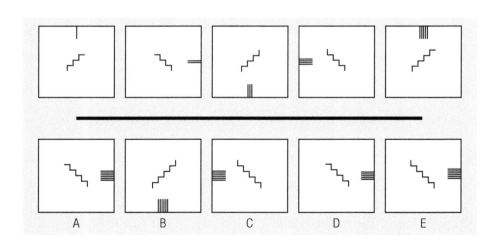

## Q5 What comes next in the sequence?

(a) A          (b) B          (c) C          (d) D          (e) E

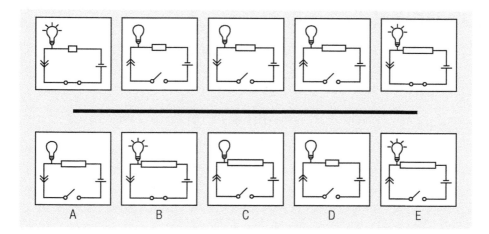

## Q6 What comes next in the sequence?

(a) A          (b) B          (c) C          (d) D          (e) E

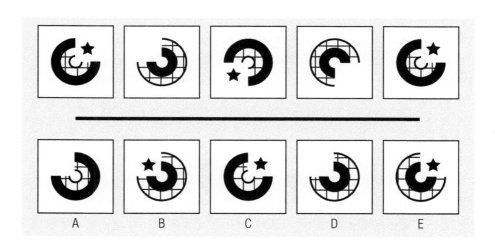

## Q7 What comes next in the sequence?

(a) A          (b) B          (c) C          (d) D          (e) E

## Situational judgement tests

The brilliant learning that you would *understand what the questions in situational judgement tests are asking you to do* and that you would *have a clear strategy to minimise your stress and maximise your performance.* Try this test, on your own, in your own time. The answers are in Brilliant answers.

### Scenario 1

You are a graduate intern on a two-year training programme at the Benign Sunshine Agency. Benign Sunshine is the UK's fifth largest marketing agency and deals with all aspects of clients' marketing, market research, PR and advertising needs.

You are a 'floating' intern and as such you are assigned to projects and to teams when they are likely to have a role for you and when they will have time to brief, coach and train you effectively in their work area. You also have a dedicated mentor to whom you can go at any time for help and support with regard to your progress, learning and work in the company.

### Situation 1

You have joined a team which is preparing to pitch to an existing client to win a contract to provide the PR for a new range of children's books which aim to teach children about environmental issues in an interesting, engaging and fun way. The client is hoping that primary schools will be interested in purchasing the series of books as one of the major topics in the national curriculum at Key Stage 2 is environmental and energy awareness.

The pitch team manager has asked you to take an active role in the pitch presentation to the client representatives. He particularly wants you to talk about your response to, and enjoyment of, the books as you are the youngest member of the team. The pitch is in two days' time.

▶

Review the following responses A to D and indicate which one you believe to be the response to the situation you would be 'most likely to make' and the response to the situation which you would be 'least likely to make'.

**Responses:**

**(A)** Prepare a presentation based on a detailed analysis of previous children's books on this topic that have done well and how they were promoted.

**(B)** Prepare a presentation based on your experiences of learning about the environment as a child and your favourite books on the topic.

**(C)** Prepare a presentation about how you felt and what questions came into your mind when you read the clients' books.

**(D)** Read the books to your nieces and nephews and prepare a presentation based on their response to the books.

## Situation 2

You have three days to go until the end of a project that you have been working on for the last four weeks in the market research team. By now you would usually have an email or call from your mentor letting you know about your next assignment location or your host team would have asked you to stay on for more time if they required you. However, neither of these things have happened and therefore you are unsure where you are going to be working next week or what your responsibilities will be.

Review the following responses A to D and indicate which one you believe to be the response to the situation you would be 'most likely to make' and the response to the situation which you would be 'least likely to make.'

**Responses:**

**(A)** Delay the end of this project for as long as you can.

**(B)** Ask your current team leader if she can assign some additional tasks to you to continue this placement a little longer.

▶

**(C)** Do nothing, as you will be able to use the 'downtime' after this project ends to pursue some personal development without having to work on a project for a while.

**(D)** Email your mentor to remind him that you think you are due to move on to a new posting or project in three days' time.

**Situation 3**

You have been asked to stay with the market research team for another project. Because of the competence you demonstrated on your last project in the team you have been given overall responsibility for a small piece of market research which Benign Sunshine have been commissioned to do by West Grimsdale Fire & Rescue Service (WGFRS).

The Service wish to find out how many households in their region currently have smoke alarms fitted and are operational and, of those who don't, how many are willing to fit smoke alarms in the next six months, either with or without incentives.

Review the following responses A to D and indicate which one you believe to be the first response to the situation you would be 'most likely to make' and the response to the situation which you would be 'least likely to make'.

**Responses:**

**(A)** Write a script for a telephone interview which your researchers will conduct with a sample of West Grimsdale households.

**(B)** Find out how many households there are in West Grimsdale and into what social categories they fall.

**(C)** Book some telephone researchers for three days next week to call households in West Grimsdale.

**(D)** Ask your team leader if you can have a meeting with the key contact at WGFRS in order to gain clarification on the detailed objectives of the research.

▶

### Situation 4

Over the last few weeks you have had sole responsibility for a market research project being conducted by Benign Sunshine on behalf of West Grimsdale Fire & Rescue Service (WGFRS). You have been doing your best to run the project according to the client's requirements but the key contact at WGFRS, Hector Jones, Director of Community Safety, has been a difficult person to work with.

This morning you received an email from Mr Jones stating that he is unhappy with the number and the quality of interviews you have conducted in households in the region and that he will go 'over your head' unless things improve immediately with regard to the running of the project. You believe that Mr Jones has been a little disappointed, and felt undervalued, because Benign Sunshine have put a graduate trainee in charge of his project. This appears to have negatively affected his view all the way through the process.

Review the following responses A to D and indicate which one you believe to be the response to the situation you would be 'most likely to make' and the response to the situation which you would be 'least likely to make'.

### Responses:

**(A)** Call Mr Jones immediately and apologise that he is unhappy. Ask exactly how you can improve the delivery of the project.

**(B)** Email back and say that you have delivered all aspects of the project as agreed and attach a copy of the original project plan as proof.

**(C)** Call Mr Jones' diary secretary and ask for a face-to-face meeting to be booked in to clear up the issues raised.

**(D)** Inform your team leader that Mr Jones is being difficult and over critical so she won't be surprised if she hears from him later.

▶

# Brilliant answers

Here are the worked answers to the questions which tested your Brilliant learning.

## Chapter 21  What are psychometric tests?

The brilliant learning from Chapter 21 was that you would understand five different types of tests which are commonly used by employers. See how you got on:

21.1 **If an employer uses psychometric tests as part of the recruitment process they will use the whole range of tests available.**

False: employers only use the psychometrics which measure what is important in the job on offer; there is no need to measure anything else.

21.2 **Verbal reasoning tests only look at your understanding of the passage you have to read.**

False: verbal reasoning tests your ability to work through a problem systematically, using reason and logic to get to the only correct answer. If it is simply your reading ability they want to test, that's the test they will use.

21.3 **You will come across the same kind of reasoning tests whether the employer is in public or private sector and even across engineering and banking.**

True: reasoning ability doesn't change across employer, so you will come across similar tests irrespective of whether the employer is public or private sector or indeed whether the sector is banking or health.

**21.4 Either you get reasoning or you don't – practising won't help.**

False: practising helps you to be familiar with what the tests demand of you, so you can focus on dealing with the test rather than using up all your energy working out how on earth you're going to tackle it.

**21.5 Situational judgement tests measure skills like problem-solving and team-working, which can transfer across employer and sector.**

True: many SJTs test these kinds of skills which readily transfer across different jobs and different employers.

**21.6 Personality tests can give you a real insight into the kind of person you are so can be useful if you don't get the job in telling you something about whether that job would have suited you.**

True: this is particularly true where you get written feedback, but even where you simply do the test, it makes you think about what makes you tick – and whether that would honestly have fitted in with the job on offer.

**21.7 Psychometrics are the best way of selecting for a job.**

False: psychometrics are a good way to measure the mind, but should be used alongside other selection techniques (application form or interview) to get a full picture.

**21.8 You can't really do a situational judgement test unless you've already worked in that role.**

False: you don't need prior knowledge to tackle a SJT – but it can help to picture yourself already doing the job if you are stuck for an answer.

**21.9 Public and private sector use the same reasoning tests.**

True: that's because they both prize the ability to reason.

**21.10 Personality tests help you check whether the job is really right for you.**

True: because they are so thorough, you'll really have to think about who you are – and that helps you to work out whether you are cut out for the job.

## Verbal reasoning tests

The brilliant learning that you would understand what the questions in verbal reasoning tests are asking you to do and would have a clear strategy to minimise your stress and maximise your performance. Here are the worked answers:

**Q1 The Bilderberg Group has critics on both sides of the ideological spectrum.**

True: summarises the 8th and 9th sentences. Right-wing critics being one side and left-wing activists being the other.

**Q2 Representatives from the media are not allowed to attend the Bilderberg Group conference.**

False: while the fourth sentence states that 'Reporters, however, are not invited' the second sentence states that conference participants include 'newspaper editors'.

**Q3 The Bilderberg Group was created as a private forum to set Europe and America's political and financial agenda.**

False: while many conspiracy theories promote this idea, the fifth and sixth sentences state that the Group was established to promote understanding and does not set policy.

**Q4 Topics discussed at Bilderberg Group conferences have included the invasion of Iraq.**

Cannot say: as the conferences are private, there is no way of knowing what was discussed.

**Q5  Because its delegates are not elected, the Bilderberg Group's activities are widely believed to be undemocratic.**

Cannot say: both sides of the argument are argued in the last sentence. We are not told either way if this view is 'widely believed'.

**Q6  Trieste, Trentina and lstria were reunified with Italy following the Treaty of Versailles.**

Cannot say: while the third sentence lists these areas as Italian territories, and the fifth sentence states that the Treaty of Versailles 'satisfied most of Italy's irredentist claims' the passage does not expressly state that these territories became part of Italy.

**Q7  Borders imposed in 1919 by the Treaty of Versailles resulted in twentieth century conflicts.**

True: both World War II and the Bosnian War were the result of irredentist claims over borders.

**Q8  Irredentist movements advocate the annexation of territories only on the grounds of prior historical possession.**

False: there are a variety of reasons given in the first sentence.

**Q9  Yugoslavia was created following the Second World War to provide a homeland for Bosnians, Serbs and Croats.**

False: Yugoslavia was created after the First World War. All the examples in the second half of the passage pertain to the Treaty of Versailles.

**Q10  Although originally an Italian movement, irredentist claims are now being made in other countries.**

True: the last two sentences mention irredentist claims in East Africa and the Near East.

**Q11  The global water crisis has resulted in less of the world's population having access to fresh water.**

Cannot say: the second sentence tells us that more people in developing countries have access to clean water than before (2 billion more than in 1990), however we are not told if more or fewer people in developed countries have access to fresh water. So we are not given the whole picture and therefore we cannot say.

### Q12  The irrigation of crops comprises the majority of groundwater usage.

Cannot say: the passage states that 70% of the world's freshwater use is for agriculture and that groundwater is used to irrigate crops. It does not follow that 70% of groundwater is used for farming.

### Q13  Despite increasing rainfall in some areas, climate change is the main cause of the global water crisis.

Cannot say: the passage does not cite a primary cause for the crisis.

### Q14  The main impediment to desalination is expense.

Cannot say: the passage states that 'The process's high costs however limit its wide-spread adoption'. However it does not follow that this is the main impediment.

### Q15  Both technological innovation and diplomacy are needed to tackle the world's water crisis.

True: the 11th sentence says 'The solution to the global water crisis lies predominantly in new technologies.' The last sentence goes on to say that 'Organising bodies and treaties are also needed . . .'. So we are told that both technology and diplomacy (organising bodies and treaties) are needed.

## Inductive, abstract and diagrammatic reasoning

The brilliant learning that you would *understand what the questions in inductive, abstract and diagrammatic reasoning tests are asking you to do* and you would *have a clear plan of attack to minimise your stress and maximise your performance*. Here are the worked answers:

**Q1** **What comes next in the sequence?**

Answer = D

Rule 1: The triangle moves clockwise 1 place, then 2 places, then 3 places and so on, around the circle.

Rule 2: The triangle alternates between shaded and unshaded.

Rule 3: The number of shaded segments in the circle increases by one each time.

**Q2** **What comes next in the sequence?**

Answer = B

Rule 1: The shape at the top alternates between the top left and top right-hand corners.

Rule 2: The number of edges of the shape indicates how many bricks should be added to the next box.

Rule 3: The number of shaded bricks per box increases by two each time.

**Q3** **What comes next in the sequence?**

Answer = A

Rule 1: The total number of edges in each box is equal to ten.

Rule 2: The last shape in each box is the first shape of the next box.

Rule 3: The shading moves one place to the right each time and then begins again from the left.

**Q4** **What comes next in the sequence?**

Answer = D

Rule 1: The minutes (long) hand rotates 5 hours counterclockwise each time.

Rule 2: The hour (short) hand rotates 3 places clockwise each time.

Rule 3: The circle at the centre of the clock alternates between black and white.

Q5 **What comes next in the sequence?**

Answer = A

Rule 1: The notches move 1 place clockwise around the edge of the box and each time increase by one.

Rule 2: The centre symbol is mirrored horizontally each time.

Rule 3: The number of lines in the centre symbol increases by one every two boxes.

Q6 **What comes next in the sequence?**

Answer = C

Rule 1: When the circuit is complete (the bottom connection is closed) the bulb lights up. When the circuit is broken (bottom connection is open) the bulb does not light up.

Rule 2: The arrows on the left of the circuit alternate between pointing up and down.

Rule 3: The box at the top of the circuit increases in size each time.

Q7 **What comes next in the sequence?**

Answer = D

Rule 1: The rings alternate between cross-hatched and black.

Rule 2: The missing quarter moves one place counterclockwise each time.

Rule 3: Every second box has a star in the missing quarter.

# Situational judgement tests

The brilliant learning that you would understand what the questions in situational judgement tests are asking you to do and you would *have a clear strategy to minimise your stress and maximise your performance*. Here are the worked answers:

**Scenario 1:**

**Situation 1**

**Responses:**

(A)  Prepare a presentation based on a detailed analysis of previous children's books on this topic that have done well and how they were promoted.

(This is the **least effective response** as this has no resemblance to the brief you were given. Also other members of the team may have been asked to look at the marketplace and competition for the client's products anyway. And finally, the client may be looking to see that you and your team can understand the uniqueness of their product rather than comparing it favourably or unfavourably to competitors' products.)

(B)  Prepare a presentation based on your experiences of learning about the environment as a child and your favourite books on the topic.

(**Not a particularly appropriate response** as you are not focusing on your client's products at all; you are presenting a 'personal' view, which may be of interest, but failing to talk about the most important thing, which is the product that you are pitching to promote.)

(C)  Prepare a presentation about how you felt and what questions came into your mind when you read the client's books.

(This is **the most effective response** as this is the brief you have been given by your team manager which is to give a personal and thoughtful view of the products; remember you are only one member of the team and therefore this will be your unique contribution whereas other team members will be able to talk about PR strategy, competition in the marketplace and to draw on more 'objective' analysis.)

(D) Read the books to your nieces and nephews and prepare a presentation based on their response to the books.

(This is **a reasonable response** as you are presenting the views of a sample of the core market for the books: however, as the client has probably done work like this when developing the book series they may be less interested in this than they are in your views on the books. After all, you may be part of the team who eventually provide PR for the product. They will want to know that you like, and believe in, their books).

## Situation 2

**Responses:**

(A) Delay the end of this project for as long as you can.

(This is **the least effective** response as you are affecting operational matters in the agency simply because of your own personal scheduling issues.)

(B) Ask your current team leader if she can assign some additional tasks to you to continue this placement a little longer.

(**A reasonable response** as you are already familiar with the market research department and will be able to contribute effectively to the team. It also buys you time with regard to seeking out your next placement or project.).

(C) Do nothing, as you will be able to use the 'downtime' after this project ends to pursue some personal development without having to work on a project for a while.

(**Not a particularly appropriate response** as you have not investigated why your next project hasn't come through – it may have been a simple oversight. You are supposed to be developing your skills 'on-the-job' and therefore you should be trying to secure new objectives and a new project on which to work.)

(D) Email your mentor to remind him that you think you are due to move on to a new posting or project in three days' time.

(This is **the most effective response** as a gentle reminder may facilitate the process. Or there may be reasons why you haven't been found a placement to move to and this way you will find out what they are and be able to act upon them).

## Situation 3

**Responses:**

(A) Write a script for a telephone interview which your researchers will conduct with a sample of West Grimsdale households.

(**Not a particularly appropriate response** as, whilst this will need to be done at some point, it is not the most urgent element of the planning process. You can't write the script until you have clarified with the client exactly what they want to find out and whether there is more information that they would like gathered during the process.)

(B) Find out how many households there are in West Grimsdale and into what social categories they fall.

(**A reasonable response**, as these are essential pieces of information required to help you plan your research and pick your sample of households to call. You clearly cannot call every household and will therefore need to select a representative sample from which you can draw conclusions about the whole of the WG region.)

(C) Book some telephone researchers for three days next week to call households in West Grimsdale.

(This is **the least effective response** as you need to decide on your research approach before you book researchers otherwise you may book too few or too many and you may not be ready to start on the interview stage by next week anyway.)

(D) Ask your team leader if you can have a meeting with the key contact at WGFRS in order to gain clarification on the detailed objectives of the research.

(This is **the most effective response** as you will need a detailed briefing from the client in order to be absolutely sure that you deliver what they want: they may have secondary information that they would like gathering at the same time as the information about the smoke-alarm fitting behaviour. Market research is expensive so the client will not want to waste an opportunity. Also, during the meeting you should be able to gather other information, such as local population demographics, which will help with your planning process).

**Situation 4**

**Responses:**

(A) Call Mr Jones immediately and apologise that he is unhappy. Ask exactly how you can improve the delivery of the project.

(This is **the most effective response** as you are acting swiftly to reduce Mr Jones's feelings of dissatisfaction and showing that you personally want to ensure his requirements are met).

(B) Email back and say that you have delivered all aspects of the project as agreed and attach a copy of the original project plan as proof.

(**Not a particularly appropriate response** as, whilst this may be true, you are not dealing with Mr Jones's views of the project. or indeed his feelings about how WGFRS have been treated.)

(C) Call Mr Jones' diary secretary and ask for a face-to-face meeting to be booked in to clear up the issues raised.

(**A reasonable response**, as a face-to-face meeting is always better than email or telephone for building relationships. However it may be even better to give an immediate (and apologetic) response to clear the air before having a meeting.)

(D)   Inform your team leader that Mr Jones is being difficult and over-critical so she won't be surprised if she hears from him later.

(This is **the least effective response** as you are failing to respond to Mr Jones very quickly and this will do little to improve your working relationship with him; it is quite a defensive response.)